I0800113

The Sufi Message of Hazrat Inayat Khan

Centennial Edition

Volume VII
In an Eastern Rose Garden

Hazrat Pir-o-Murshid Inayat Khan

The Sufi Message of Hazrat Inayat Khan

Centennial Edition

Volume VII
In an Eastern Rose Garden

Sulūk Press
Richmond, Virginia

Published by Sulūk Press
112 East Cary Street
Richmond, Virginia 23219
sulukpress.com

Cover ornament from Shutterstock.com
Cover design by Sandra Lillydahl

This edition is printed on acid-free paper.

ISBN 978-1-941810-53-8 paper
ISBN 978-1-941810-52-1 hardcase
ISBN 978-1-941810-54-5 e-book

Names: Inayat Khan, 1882–1927, author. | Inayat Khan, Zia, 1971–, author of introduction.
Title: The Sufi Message of Hazrat Inayat Khan, Centennial Edition, Volume VII: In an Eastern Rose Garden
Description: First Edition, Richmond, VA: Sulūk Press, 2025. | Includes introduction, biographical note, glossary, index.
Identifiers: LCCN 2016940929 | ISBN 9781941810521 (hardcase) | ISBN 9781941810538 (paper) | ISBN 9781941810545 (e-book)
Subjects: LCSH: Sufism BISAC: Religion/Sufi | Religion/Mysticism

Printed and bound in the United States of America

CONTENTS

Acknowledgments

Thanks are due to Anne Louise Wirgman at the Nekbakht Foundation for locating source texts in the *Complete Works* and finding the previously unpublished transcript of "Spiritual Democracy" in the Nekbakht Archives in Suresnes. Thanks as well go to Sandra Lillydahl for her design, to Beatrice Upenieks for scanning and preparing the texts for editing and for laying out the pages, and to Dorothy Craig for proofreading.

Cannon Labrie, editor

INTRODUCTION

In 1921 the world was recovering from the unprecedented catastrophe that was the First World War. The old thunderclouds were abating, but new storms were brewing. Worldwide, it was a year of peace treaties and truces, but also of invasions, riots, and massacres. Freud wrote in that year about "mutual induction," the group dynamic by which people amplify each other's emotions. In the age of total war, the stakes of thought patterns were becoming clearer than ever before. But how could minds, individually and collectively, realize peace and amity without sacrificing the creative energy that makes art and science possible?

In an Eastern Rose Garden was compiled by Dr. O. C. Gruner, an English murid (disciple), and published by the Sufi Publishing Society in Southampton, England, in 1921. Dr. Gruner had previously compiled *The Way of Illumination*, which appears in the first volume of the present series. He would go on, in 1930, to publish a notable study of the medical legacy of Ibn Sina entitled *Treatise of the Canon of Medicine of Avicenna*. Dr. Gruner's treatise features an illustration depicting a quartet of figures consisting of Ibn Sina, a Chinese sage, Saint Thomas Aquinas, and Hazrat himself.

In compiling *In an Eastern Rose Garden* Dr. Gruner dispensed with thematic unity in favor of bricolage. One could say that not only does this rose garden contain roses, it also harbors tulips, narcissi, poppies, and many other flowers. While there isn't an obvious thematic focus linking the chapters, there is nonetheless—as there is in the best gardens—an intuitive rightness to the total composition. To spend time among the parterres of this book is to come away refreshed, inspired, and grounded anew.

Perhaps the leading idea of *In an Eastern Rose Garden* is the idea of freedom. All beings pursue freedom since freedom is an essential quality of the soul. Too often, however, one person's ostensible freedom is achieved at the expense of that of someone else. A truer freedom arises from the realization of interconnectedness. Hazrat writes, "When people see that the ideal of every soul is freedom, and that they cannot enjoy their own freedom unless they have shared their freedom with others, then and only then can it be that troubles and unhappiness will cease." Hazrat calls this ecological vision of life "nature's religion of freedom."

Ultimately, freedom flowers in the soul's awakening. Creation is the story of spirit's discovery of itself. A person thinks this or that circumstance will provide the freedom they crave. Little is one aware, what one is actually longing for is the revelation of one's own true nature. To attain this disclosure one must die to the fiction of the conditioned self and undergo rebirth in the light of the soul, which now reveals itself as a ray of the universal Intelligence.

In two essays in the volume, Hazrat presents an inspiring elucidation of the meaning of friendship. Key features of friendship according to Hazrat are wordless mutual understanding, an absence of self-interested maneuvering, and a constant readiness to see the best in each other.

On the surface, freedom and friendship might seem unrelated concepts, but in fact the two phenomena are siblings. In English, both words derive from the Proto-Indo-European *priHós,* meaning "pleased" or "loved." To be a genuine friend to someone is to wish for, and work for, their freedom. It is by going down this path, as Hazrat says, that a person comes to know the friendship of God.

In the end, *In an Eastern Rose Garden* is a book about human wholeness. Peace and creativity, freedom and friendship, aristocracy and democracy, the inner and the outer—in the reconciliation of each of these pairs of seeming contraries lies the realization of the purpose for which we were created.

In the rose garden, with all its blossoms and all its thorns, the opposites meet in the essence of the human being, which touches divinity and is therefore a source of endless beauty: "What do we want? We want human beings. It is not necessary that all people must become most religious or most pious or too good to live. We want wise people in business, in politics, in education, in all walks of life—those who do not only live on the surface, and those who do not only show belief in matter, but those who believe in life within and without. It is such souls who will produce beauty."

Such is the loveliness of the garden in spring.

Pir Zia Inayat Khan

1

LOVE, HARMONY, AND BEAUTY

How the words *love*, *harmony*, and *beauty* delight the heart of everyone who hears them! One may wonder what it can be in these words that should be able to exert such a natural power upon the human soul.

The answer is that if there is anything in life that appeals to the human soul, it is love and beauty. If you ask, "And what besides this?" then the answer is, "Besides this, there is nothing else." Why is this? Because it is the very nature of life. Love is the nature of life, beauty is the outcome of life, harmony is the means by which life accomplishes its purpose, and the lack of it results in destruction in life.

When we reflect upon this whole creation we cannot but see that its purpose is to express an ideal of love, harmony, and beauty. Love could not have manifested itself if there were nothing to love, eyes could not have seen if there were nothing to see. What could love have done if there were no beauty? Love would have been silent. Love can only be said to exist after it has passed from silence into expression.

Now comes the question, "What has made beauty?" The answer is that it is love that has made beauty. When a Sufi calls you "Beloved Ones of God" that one has this idea in mind. Whatever God has created, God has created out of love, God has created for God to love, and therefore whatever God has created and all God's creatures are God's beloved ones.

We human beings have our prejudices; we like one, dislike another; we consider one worthy of high estimation, another only worthy of low esteem, but to God they are all alike, they are God's creation. It is just as it would be for poets to have the little scrap of paper on which their song was written thrown away, or lost and disesteemed. How could they sing without their voice? So it is with the Creator; who cannot be pleased when little scraps of paper are disesteemed.

God is love, and God has created humans out of that love. How then can God be pleased if you have hatred or prejudice against a fellow human being through forgetting that, however unworthy a person may seem to be, that one is nevertheless the beloved one of God? God has created that person to love him or her. Therefore God, the Father and Mother of all beings, is equally pleased with all God's creatures.

But is not one thing more beautiful than another, one person more than another, either in external or in internal being? What is the reason of this?

The reason is found when we consider the work of an artist, of a poet, of a composer of music, of a writer. We can see that one composition is much more beautiful than another. One picture may perhaps be the best the artist has painted in all their life. The poet may wonder, "Have I written this verse? Where can it have come from? It is so superior to all others; it is marvelous how these words came to me."

Just as we see this in the individual, so also do we see it in the work of the Creator. At the same time, love is the only power that has created, or that can create.

In this way God becomes the lover and the manifestation or object of love at the same time. In the Sanskrit language this is called by mystics Shiva and Shakti, or Purusha and Prakriti, or Ishvara and Maya—these three pairs of words. The one part is love, and the other part is beauty. Love has created beauty in order that it may be able to love. God is love; that is why God is called the Creator. The lover alone has the power to create, and that which God creates is for the purpose of receiving God's love.

The Prophet has said, "God is beautiful and loves beauty."[1] Now, the word *beautiful* does not refer to the form of God. God is formless. God has no personality until God self-manifests. Therefore it is not God's personality that is beautiful, for God is beyond that which in the ordinary sense of the word is called personality.

What then is the source of the beauty? God is beautiful because God has created beauty. If there were no beauty in God, there could have been none in God's manifestation. If there were no beauty in the thought of the poet, he could not write beautiful verse; if there were no beauty in the thought of the artist, she could never have painted the picture. One cannot see the beauty in the heart of the painter except in the beauty of the picture she has made. It is not the picture alone that is beautiful; it is the heart of the painter that is beautiful first. Consequently we become able to see the beauty not only in manifestation, but also before it was manifested; and before it was manifested it existed in love. In other words, we can see that the beauty was hidden in love; beauty is hidden in love, and the beauty that love has before it to love is its own beauty. Therefore, to whatever extent beauty is beautiful, so is love beautiful; nay, even more so, because the Creator is more beautiful than the thing the Creator has created.

All things that we make are the work of our hands. We are their creator, and we are greater than our hands. So it is with love. Love is greater than beauty, because love is the creator of the beauty that love loves in its life.

No doubt by loving, love becomes limited—limited as beauty—but then that is the purpose of love. If there were no beauty,

1. Hadith.

God's love could not have realized the latent joy of its own nature. The joy of its existence would die out.

As soon as we can think in this way, we come to see that the lover is vaster, incomparably vaster than the object that is loved. The real love, the real beauty, is in the lover. The object that is loved is much smaller, although for the moment the lover is not aware of the difference. "You are the object before which I bow. You are the object of which I think day and night, before which I am helpless. You are the object that I admire, that I adore," so thinks the lover. Yet the lover does not realize the vastness of his or her love, and indeed, strictly speaking, love is vaster than the lover.

When people begin to learn the lesson of love they are apt to become frightened at the pains and difficulties and troubles that they will have to meet on behalf of love. When they compare their condition with that of the beloved, they think the beloved is much better off than they. "The one who takes my thought, who gives me pain, who wounds my heart, is much happier. When I compare myself with the beloved I think that one is much the happier." And the lover goes on to think, "If I were the beloved, it would be much better." Every soul experiences that thought, but once one has risen beyond it, then one begins to know love. The soul that has not escaped from this fails to realize the fullness of love.

There is another side to love, and that is selfishness, and one must escape from this. The true lover says, "I will give everything, I will endure all things, all tortures, all torments that may have to be faced in life. I will bow in humility before whatever befalls me. I will give all that I have. I will bear all things, believe all things, hope for all things, and endure all things." But the other side of love says, "Are you crazy? Have you lost your senses? You are foolish. Why this complaining? See how happy the beloved is. Be happy like that one, and be in the beloved's exalted position, instead of in this humility and degradation. Enter into this greatness and not into that destruction."

Then the lover proceeds to reason, and at length understands. The one thing leads to destruction, the other promises safety. But in destruction there is the hand of God, while in safety there is the hand of Satan. All things that are selfish are taught by that power and by that knowledge that is the enemy of mankind. He is an enemy because he leads one away from the purpose of one's life. Satan is he who leads you astray from the purpose of your life. He seeks to make the lover change places with the beloved, saying, "Your position is better than mine; now I would like to be like you." And perhaps one will wait all one's life to gain that coveted position, and it never comes because the beloved would not surrender the wealth when the chance was there.

The life of a person would be quite changed after being melted in the fire of love. The fire of love will exalt one, even so that with animals and birds one's power will have influence, both the wise and foolish alike will be attracted to one. Once one is purified, burned in the fire of love, one will become the attraction of every soul, of every being, invisible as well as visible. It is only the advice of Satan that keeps one from that. The master is one who suffers. Many times do we reflect how Jesus Christ washed the feet of his disciples. What beauty there is in that service, in that humility! Can you see that beauty in a proud person? Can a proud person win the hearts of the world for centuries and centuries? The proud person is led by Satan—egoistic, selfish, cold; everyone in their presence will freeze, for their presence is as ice and cannot impart comfort.

But how forgiving becomes one who has been through all suffering! Was there anything else in Christ's life but forgiveness and tolerance? "Always forgive, always forgive, always tolerate," he said. It was because the love in the heart of the master was so great that it appealed to everyone. Love was all the philosophy that his fishermen could understand, and if love were placed before philosophy and religion, how devoted would the devotees become. The animals would become attracted, the birds would become attracted by the power of a person's heart aflame with love.

As it is, a person only frightens love away on the least suspicion of its appearance, and love never wants to come nearer.

How often is the word *love* used in everyday life for what is nothing but an amusement, a pleasure, a pastime, a degraded thing. Love is so much higher. It is not a thing that you can give to a person, or of which a person may say, "I can develop it." One cannot learn it, one cannot study it in a book; there is only this one thing to be done: to allow it to grow in the heart. A person cannot live without a heart, and the heart cannot exist without love. However loveless and cold a person seems to be, however wicked and cruel a person seems to be, he or she nevertheless has love, though it is hidden. There is a thick wall built round it. It has no means of coming out; it is continually kept within this shell, and it is uneasy and restless. That is why people become cold and unhappy, always wanting they know not what, because they do not understand the only true inclination. The love power has become captive in a thick shell, a shell of coldness, the frozen part of love, and this shell refuses outlet to the stream of love, the divine power that seeks to emerge through the heart. When one does not give outlet to this love one becomes a burden to others; one's presence becomes disagreeable to one's surroundings, one's influence becomes a burden to oneself. Many times it is this that has caused people to be disagreeable in nature, and even for this reason some persons go mad. Not knowing what they want in life, they always blame others for not having loved them, or sympathized with them, or been kind to them. They do not realize that the key lies in themselves; in their heart lies the power to open and melt anyone's heart. It is our own power that can bring another to our feet.

Whoever learns this truth ceases to blame a person for being cold to one, unkind to one, unsympathetic toward one. One finds that it is within oneself that the cause lies. By seeking the sympathy and good feeling of another person one covers one's own heart and stops it from expressing itself. The love power is ever wishing to come out to impress itself upon its surroundings, and yet it is as if the doors were being ever closed to prevent God from coming out to fulfill the purpose of God's own creation.

How beautiful are the words of the Prophet when he says, "The shrine of God is the human heart."[2] How true that is! Is God to be found in a mosque, or temple, or church, or in any place where people sing hymns and offer their prayers? Can God be found where there is no love? God is not to be found in the houses that people have made for worship. These are only schools for children, and their playgrounds. Children like playing with toys, and yet they are preparing themselves for something else. When one has come to know the real beauty of God, one will find that it is only in one place—namely, the human heart. God is love, and God is found in the human heart.

One who understands this can even worship God in the human, for in abiding by this philosophy one is always considering that in every aspect and at every moment one may be injuring or hurting the feelings of God; one is in danger of breaking the shrine of God in breaking the heart of one's fellow human.

It might be thought that the philosophers and mystics and sages, who are so near and close to God, may take too much freedom with the world. But they are, on the contrary, the most tender and delicate of humankind. They are ready to share anyone's trouble, to share anyone's sorrow, to share everyone's depression and despair. They are ready to console any and every person with their words, and to help with their service, and to give their sympathy always to those who require it. They shrink at no sacrifice of time, money, pleasure, or comfort. As Christ teaches, "Whosoever shall compel thee to go a mile, go with him twain."[3]

2. Hadith.
3. Matthew 5:41.

What does all this teach us? It is all a lesson in sympathy with one's fellow humans, to share in their troubles, in their despair. For whoever really experiences this joy of life, it becomes so great that it fills their heart and their soul. It does not matter if one has less comfort or position than many in this world, because the light of one's kindness, of one's sympathy, of the love that is growing, the virtue that is springing up in one's heart—all fill the soul with light. There is nothing now that one lacks in life, for one has become the king of it.

Such persons become healers, real healers. They heal a person with their glance, with a kind word, with their hand, by their comfort, by their nature. What a healing that is! Unpretentious, unassuming healing. The real healing is when a person is in sympathy with another's trouble and gives the other a helping hand. Those are the possessors of the true wine. Those who can send from their eyes the glance that proves the sympathy and help they are anxious to give, what a healing power they have! Is it not as when a bird is taken in beneath the brooding wings? There cannot be a more beautiful process of healing than this among all the different methods with which people have endeavored to heal.

People may question, "What should be the object which we should love in this life?" Is there any particular object that one can be recommended to love? Is it best to love the parent, or friends; to love one alone, or to love just one beloved of the opposite sex; should one love something in the abstract, some spirit, some ideal, some name, or something that is beyond one's nature? Or should one love something that we idealize as the God whom we worship? There are many who say that there is no other love that is useful but the love of God; all other things are worthless. Another says, "I can love no one who is of the opposite sex." Why? "Because I was once disappointed in one." Another will say, "I will love no human being; I can love my dog or my cat better. They do not disappoint me, whereas I was once disappointed in a person." Another says, "I love my money, because if I am in need that is the only friend that comes to my rescue. The deposit I have in my bank does more for me than anyone can do. Why then should I not love my money?" Another person says, "If God is all, if God is to have all love, then why not love the chair, or the table, or a book, or the work that a person does—a work of art, a piece of music, or sculpture—is it not the same?" But all these questions are voiced by hearts that have once been disappointed, once broken. They broke and became closed, and once the doors of the heart are closed there is no light to guide its path. That is what is so beautiful in the little English song, "The light of a whole life dies when love is done."[4] There is no light when love is done. When love is done, the heart is closed.

So often does one meet with people who complain that the love on the part of the lover failed to satisfy and caused their despair and distress. What does the Sufi learn, what does the sage learn from this? They learn this—that it is those who love who gain. Those who have loved and not gone forward are those who have lost. The reason why they have gone back before reaching their destiny has been that they were dependent upon the object of love that disappointed them. The Sufi is aware of this great pit on the path. Whenever lovers, who were attracted by beauty, fall from their love, it is because they depended on the beauty. It was the beauty that they loved, and they could only stand as long as that beauty remained their ideal. The lovers rise again when they consider within

4. Francis William Bourdillon, "The Night Has a Thousand Eyes" (1894):

> The night has a thousand eyes,
>   And the day but one;
> Yet the light of the bright world dies
>   With the dying sun.
>
> The mind has a thousand eyes,
>   And the heart but one:
> Yet the light of a whole life dies
>   When love is done.

themselves and say, "I will make an ideal such as shall allow my life to become self-sufficient. The ideal will be my excuse, but in reality I will raise my love. Whenever love was broken it was only because the ideal did not prove to be what the lover expected it to be. I will therefore avoid blinding my eyes with the external life, but will build the path on which to travel in my own heart. That ideal will suffice and fill everything that the beloved may lack." These lovers are the real lovers, because love has a beauty too, and these lovers produce from their own love the beauty that perhaps the beloved lacks, and they no longer notice the lack in their beloved. From this time, the beloved becomes their love because they have made a beloved in their thought, in their imaginations, and they can continually add to the beauty of the manifestation.

In this manner it is that the song of love and beauty has been sung in all periods of history. Saʿdi of Persia, Dante of Italy, and all the great ones who have loved and appealed to the human heart—all of them have left words that pierce through our heart today because of the greatness of their ideal. They have themselves created their ideal in their own heart. For all such there can no longer be a question of the beloved proving unworthy of love. The lover has become the creator of the love. Did not God create love? Have you not inherited this beauty of God? Can *you* not create love also? That which you can create can always be depended on.

There is another side: the ideal of love that is created by humans is according to their evolution. If they are material, they will appreciate material beauty in a person or object. They cannot help this. It is not their fault. It is right for them to admire that which directly appeals to them. Some will prefer beauty of mind, of virtue, of personality, of some good manner, of some goodness that appeals to them; they value a beautiful personality, a sympathetic presence. Others will perhaps like the soul in the form of inspiration, intuition, peace of mind, joy. They find their ideal in that.

Therefore one cannot point to any particular object as the only object worthy of love, because beauty is only according to a person's evolution. One who is of lower evolution cannot love a higher object. But a person of higher evolution can love the lower as well as the higher. One who once loves cannot hate. One who hates is one who cannot appreciate. Hatred is found in the lower grade of evolution, not in the higher. And the higher the evolution proceeds, the less does the hatred and prejudice become. In the higher realm there is no poison, for the object is higher, the standard is higher, the sphere is greater. As high as you set your ideal, so high do you attain, and it is by raising the standard of beauty step-by-step that one rises up and up into the highest heaven.

It is by walking along and keeping ever on the path of love that even from the lowest depth the soul can reach the highest heaven. One can ever raise one's ideal to that height in which one becomes able to love God the Formless, God the Nameless, who is above all goodness and virtue; not even God can be restricted to virtue, for God is beyond goodness.

There are sages who are moved to tears just by saying to themselves one word of essential truth, of abstract truth. What is it that should have this effect? Is there some pain concealed in it? Is anything said to evoke sympathy? No, it is their ideal that is so high that they see the ideal beauty in the truth. The truth of being has become beautiful to them. Their beloved has become God, and when a word of truth is spoken in their hearing they are moved to tears. To these sages everything is a real manifestation of the beauty of God.

If they go to hear music, in that music they feel God, in that music they see God. If they are standing before a picture, in the beauty of that picture they see their Beloved. If they are standing in a crowd, with all manner of faces, to them the whole picture is one harmony, one vision of the sublime, and they can see the whole beauty there. Whether it be desert or sea or sky or land—whatever it is that is before their eyes, all has a vision of beauty to offer to them. And it is in that way that the whole manifestation has become for them an immanence of the beauty of God.

2

NATURE'S RELIGION

Although it is no exaggeration to say that there are numberless religions in the world, and every religion has so many different sects and churches and chapels that this life is not long enough to study them—indeed it would be impossible even to count them in one lifetime—yet that which is really to be studied proves to be a very different thing, for the thinker perceives that many different religions have sprung out of one religion, one church. The religion may begin in the East or the West, in the South or the North, yet it will end in many religions. The more we think upon how all can come from one, the plainer becomes the fact that all are expressions of one religion. And this religion is nature's religion.

The question what exactly this religion can be, and in what manner it may become known, can only be answered by those who have raised themselves beyond the limitations of ceremonial and dogmatism in which they are always first instructed. But rising above a religion does not mean giving up the religion. It means being fully benefited by the religion. Those who say they have given up their religion are not above it. They alone are above it who have arrived at full understanding of the spirit of religion. As soon as the spirit of religion has become manifest, then indeed are the eyes blessed. The distinctions and differences of castes and creeds and religions all vanish away in one moment of time.

Once this is perceived, there ceases to be anything to criticize; it is all one what form of worship is to be used, what church is to be attended, what book is to be read. From this time it is seen that there is no such thing as a heretic, no such thing as a heathen, no difference between Kafir and Muslim. But until this truth is perceived there is always the thought, "Whatever religion, or belief, or faith I have or hold, the scripture that I read, the church that I visit—that is the only scripture, the only church, the only faith; this that I have understood and regarded as mine all through my life, this is the only path."

It is as when one is in pursuit of a bird. One looks at the branch of the tree that is still shaking after the bird has flown from it. One says, "Oh, here is the bird"—but one is only looking at the branch trembling hither and thither after the bird has sat there just for a moment. One calls the branch the bird. Another person may see a branch moving, but this time the branch is so strong that the bird could not possibly have moved it. Not understanding this, the person thinks the bird used to sit on that branch. "That is where the bird sat," the person thinks. Thus it is with the Truth.

Instead of understanding the spirit of the Truth, people have taught that religion lies in the name of the teacher. Importance is given to the name of the teacher, to the scripture, to the house in which worship is customary, to the priests or clergy who officiate. Prominence is given to being Brahmin or Buddhist, to belonging to certain communities formed in the name of the particular religion, to the castes set up, to the families formed, to those associations made in order to follow one particular creed, or ceremony, or law. Finally the loyalty to that particular religious system becomes its life, and this leads to the neglect—not only neglect, but actual hatred—of the religion followed by others. It is in this way that all wars, all differences that have existed from all time, have arisen.

When one studies nature, one finds that nature cannot create itself without expressing its religion. The origin of all religion is love and beauty. If there were no love or beauty religion would never have come, because beauty is the beginning of worship and prayer. The beginning of prayer is admiration. The first step of worship is admiration.

A child knows nothing about religion, and from the very first it is attracted to something that is beautiful, something that it can like. As it grows older it is only the form of its wants that changes; it still seeks to acquire the object of beauty. As it grows older still, it comes to recognize beauty in intellectual things. It is beauty that a person bows down to. When one gives honor and respect and reverence to another it is still because of the beauty that one perceives in some form or other in a person, and one has a natural inclination to bow before this beautiful living thing. Prayer and worship are acts of bowing to beauty, acts necessary to satisfy the predisposition with which every soul is born—the predisposition that is called love. And it is the innate desire of love to satisfy itself by admiring and bowing before someone, to respect someone, to have veneration for someone, to worship someone.

People go step-by-step from simple worship to the worship of the Most High, as they realize a higher and higher ideal. We can see this when we study the history of religions. It is the desire to pay respect, the desire to idealize, that has made people worship idols or worship trees. Some people consider a certain tree sacred. And even in bowing before trees the desire of love is satisfied, its desire to humble itself, its desire to pay respect and reverence; and by this means the love of the heart has its outlet. Such people are not evolved enough to know where God is; God is not before their eyes as this idol is. How can one be known who is not seen? Therefore people bow before beautiful flowers, beautiful herbs, beautiful trees in the forest. Others bow before rocks that have a certain form that attracts them and produces in them the desire to use this particular rock as the object to bow before, thus bringing satisfaction to the soul's desire to bow and pay respect.

Then, as intelligence developed still more, people would perceive that sometimes they were higher than the rock before which they previously bowed. They thought, "That rock is low; we can touch it; we can reach the top of it; there are a thousand others like it." Therefore they came to think, "It is best to worship the sun, because there can be nothing higher than the sun. We cannot get near it. There is nothing as bright as the sun. When the sun appears, does it not take away all our gloom, and worries, and all the fears of the dark night also? It takes away all the conditions of death and destruction, as thieves, robbers, tigers, and lions in countrysides and villages—all clear away when the sun rises; and then a new life begins, strength comes, vigor comes, energy comes, enthusiasm to go out in the world comes. This is the one object that takes away fear, and this is what, when it goes away, allows us to be afraid again and hide in our little villages."

And this worship of the sun lasted a long time. In places like Persia and in places like eastern Russia, where there is always sun but always need of a fire, the people sought refuge from the cold weather by sitting near the fire. The light of the fire becomes company in loneliness, the heat of the fire brings comfort, the light takes away fear, the heat purifies everything that comes into it. So that is how in those countries where there is cold they call fire sacred, and bow before it in obedience to the same innate yearning to bow and pay respect.

But people ascended still higher until they began to think, "No, no; the sun that goes away and comes back, appears and disappears, this is not constantly with us. So I will seek something that is constantly with us." And what is that? Surely it is the imagination. Surely it is a spirit that is God. In Mongolia and China and in all those Eastern countries where there are numberless gods worshipped, they say "That one thing that lasts through day and night, through trouble and sorrow, through joy and sadness, that thing, that spirit—that is God."

Then comes the time when the ruling power is seen in every object, in every being, in every plant, in every star—a controlling power ruling so many diverse objects. Thus it came about that the heroes were respected, rulers were worshipped, and even every planet or star was thought to represent a separate god. This ideal of worship was developed among the Greeks and Hindus.

Then we come to the Semitic race, the race from which the beginning of the Bible is to be traced, the children of Israel. Abraham noticed people around him worshipping idols, people worshipping symbols, and people worshipping sacred cows, or beasts, or birds. He pondered about God, thinking, "No, if you are anywhere, you must be somewhere within me, and I want to find you." Once, lying awake, he repeated God's name, and as he thus thought about God he sought some sign of that One who is really worthy of worship. Again, in his visions, he saw the star, and arose to ask, "Are you the God?" And the answer came from within: "It is not God. It comes and goes, for it is not stable nor steady. An object that is worthy of worship must be constantly before me." Then, next day, he saw the moon and asked, "Are you the God?" And the answer came, "No, for the moon takes its light from the sun." Then he saw the sun and asked the same question, and the answer came, "No, that which appears or disappears, however perfect in its light and form, cannot be the eternal God." And thus he perceived that God is a higher ideal than the sun, or moon, or anything that words can ever express; a God who is unseen and without form and without name, altogether beyond human conception. That is how that ideal of "one God" began.

This great ideal came through different prophets, and was expressed in different ways. If Moses said, "One God; no other gods but me," Jesus Christ said, "Not only one God, but one Life also; the whole manifestation is one."[1] The sun is not what we see; there is the sun, there is the manifestation that we see, and there is that which proceeds from the sun—all three aspects of the one. "I and my Father are one." "That which proceeds from the Father and the Son is one"[2]—all three aspects that create a puzzle in the human mind; one can remain in this puzzle all one's life. There is the thing itself, there is its manifestation, and there is that which proceeds from it, always this trinity in one. In all ages the message was given with truth and wisdom as each messenger came, but how could all understand the truth when not everybody has been able even to understand another? Language can hardly express it, and it is hard to understand.

The same difficulty arose at the time of Muhammad. He said to his people, who were the worshippers of so many gods, "There is no god but One God." They asked, "Where is God? Is God in our temples? Is God in the Kaʿba?' He said, "No, God's temple is in the human heart."—"How far away is God?"—"God is nearer to you than yourself."—"In what can we find God?"—"In all things and all beings."—"What is God's sign?"—"God is beyond all signs and yet all are God's signs. God cannot be restricted to one center, or one form, or one name, because all names are God's names, all forms are God's form, all in heaven or earth are God's beings, and there is only One!"

If you want to find God you will find God in the higher intelligence. When intelligence manifests itself on the surface, that is God. In manifesting God's being, God has assumed various forms; through each of these God seeks gradually to attain to the same state of absolute being. Every form—rock, animal, bird, human, everyone—is always striving to climb to the surface. The Bible says, "Raise your light on high; it is covered

1. See 1 John 1:2.
2. John 10:30; 15:26.

under a bushel."[3] The bushel is the manifestation of our life; all these forms that cover the inner intelligence, which in its original aspect is the root of being, are the bushel. The inner intelligence, the light, has become veiled under the manifestation, and it is the desire of nature to unfold it again, so as to allow it to behold its original being, which it does by all changes that take the form of death and destruction.

This great truth, so difficult to express, must needs be uttered by every prophet, every teacher, every saint who has brought the message, in that language that the hearers could understand. If the teacher perceived that the method used by the hearers was good, that teacher would advise them to continue in the same mode of worship, to continue to go into such a temple, or such a church, until they were able to perceive what is the real truth hidden behind all these things.

Having grasped the idea of God, there comes the question of the mode of worshipping God. Religion offers many ways of worship. Various religions offer many modes of worship that have become the law of each religion, and how can that law be obeyed by the whole world? Let us ask the ministers of any religion—of Islam, of Christianity, of Buddhism, of Hinduism—whether their own law can become the law for the religion of the whole world. Though each one of them will say yes, yet surely it is not meant to be so. All are not alike; the tendencies of each people are not alike; their habits are not alike. For instance, the law of the Hindu is to go to the Ganges in the morning and bathe in it. How would that do in London? How would one bathe in the Thames in December before offering one's prayers? You will perceive at once that no one could do such a thing. Again, Muslims obey the law of leaving their shoes outside the mosque, and then go to wash their hands and feet, and make their ablutions in running water; then they go and stand on the marble floor of the mosque, and offer up their

3. Matthew 5:15.

prayers. If the same mode of worship were to be the law for Russia, where there is so much cold and snow underfoot that to prostrate oneself on the marble would mean to be frozen to death in one day; and then one would never live to take the name of any religion again.

In this way we see that it cannot be that the one faith and religion and law can be promoted and advocated in all the different lands and places alike. The different faiths are bound to become unrecognized and forgotten, and those who wish to promote their own customs would cease to imagine such a thing, could they realize that every person has a different temperament, that every form of religion is a form of worship of the same God. Nature teaches every soul to worship God in some way or other, and often provides that which is suitable for each. Those who want one law to govern all have lost sight of the spirit of their own religion. And it is in people who have not yet learned their own religion that such ideas are commonly found. Did they but know their own religion, how tolerant they would become, and how free from any grudge against the religion of others!

So it is, too, with the manner of worship. It does not matter in what way people offer their respects and their reverence to the deity they worship. It only matters how sincere they are in their offering. In the one house of God we find people are without their hats; in Hindustan, Persia, and Arabia, they put on turbans to go to the mosque. That is their custom. It makes no difference whether some people pray standing, some sitting, some kneeling, some prostrating themselves, some in company with other people, and some alone. All that matters is that the heart of the worshipper is pure, that the mind is connected with God, that there is sincerity and earnestness.

There is a story that a farmer's boy, who was taking care of his father's cattle in the jungle, had heard a teacher of religion in his village. This teacher was teaching about God and glorifying the name of God. The young boy was so impressed that when he went to the jungle next time, he experienced that innate tendency to worship someone, and so, in the jungle, he began to say aloud, "Oh, God, I have heard so much about You; You are so good and kind that I feel that if You were here by me I would take such good care of You, more than of all my sheep, more than of all my fowls. In the rain I would keep You under the roof of my grass shed; when it was cold, I would wrap You in my blanket, and in the heat of the sun I would give You a bath. I would put You to sleep with Your head on my lap, and I would fan You with my hat, and I would always watch You and guard You from wolves. I would give You bread of manna, and would give You buttermilk to drink; and to entertain You I would sing and dance and play my flute. O God, come and see how I would tend You." Then Moses, the messenger of God, came up, and heard all that the boy said, and answered, "Oh boy, how foolish is this conversation! God, the Unknown and Unseen, who is in the heavens, the One before whom there is no might, no strength that can stand, that one is almighty; the might is all God's. God is beyond form and name and color; God is beyond human perception and comprehension."

The boy was disheartened, and afraid of what he had done. But the next message from God to Moses was, "We are very displeased indeed with you that you have separated a devotee who did not know us. If he did not know us as you do, at least he knew us as far as his mind could grasp. All our devotees picture us in different forms and according to different qualities of love, and we receive their love through whatever form or garb it is directed to us. They are all our creatures, and we receive it even if they worship the sun. We have sent you to unite our children to us, and not to separate them from us."

How we would keep our wisdom covered, did we only realize that the first step of approach to God is sincerity and earnest love for God! We should never call anyone heathen or pagan. We should never consider anybody in this world as unworthy. We do not know in what form a person is worshipping God.

We do not know the earnestness in a person's heart; yet that is the real thing.

Now, coming to the law about right and wrong, it is not only the learned, or so-called educated and enlightened persons who perceive the meaning of the law of right and wrong. Even among savages there is some sense of it, because it is an instinct; it is the law by which the savage lives. We may think many people are doing wrong, yet we do not know what is wrong for them and what is not wrong; we do not know what is right for them and what is not right. We ourselves may be doing many things that we think right, but really are wrong to others; and things that appear to us to be wrong others do, and yet are acting rightly in their case. It is just a matter of looking at it from the point of view that the other has.

How few there are in this world who stop to think whether the actions of another are right for that person. We are so ready to accuse another, and we are so ready to hide our own faults. Did we but apply to them the decision between right and wrong from *their* standpoint, we should find that the meaning of right and wrong would change. It is wrong for a little child to go out without asking its parents, because perhaps it will meet a motorcar from which it cannot protect itself. But can the same thing be wrong for a grown-up? It is only during the age of childhood that the act is wrong, in the later age it is right.

Did we but study the object of life, we should come to understand the nature of right and wrong; and once we knew the nature of right and wrong we would not need to consult the law of scripture, for that law of scripture would itself then begin to reveal its own truth to us. Nature herself can tell us what is right and wrong for us and for another.

The secret of it all is found in the answer to the question: "Why are humans here?" The answer is, "They are here to attain the satisfaction of their innermost desire." And what is that innermost desire? It is first joy, then peace. But the attainment of each is contrary, because joy comes from activity of life, and peace comes from rest.

All this activity that persons experience and enjoy by their senses is a glimpse of joy. The greater joy comes when they can experience through their inner self also, through their mind. For there is another joy, that of the mind when it is delighted with a thing of truth or delicacy, or a beautiful thought. Beautiful music, beautiful verse, beautiful imagination—all bring delight. It is perhaps a greater joy than the joy of a delicious dish, for some persons would give anything for a verse that they would never give for a delicious dish.

But there is a still greater joy, that of the heart, the innermost being of a person—the joy when this heart can express itself and experience love. There are many in this world who only live in the body; their heart is dead, their mind is dead; they seek their highest joy only in the body. But there are others who live in mind as well as in body. It is like the difference between a thoughtful person and an ordinary person. When one is thoughtful one has become a different person. This view is expressed by the words *gentleman* or *gentlewoman*. There are very few who could be truly called such, though many pass for such. The gentleman or gentlewoman is one who is beginning to live in his or her mind, whose mind is becoming alive, who enjoys life too, yet is not delighted merely with the experience of the senses.

But one whose heart is awakened is higher than a gentleman or gentlewoman. Such a one can sympathize with another; their sympathies are awake to consider another, to think for another, to serve another, to sacrifice for another. They are not merely gentlemen and gentlewomen; they are saints. The power of sympathy and love takes away the gross self that used to demand all for itself. Once that is taken away, a person thinks far higher. "Whatever I can do for another, that will I do; I will sacrifice all I have; the loss is no matter; it is a satisfaction." To satisfy the heart, what a thing it is! This also is a part of joy, but it is not peace.

Joy is the desire of attainment by the world; peace is the attainment of heaven. In the ordinary sense we call it peace to be at rest in an armchair, on cushions, or in bed. But when the body is on a beautiful couch, does that mean that the mind is resting on cushions also? Cannot the mind go through torture at the same time? If that be the case, of what benefit is the peace and comfort of the body? The whole being must have peace. The mind must have peace from anxieties, worry, the greed that gives us ambitious desires and that we call "wrong" and "sin." When all this has gone, the mind is at rest. Then, when the heart is at peace and has done its work of love, the heart has enough; it ceases to be interested in any particular object in life, but is equal toward all. When there is no demand there is peace, and this peace helps toward peace of the soul.

These are the two desires that we hold. It is when we do not know the manner in which to attain these two desires that sometimes the joy of one part of our being takes away the peace of the other; the peace of one part of our life takes away the joy of the other part of our being. It is when one once knows this that one is able really to master oneself, to manage one's life's affairs as one wishes, to have a better idea of what is right and what is wrong, what is sin and what is virtue.

This knowledge is gained through a study of life rather than of books. If we only knew how much the study of life can tell us! One could go into the British Museum and read every book in the building, and yet might not obtain satisfaction. It is not study, it is not research, it is not enquiry, that gives this knowledge; it is actually going through the experiences of life, witnessing life in its different aspects and in its difference phases or spheres—that is what reveals the ideal of life.

One may know about the whole world's doings, saying to oneself, "In the morning I will go from my home to the office, and shall find out all about the world from my paper before

I go." But all one has learnt is what the newspapers feed one with; for next day, how often is the news of today contradicted! Still one is satisfied, thinking one has learned so much about the world in the morning. And in the evening one is ready to discuss topics at the dinner table. And next day there is again something fresh. But is that knowledge?

How wonderful is the sight that is given to us, how marvelous is the mind, how great a treasure is the light of the soul! Can this be intended only for things like that? If we only knew the value of our life, the value of our soul, we would give the precious time that is ours to keen observation with calm perception, combining the attitude of a student with the care of a scientist.

Look not on life as a person would watch a play on the stage; rather look upon it as a student who is learning in college. It is not a "passing show"; it is not a place of amusement in which to fool our life away. It is a place for study, in which every sorrow, every heartbreak brings a precious lesson; it is a place in which to learn by the suffering of oneself by the study of the suffering of another, to learn from the people who have been kind to us as well as from the people who have been unkind to us; it is a place in which all experiences—be they disappointments, struggles, and pains, or joys, pleasures, comforts, and everything of the kind—contribute to the understanding of what life is, and realizing what it is.

Then do we awake to the religion of nature, the only religion. And the more you understand it, the greater your life becomes, and the more blissful will your life be for others.

3

THE PERSONALITY OF GOD

That ethical view of God that conceives of God as a personality is really a conception of the self; the divine love, power, and inspiration are really within oneself. But when those who have not truly studied and understood the subject of God's personality begin to talk about it, they are apt to destroy the religious beliefs of many besides their own. Not only are they apt to go astray themselves, through failing to assimilate the knowledge from the ethical point of view, but they will also confuse others in their faiths and beliefs.

After reading a few ethical books and after considering the Christ-idea from the ethical point of view, and the idea of God from that point of view, a person may go and tell a friend who has simple faith in Jesus Christ and has never considered "ethics" or science or philosophy, but has always held a picture of the Lord before him or her, fearing to displease the Lord, being devoted to him—such a person may go and tell this friend, "There is no such thing as Jesus Christ; he never came on earth; it is a myth; it is an ideal; it is an ethical ideal." What happens? The plant of devotion, the ideal in the heart, the plant that leads one further and further in development, is broken by this person, and the friend is driven either to shut the doors of the heart, which should be kept protected, or must give up his or her faith. To yield is to go astray, and yet not to yield may be to go astray also.

There is a danger, then, of an ethical point of view destroying one's own religion and understanding; and there is a greater danger of its doing so in the case of the religion of others.

The Sufi always tries to keep the ideal of God, not only as a philosophy, but as a religious philosophy. It has always been garbed with religion so that it might not be a bare truth of the ideals of a master, a savior, a god. For of all those who have the ethical point of view there may perhaps not be one in a thousand who has experienced trouble, distress, sorrow, and the pains of life in such a way as to be able to use this ethical knowledge in his or her life. The majority of people with an aptitude for study obtain the ethical knowledge, but proceed to criticize their own religion or that of others, and endeavor to destroy the faith that others have—such is human nature.

It is human nature to take others and lead them astray from their path. It is rare for one to ask oneself, "Have I gone astray? I will at least not mislead another." The true parent would think like that. He or she would say, "My children shall be happier; they shall not make the mistakes that we have made." So, once the love of humankind has developed in one's heart, one begins to understand other people as parents do their children, and to say to oneself, "If others lead you astray, at least I will not do so."

In reality, the ideal of God is a bridge connecting the limited life with the unlimited. Whoever travels over this bridge passes safely from the limited to the unlimited life. The bridge may be taken away, it is true, and yet one may swim across the chasm, but one may be drowned too. The ideal of God is a safe bridge that takes you safely to the goal.

There are four paths or stages that lead a person into spiritual knowledge from the limited to the unlimited.

The first stage is *shariat*. This is where the God-ideal is impressed upon humankind as authority, which refers to fear of God. This really means conscientiousness, not fear, as is usually thought. If you have love, you do not wish to displease; love does not force you to an act, but it asks you to be conscientious and take care not to cause the least disharmony with the one whose happiness you want. The first lesson is to idealize someone who is beyond the personalities of earth, more than mortal, a protector more than a father, guardian, king; mightier than the nations; richer than all the supermillionaires in this world. Wonderful though the goodness is that one sees in a mother, causing you to say, "Yes, she is kind and merciful," it is nothing compared with the perfection of kindness and mercy in God. That which attracts you to the mother is limited; unlimited mercy and kindness are only to be seen in God. We perceive that all things that give protection, peace, fear, or love are only found in their perfection in the one ideal, that is, in God.

Such persons offer their prayers, worship God, think of God, hold the ideal in their mind; and a kind of connection comes to be established between them and the ideal, so that in times of depression, of despair, of sorrow and helplessness they have the ideal within immediate reach. They can say, "I know someone greater, a greater friend than anyone in the world, to whom all respect and worship and humility is due."

This stage of shariat is where people think, "What will please God, or displease God?" They learn their religion from their parents, their friends. A good action pleases, a bad action displeases, and pride displeases most; they learn everything very easily by what displeases another. How easy it is; and still they go to a clergyman or to a priest to ask, "What pleases God?" And all the time it is just what pleases them that pleases God, and therefore if you please all around you, you please God; if you displease them, you displease God. Such persons realize what reward comes to them when they please the world, and what happens when they do not. Just think of the peaceful state of those who have done some good to another, what condition is theirs when they retire to bed at night, what joy, what peace, what sense of safety! Whereas those who have harmed another, stolen something, caused trouble or pain, their punishment is with them also. The reward and the punishment can be seen in one's own day; there is no need to wait for heaven or hell; every day is heaven or hell once we realize what reaction one's own works bring on oneself.

The next stage is called *tariqat*. In this stage one finds what it is that really matters; what it is that is really wrong, and what it is that is really right; how some wrong is hidden under what people call right, and right is hidden under what we call wrong. It is now that a person begins to understand the nature of things. What the whole world calls wrong may be right. Although one pleases the world, at the same time one thinks of the pleasure of God first. One goes on until instead of finding the pleasure of God in the world, one also finds it in one's own being, by one's own conscience, by one's own intelligence. One also begins to be able to say, "Yes, it is true there is a Creator, it is true I am a creature; but at the same time where has God created me from? Whence has God created the whole world? Is it from God's own self or from substance, and if substance has existed, where did that come from?

Having begun to think in this way one begins to find that if there is any substance, it is something that God made out of God's own self. One can see that by considering one's own thoughts. When one notices that a thought has come to one to do such a thing—where was it before? How did it arise? Surely, your mind has in that case created something out of nothing, or out of yourself. Mind is one thing, thought is one thing, but at the same time, the thought is of the mind, the mind has created the thought, and yet the thought is not another substance, it is the substance of mind itself. But the mind as the knower of the thought and the creator of the thought stands at the back of the thought, and when the thought has disappeared the mind is there just the same. When the thought has gone the mind is still there. So it is with God. God has created all things; they are sustained a certain time and then lost from human sight, but at the same time they have come from God, they are lost from God, and God remains the same.

This then is the second stage, where the person understands the Creator.

The third stage is that of *haqiqat*. It is in this stage that one begins to realize the truth of the whole being. "The one whom I have called God, and whose personality I have recognized and whose pleasure or displeasure I have sought," this one—one begins to discover—"has been seeing life through my eyes, has been hearing through my ears; it was God's breath that came through my breathing, God's impulse that I felt, and therefore I know that this body that I had held in my mind to be my own I really find is the true temple of God. I did not realize that this body is the shrine of God." Not knowing that God experiences this life through the human being, one is seeking for God somewhere else—in some person aloof and apart from the whole world, whereas all the time God is in oneself.

It is not meant that such a person is to set to work to break people's beliefs, and say that God is both in heaven and in the human body. People would answer, "If God is in my body, I will no longer worship that God. I thought God was pure and in the heavens, and if God dwells in my body, that idea I cannot bear for one moment." That person will be frightened and go astray. That is why in India it is considered a great sin to awaken anyone who is asleep. If a person is asleep, do not wake them; let them sleep; it is the time for them to sleep; it will not do to wake them before their time.

So, too, a mystic understands that those who are taking their time to awaken must not be awakened to give them the mystic's idea; it is a sin, because they are not prepared to understand it, and their beliefs would be shaken. Let them go on thinking God is in Benares; let them think God is in the temple of Buddha; let them think God is in heaven; let them think God is in the seventh heaven above the sky. It is the beginning; they will evolve in time to arrive at the same stage. The rest they are having just now is good for them. The awakening comes, all in its good time.

This explains what is meant by saying Sufism is a religious philosophy; the philosophy is garbed with religion, that it may not break the ideals and faiths and beliefs of those who are beginning their journey to the goal. Externally the religion, inwardly the philosophy. The one who wants to understand will understand. "He who hath ears to hear, let him hear."[1]

It also explains why people in the past have pictured their philosophy as myths, as did the Hindus and the Greeks in their stories of gods and goddesses. And even in the carvings in wood and stone, as at Elephanta and elsewhere, truths are represented in pictures, which convey to the seer and the reader the truths underlying all religions.

The fourth stage is *maʿrifat*. This is the knowledge that enables those who have arrived at it to call God "Truth." They apply no other name to God but only truth; in the end of their journey they have found the divine light that is truth, the light illuminating their whole being, the whole universe; and even if a thousand universes were there, they would be illuminated by it.

In the Bible it is said, first there was the Word, and there was Light.[2] That means that the first or highest knowledge is the truth. Light gives knowledge, words give knowledge; in fact, it is knowledge. The Qurʾan says, "Allah is the light of the heaven and the earth."[3] That means that illumination to which one reaches.

The story of Aladdin, who went in search of the lamp, teaches the same lesson. In the end you arrive at the stage where in the shrine of God you find the light, the light of truth that illuminates all your life, the light that suffices the whole being. When this light comes, all the fear of God, the confusion, the

1. Matthew 11:15.
2. See John 1:1–5, and Genesis 1:3.
3. Qurʾan 24:35.

puzzle are gone, because all such things are due to the lack of light. Whatever difficulty there was before us would not disappoint us if there were a light for us to see through it. That which breaks the heart or brings despair is a difficulty or a trouble that we cannot see through; that means that our trouble in life is always the lack of light and nothing else; that every difficulty can be solved, and if we understand the nature of our difficulty, we can see our way through. It is the lack of light that keeps us from seeing into our trouble, as well as the way out of it, and it is the light that gives us the power to see into our difficulty as well as shows the way out of it.

Therefore what we need in our life is the lamp of Aladdin. That is what is gained at the fourth stage of development, which is called *maʿrifat*.

4

SILENT LIFE

When we look at the universe we find there are two aspects of existence: first, life, and second, the condition that, compared with what we call life, seems to be lifeless. The one aspect of existence we call life, the other aspect we overlook. We divide it according to periods and call it time, or we compare it with objects and call it space.

We say, "This is alive," when the object shows some activity and consciousness, meaning that it can move and see and think. An object that cannot see and is not active we call dead. Whatever it is that seems to be void of activity and consciousness is called a thing; when it has consciousness and activity, it is called living.

Where is the source of this consciousness and activity? The circulation of the blood, the energy of the movements of the body, the activity of the nerves and muscles—if we could only know what it is that keeps them in action. A person may say it goes on mechanically like a clock; but the clock is not the source of the movement. The mind is the source of the clock; the mind has made the clock, has thought about it, has wound it; it continues to depend on the human to keep it going. Therefore behind "clock" is a "human." Even if it only wants winding once a year, still there is a human behind it, whom you do not see.

It is the same with the whole mechanism of nature—all is mechanical and runs according to certain laws, and yet there is a source or origin of things hidden behind it all. As artists are hidden behind their art, as scientists are hidden behind their inventions, as the mind is hidden behind the body, as the cause is hidden behind the action, so there is one aspect of life that is hidden behind the other aspect of life, which alone is recognized as life.

Both science and religion show that consciousness has evolved through different stages, from mineral to vegetable, from vegetable to animal, and from animal to humanity. It is regarded as the achievement of modern science that this thought has been reached, but its source lies in the traditions of the past. Rumi's *Masnavi* tells us about the experience of consciousness from the mineral up to the plant:

> I died as a mineral, and rose a plant,
> I died as plant, and rose again an animal,
> I died as an animal, and rose a man.
> Why then should I fear to become less by dying?
>
> I shall die once again as a man,
> To rise an angel, perfect from head to foot.
> Again, when I suffer dissolution as an angel,
> I shall become what passes the conception of man.

Science stops today at the human, but the poem says, "From man I shall rise to an angel, and from angel I shall ascend to that stage of being that passes human comprehension." This poem was written in the thirteenth century.

That proves Solomon's saying, "There is nothing new under the sun."[1] We discover something today, but in reality we only bring to light something that existed in the past, either as history or as tradition. Even before Rumi, the idea was in the Qur᾿an.

1. Ecclesiastes 1:9.

What can we learn from this? Every activity that we call "life" has sprung from a source that is silent, and will always be silent; and every activity that is different in its aspect and peculiar to itself and different in its effect, is still the activity of a tiny part of that life that is as wide as the ocean. Call it world, universe, nation, country, race, community, or one individual—or only a particle, an atom—its activity, its energy springs in each case from one inseparable and eternal silent aspect of life.

And it has not only sprung from it, but it resolves itself into it also. You throw a pebble into the water, water that is still and calm; there comes an activity, it comes for one moment, and then it vanishes. Into what does it vanish? It vanishes into the same silence in which the water was before; and as the water is a substance that is active by nature, and the silence, the stillness, the calmness that it shows is just the original state, the effect of its original source. This means that the natural inclination of every thing and every being is silence, because it has come from silence. And yet it is active, because it is activity that produces activity; and its end is silence.

Therefore, sages, mystics, and philosophers who have probed into the depths of life have seen that what we call life is death, and that what we call no life is the real life.

A Hindustani poet says, "Raise your eyes, friend, from this that you call life to that which perhaps you do not recognize as life, and then you will find that what you had once called life is nothing but death, and what you thought was nothing, in reality, is life."

When you come to the essence of the teachings of Christ you will see that from the beginning to the end the whole attitude of the teacher is to tell humankind that there is a life beyond—higher than this life, higher in quality, not beyond in time—that which you call life and yet is not life.

The life you recognize is only the mortal aspect of life. You have never seen or been conscious of the immortal aspect at all. Once realize life, and what you have hitherto called life is found to be only a glimpse or shadow of the real life that is beyond comprehension. To understand it you will have to raise your light high from the cover that is covering it like a bushel. This cover is one's mind and body; it is a cover that keeps the light active on the world of things and beings. "Do not keep your light under a bushel"[2] means that we are not to keep the consciousness absorbed in the study of the external world, and in its pleasures and enjoyments. People are always apt to say religious thinkers are dreamers, lost in vague ideals, having no proof for what they believe, far from what they themselves would call the reality. They never think that what they call real has in its turn become unreal to those to whom the silent life has become reality. Can you call this life real that is subject to such changes every moment? Every activity and the object of everyone's life—riches, power, love, friendship, childhood, youth, health, pleasure, displeasure, happiness, poverty—all are changing, in some cases soon, in others late. Can you think such things are the reality? What can you call all this that is subject to change, whose source is unseen and whose end is unseen, subject to death and destruction, after which it is seen no more? Can you call it reality? Or are not the realities perhaps really behind the scene, from whence it came, and to which it goes?

Perhaps many of you have experienced at some time or other, in your own home, or in a church, or in a temple or other religious place, how there is a kind of silence as you sit there. Compared with a bazaar or market or factory there is no activity. Have you, under such circumstances, noticed the condition of your own self, of your mind, of your thought, of your body? If you have felt any comfort, have you thought why you feel comfort and rest? Then, take another experience. One may be a few moments or a few hours in the woods, away and apart from everybody. It may seem as if even the trees and the leaves

2. See Matthew 5:15, Mark 4:21, and Luke 8:16.

are keeping silence. The feelings that you have at such a time cannot be expressed in words. The feelings cannot be called pleasure because that which we are accustomed to in pleasure or in joy are not the same. You could only say, "That peculiar pleasure, that peculiar joy." There is no name for it, and yet it is a true experience of the soul.

Then there is a still greater and deeper experience: when a person is in a wilderness, near rocks in the desert, where there is no sound even of birds or beasts, when there is absolute silence. In the East, all the prophets from the time of Abraham, Moses, David, and in the time of Christ and Muhammad, all the prophets of the Old Testament and the New, and of the Qur᾿an, did they not receive their inspiration from the same source? The history of Moses on Mount Sinai, the Prophet of Nazareth in the wilderness, the Prophet Muhammad on Ghar-i Hira—did they not all drink from the silent life? Though God is in all activities and forms and names, it is in God's other aspect—solid, firm, eternal, all-sufficient and powerful, all-intelligent, undivided and inseparable—from which the inspiration came as a perfect inspiration, so that the world could take it as the sacred Word, in all ages and in all times.

Then, coming to the cause of idol worship, a person might think of the old custom of Brahmins and Buddhists, who went into the temple of Buddha or Krishna, and sat before an idol that neither spoke to them nor took notice of them—that person might think, "What could they gain? It has a mouth and speaks not, it has hands yet cannot move." And so people mocked at them, scoffed at them, and called them heathen and pagan. But they did not know of this silence that was impressed upon the worshipper. This human form sitting before them, silent and quiet, and not speaking, or hearing, or thinking, absolutely quiet—just think what it means.

When one is among friends one may get tired; sometimes one enjoys their society, but when one does not enjoy it, one thinks, "My life has gone from me." Why is this? It is the impression of their minds that has been produced in one's mind. Perhaps someone has insulted one, or snubbed one, or told one this or that, and one goes among friends bringing all one's troubles with one; and so one goes away still saying, "I am tired." If you are working in a factory, it is reasonable to be tired in body; but why should one be tired in society where people are laughing and chatting? It is because their condition of mind is not like yours.

But before the idol god there is perfect harmony. See, here is someone sitting and quiet. A quiet human form that does not speak, what rest! It may not help, but it does not disturb. It keeps you silent. That was the idea.

What do we learn from this? Every effort was made by the teachers of religion to waken people to that aspect of life that is overlooked in the ordinary life that they call "life." Concentration, contemplation, meditation—all that is the essence of religion or mysticism or philosophy—is nothing but this one thing: to attain to that depth of life that is the root of our life.

A Marathi poet has said, "O mind, my restless mind, my mind with its thoughts of a thousand things that it supposes will make it happy, saying, 'If I had that, I should be happy; if I had this, I should feel life was not wasted.' O, my mind, will you tell me who in this world is happy?" The mind says, "If I had the wealth that I see others have, I should be happy." But are they happy? *They* say, "If I had something still higher!"

The secret of happiness is hidden—hidden under the cover of spiritual knowledge. And this spiritual knowledge is nothing but this: that there is a constant longing in the human heart to have something of its origin, to experience something of its original state—the state of peace and joy that has been disturbed, and yet is sought after throughout one's whole life, and never can cease to be sought after until the real source has at length been realized. What was it in the wilderness that gave peace and joy? What was it that came to you in the forest, the solitude? In either case it is nothing else but the depth of your own life, which is silent like the depths of the great sea, so silent and still. It is the surface of the sea that makes waves and roaring breakers; the depth is silent. So the depth of your own being is silent also.

And this all-pervading, unbroken, inseparable, unlimited, ever-present, omnipotent silence corresponds with your silence like the meeting of flames. Something goes out of the depths of your being to receive something from there, which comes to meet you; your eyes cannot see and your ears cannot hear and your mind cannot perceive, because it is beyond the mind, thought, and comprehension. It is the meeting of the soul and the Spirit.

And therefore the idea of understanding the spiritual ideal is to attain to that state of being, of calm and peace and joy and everlasting happiness, which neither changes nor ceases to exist. It is to realize what is said in the Bible, "Be ye perfect even as your Father in heaven."[3] Those words do not tell us to be yet imperfect as everybody on earth. No, they mean the idea of all perfection, all unity, no separation. It is the opposite of the idea that religion should keep part of humanity separate, saying, "Do you belong to our church, our mosque, our temple?" It is the opposite of loyalty to this particular sect or community, to this particular sacred book, to this particular teaching, to this particular truth. The source of all truth, is it not hidden in every man's heart, be he Christian, Muslim, Buddhist, or Jew? Is each not part of that life that we call spiritual or divine? To be just this or that is the same as not going further than this or that. The bliss found in solitude is hidden within every human being; each has inherited it from his or her Heavenly Parent. In mystical words it is called the all-pervading light. Light is the source and origin of every human soul, of every mind.

Sufis look upon life as one life, upon all religions as their religion: call them Christian and they seek to be that, call them a

3. Matthew 5:48.

Muslim and they are that, a Hindu and they are that; call them whatever you like, they do not mind. It is not the thought of Sufis to be called anything. Who calls them Sufis? It is not them. If they do not call themselves something, someone else is sure to find a name for them. Cats and dogs do not declare their names; it is the human that gives them a name. If you call yourself "New Thought," it will be made into the name of a new sect some day; if you call yourself "Higher Thought," that will be a sect one day, if you call yourself what you will—philosophy, theosophy, religion, mysticism—it is only the one thing, it is nothing but the constant longing of the soul of the human being. After experiencing all different experiences of life, the life of activity, it is the longing to attain to that state of peace or calm that seems to be the only object that, in the end, the soul wishes to achieve.

A person may keep thinking, "Perhaps I shall be happy when I am a king, or rich, or an officer; then I shall gain my desire." No, as long as one has not got it, the sweetness of the thought lies only in the hope. As long as there is hope there is sweetness; after fulfilling the desire, the hope has gone. Then one hopes for something else. It is hope that is sweet, not the object. The object is never sweet; it is the sweetness of the hope that seems to make the object sweet. The whole sweetness is in the hope.

"If I could reach that height," one says. So long as one has not reached that height, the dream of reaching the height, of one day experiencing that position, experience, or imagination, the dream of being comforted with it, so long has one the sweetness of the hope. But when it has come, it has finished. Then begins a new hope, always hoping, hoping. And still behind it all is that one inclination, common to all, the inclination of which one does not know the nature. No person would live did they not have the hope of something for which they are waiting.

Hope is the only food of life. Then reason says, "Yes, I am looking forward to my change from this place to the next; to get my inheritance some day; then I shall be all right; I shall be all right when I get that position, that house, that comfort." It is the thing one has before one, imagining, building, preparing, and holding it in the mind all the time, and yet when one does get it, there is always another hope.

It is only those who are blessed by perceiving the origin and source of all things who awaken to the fact that the real inclination of every life is to attain to something not to be touched or comprehended or understood. The hidden blessing of this knowledge is the first step to perfection. Once awake to this fact, the person sees there is something in life that will make them really happy and give them their heart's desire. They can say, "Though there are many things in life that I need for the moment, and for which I shall certainly work, yet there is that one thing, the only central thing in life, the spiritual attainment, the religious attainment—the attainment of God, you may call it, perhaps—that will satisfy me." Such a one has found the key to all happiness, and has found that all the things one needs will be reached because one has the key of all. "Seek, and ye shall find; knock and it shall be opened to you. . . . Seek ye first the Kingdom of God, and all these things shall be added unto you."[4] This kingdom of God is the silent life; the life inseparable, eternal, self-sufficient, and all-powerful. This is the life of the wise, whatever be the name given to it; this is the life that the wise contemplate. It is the face of this life that they long to see; it is the ocean of this life that they long to swim in; as it is written, "In Him we live and have our being."[5]

These are the ones who are really happy, who are above all unhappiness, above death and the destruction of life.

4. Matthew 7:7, 6:33.
5. Acts 17:28.

5

THE WILL, HUMAN AND DIVINE

The will is the same, whether it be human or divine. The only difference is that in one aspect it is the whole, in the other aspect it is a part; in one aspect it is almighty, in the other it has only a certain might, or a certain power; in the one aspect it is unlimited, in the other it is limited.

The difference between the divine and the human will is like the difference between the trunk of a tree and its branches; and as from the boughs other branches and twigs spring, so the will of one powerful individual has branches going through the will of other individuals. In a tree there is a trunk, and there are some prominent or large branches; from these there spring many branches. So there are the powerful beings, the masters of humanity. Their will is God's, their word is God's word, and yet they are branches, because the trunk is the will of the Almighty. As the branches grow, so we too grow; as the branches develop, we develop; as the branches flourish, we flourish; as the branches bear fruit, we bear fruit; as the branches are capable of rising, we too rise. Whether the branch be large or small, every branch has the same origin and the same root as the stem. Therefore, whether a person be holy or wicked, wise or foolish, they have in their innermost spirit the same essence and the same power that the wise have. Therefore, there is no reason for people to feel discouraged by their weaknesses or deficiencies, or by their actions that have dissatisfied them, or by anything in life that has failed. They should forget the past that has failed them, and begin to construct and mold their future as they would wish it to be—considering that as a branch is not separate from the bough, and the bough is not separate from the stem, so with all our limitations we are not separate from the will of the Unlimited One.

In Sufi terms these two aspects of will are called *qaza* and *qadr*. Sometimes we think, "If we could see that friend it would be so pleasant," and at the same time there comes a desire, "If we could have some nice flowers," and then a friend comes bringing a bunch of our favorites. We desire to have fish to eat, and the cook brings a savory dish of fish. Sometimes this is due to the strength of one's own will, and sometimes it is the soul working in harmony with the divine will. One only knows when it is in harmony with the divine will and when not by noting the results, and the one who knows beforehand is the seer. Sometimes things are accomplished without the least effort. When it is the divine will it is like something floating on water; it advances without effort. Problems and actions may be achieved in one moment's time then, while at other times the smallest problem cannot be solved without great difficulty. In the case of some persons you find that they are very clever and experienced in industrial work or in politics; and they have striven very hard to attain their goal, and yet have accomplished nothing—they are always a failure. And there are others who take up a thing, and without much effort, without much worry on their part, they have finished and attained their goal. All this is accounted for by harmony with the divine will, everything is there; you just cast a glance toward the thing, and it is found. As there is a saying, "Word spoken, action done." When we strive with all the material in our hands, and yet cannot achieve our desire, that is when the matter is contrary to the divine will. Our success or failure all depend upon the harmony or disharmony of our individual will with the divine will.

But if our individual will is a branch of the divine will, if its source is the same, how can it ever be out of harmony? At some times the hand sympathizes with the foot, at other times it does not. We hurt ourselves many times just because of disharmony; we may cut ourselves—our fingers, for instance. If then, I, who am one person, can cause harm to myself, and suffer thereby, why should it not be possible that the human will should be out of harmony with the divine, so that the divine suffers thereby? It is possible to act contrary to the divine will, even though one is only a branch of it. In a fountain there is a big stream that flows up and then breaks into many drops. The stream is like the divine will, and the different drops like the wills in us. One drop goes higher, another lower, one falls to the left, another to the right, one goes north, another south. But the source of all this activity is one; it is one thing that turns into so many, scattering into all directions. Thus from unity there has come variety.

The sages have therefore taught the part played by contentment. It is said, "Resist not evil," and yet how many give in to evil instead. The real meaning of the scripture is this: suppose a person is angry with us, if we partake of their anger we resist them; the fire that they set alight in our minds we allow to become alight in ourselves, and we have resisted. Do not resist evil in that way. Do not partake of the evil of another. If you are quiet and calm, your calmness and quietness will make a greater effect on the other than their anger, so that true resistance is practice of contentment. Patience is the best quality that a person can cultivate. We are always apt to become excited or annoyed because another person does not understand us. Why get excited if they cannot understand us? If a person is foolish or cannot do things right, by becoming excited we make them still more foolish, still more stupid. We cannot help them in that way, and we partake of their quality by allowing ourselves to oppose them. If we kept our mind tranquil, if we had patience, we should keep in harmony. Harmony is the greatest thing to learn in life. All the disagreement between couples, friends, people in business, and politics—all comes from lack of patience. If we just had patience and contentment, we could teach ourselves much better.

Contentment teaches resignation. But this resignation is not exactly what people mean by fate. The true recognition of fate is as the drop realizing that it is foolish to fight against the ocean. The drop is part of the ocean. Why want to fight it? If the drop does not resign itself, of what profit will it be? Why think, "What I think is right, and no one can rightly think otherwise"? We should remember that another person does not see as we see, because people see only a reflection of the highest ego that works unconsciously in them. To that one it is right, but in the view of the other it need not appear right. It is only right for the one person, for that one moment; later it may not appear so. The limited being cannot claim the perception of the Unlimited. Therefore we cannot regard our own will to be the universal will, unless our will is harmonious with the will of God. We should therefore practice harmonizing our will with that of our fellow humans, by tolerance, patience, endurance; because in this world every ego is working for itself, however near or dear another may be. Everyone thinks, "What can I make another person do for me?" They want everybody to be harmonious with their way in life. That is why there is a world full of rebellion, like the thorns in the rosebush.

It may seem a great sacrifice and torment to do the other way, but it is the only way to get out of the whirlpool; it is the only way that one can conquer life's difficulties. If anybody has ever conquered, they have only done so by this means, never by the means of resistance, but always by the way of resignation. All teachers have taught this way, saying, "Prostrate thyself on the ground; prostrate thyself before God; kneel down." Some of us neglect to appreciate this, but the messengers do not leave anything unspoken; it is we who do not understand what they say. People fight for their religions; if we were just to learn the *one* instead! The question should always be: have we learned our own religion? To have learned it means to practice it and see its benefit. However you may try to run away from it, you will still find this lesson to learn. You have to make yourself strong and prepared to withstand all that befalls you. Therefore develop your willpower first by such morals, and be able to harmonize your will with the others. One thinks one can develop willpower by fighting, but that is not so, because by fighting you make very little progress; by fighting with yourself you progress a hundred times more. Your greatest enemy is yourself. All weakness, all ignorance keeps you from the truth of your being, from all the virtues hidden in you and all perfection hidden in your soul. The first self we realize is the false self. Unless the soul is born again it will not see the kingdom of heaven. The soul is first born into the false self; it is blind. In the true self the soul opens its eyes. Unless the false self is fought with, the true self cannot be realized. Therefore endurance is necessary, patience is necessary.

If we could fight with ourselves and make ourselves such as can give pleasure! Sages are as harmonious to a pious person as to a wicked one, as harmonious to a wise person as to a foolish one, to a rich person as to a poor one. We feel friendly toward some, not toward others; we get on well with some, but with others there is always disharmony. With some, everyone feels peaceful and happy.

The lions could not harm Daniel because of the harmony of his will with the universal will. The lions represent the destructive elements in the human mind. They represent wars, disappointments, rivalries, jealousies, envy, passions, and so forth, in different horrible guises. Our ego is the lion of lions, and if this is conquered, then these external lions—the different egos around us—are conquered also; and wherever you go, with all, whether foolish or wise, good or bad, you now have rest.

To learn the lesson of how to live is more important than any psychic or occult learning. Every day we think we have learnt the lesson, but if we knew it, the world would have become a heaven for us by now. We may seek the higher knowledge or the higher things, but the very smallest thing, the control of all the creatures of the mind, seems as nothing to the higher knowledge, yet once learnt and acted upon would be greater than all. This is a great step. How difficult to gain this, how reasonless it seems! But when we pause to think of the difference between ourselves and animals, we see the greatness in this simple thing of yielding the will. If there is one animal in a place and another one comes to it, the first one wants to bite or bark, or even drive the other out of its sight. A dog will do that even though it has finished its dinner and does not want to eat the food that has attracted the hungry dog to the place.

There is an Eastern parable of a dog traveling to a certain town. His journey was a very long one, taking two or three days as a rule, and yet he arrived before sunset of the same day. They were all very surprised to see him so soon. (In India the dogs live together a great deal, without belonging to anybody in particular; this is possible because of the kindness the people show them.) "Yes, it is a very long journey," he said, "but I attribute my speed to the kindness and help of my fellow dogs. Since I left home, whenever I felt tired and tried to stop a moment to rest, four or five would run up and bark at me and want to bite me. So I had to run on without staying to rest in that place, or to search for food. And so it went on at every place I came to, until in the end I have arrived here at my destination." This illustrates the animal nature. A human's selfishness shows itself in wanting to get the better of one's fellow humans. If we developed humanity we should do differently. We should be satisfied with a slice of bread if there were another in need, but as it is, it happens that even when we are fed ourselves, we do not wish anyone else to share the food. The human heart can only be satisfied by knowing that the other person is happy. True pleasure lies in the sharing of joy with another. From that day, we begin to act as human beings; and hitherto we have not done so even though we have human forms.

Sages have always repented of all things that make them animal. It is human beings that repent; it is the animals that are pleased with everything that they do. The Bible says, "Repent, for the kingdom of God is at hand."[1] This has to be done all day long. Once realize that, and the kingdom of God is at hand. Sinners can become righteous at any moment if they make up their mind; the difficulty is to make it up. The next thing is to carry it out. Revolutions and harmony, war and peace—all are parts of a whole being. But contentment and perfect resignation open up a harmonious feeling and bring the divine will into harmony with our own. Our blessing now becomes a divine blessing, our words divine words, our atmosphere a divine atmosphere, although we seem to be limited beings; for our will becomes absorbed into the whole, and so our will becomes the will of God.

1. Matthew 3:2 and Matthew 4:17.

6

MIND, HUMAN AND DIVINE

The mind is not the brain, but that faculty, that intangible and unperceivable activity of which the brain is merely a vehicle. Humans limit things that are unlimited and beyond their power of measurement, and therefore they have pictured God in human form or given a sacredness to the forms of animals. A person of larger mind has a larger view, and perhaps sees good in everybody, whereas one with a mind always desiring to find some evil will be able to find a spot of evil even in a good person. That means, from childhood onward people are accustomed to measure and understand things from their way of understanding, and to examine them in the limited way peculiar to themselves.

"There is nothing new under the sun," said Solomon.[1] People keep claiming to have found something new, but it may have been discovered and rediscovered a thousand times in days gone by.

The Vedantas, which represent the ancient philosophy of the Hindus, using Sanskrit, the mother of languages, employ the word *manu* or *manushi* for "man." *Mana* means "mind." The English word *man* has the same origin. This shows that the origin of a human's being is their mind; and their external form

1. Ecclesiastes 1:9.

is so much before their eyes that it hides the other aspect of their being, which seems, in comparison to this, to be invisible. Their body is here, but their mind may be in China; the real *person* is not here.

The life of the Prophet relates his journey to Heaven. "A heavenly animal came down to earth and took the Prophet to heaven." This means that the Prophet visited heaven in his mind. It is the state of mind that is heaven; it is the state of mind that is hell; it is the state of mind that makes you great, or feeble, or insignificant, strong or weak.

In the Hindu writings, it is said, "Your success or failure depend entirely on your mind. If your mind has failed, no one can bring success, and even if everything has gone wrong and your mind is in success, the success is there!"

The more we think of mind, the more we understand the nature of the human being. The tendency to sin or virtue, the temperament, the attitude toward right and wrong, failure and success—all changes in life are entirely dependent on the condition of the mind. The dream tells the state of the mind at the time; the mind is in full play when a person is asleep. It is not free during the waking hours because of the occupations of the day. The dream will show the state of a patient's mind. It is a disturbance of the mind that produces coma.

Whatever a person desires, that desire informs us of the state of mind he or she is in, and those who understand mind easily know the mind of another just by studying and knowing the desires and tendencies of life. Love of a rose, a lily, a jasmine, of sweet, sour, salty, or savory things express the particular tendency of a person's mind, the mood in which he or she is in. Modern education omits the study of the truth of unity from the nature of variety, whereas the sole aim of the mystic is to keep near to the idea of unity and find out, "Where do we unite?"

In the Arabic language it is written, "If you wish to know God, you must know yourself."[2] How little one knows while one is in the intoxication of individualism. One thinks, "I am a separate being; you are another; there is no connection between you and me, and we all have our own joys and free will." Did one but know how much one's life is dependent not only on the objects and things that keep the body alive but also on the activity of a thousand minds in a day. Every time a person laughs it is the reflection of that person's mind, controlled by the power of another person's mind. Why does one feel sometimes sad, sometimes glad, sometimes cheerful, sometimes enthusiastic, sometimes tired without reason, sometimes depressed and exhausted? We meet so many minds throughout the day and night that are reflected on our own mind; and so the thoughts are changed, seemingly without reason, yet the whole activity of life depends on these thoughts, and is changed according to them.

Who then can say, "I am an individual, independent and free. I can think what I wish, and I can do what I wish"? You are not doing what you wish; you are not thinking what you wish. There are various thoughts around you in the form of people and animals and entities who influence your mind and feeling and thought; you cannot escape them. No one can escape being affected by the effect of another person's mind. There is always some person stronger than you, and always someone weaker than yourself. We are connected with one another. Our lives are tied together, and there is a link in which we can see one current running through all. There are so many globes and lamps, and yet one current is running through all.

Mystics seek to realize this constantly and impress it on their mind in whatever they may see. What, for them, are the waves of the sea? Are they not in the sea? Their individuality is only so far as one wave rises and falls. It rises and falls, but it merges

2. Hadith.

into the sea. The new wave is a different wave altogether. What, for them, is the tree? There is one stem; the leaves spring from it, change their color, and drop off. But at the same time the life of the whole tree depends on the root and stem, and any damage done to either of these affects every branch and bough, every part of the tree. What, for them, is the body? Eyes, nose, head—which of them is self? The hand has a separate name, the fingers have separate names; every part has a different name. Myriads of thoughts, myriads of imaginations, myriads of feelings! Can we ever number their variety? The different emotions, the different kinds of sorrows, the different grades of joy—can we ever distinguish them or classify them? Our being has so many aspects, and what is it after all that calls oneself "I," "me"? It is one, not many. It is simply that if we had no body or mind, we could not realize that we exist. Through all this variety one realizes, "I am one."

It is the same things working further in mind, until one finds that oneness that exists behind all these numerous names and forms, and in which one will unite with one's God.

This shows, that the experience of individuals—the thoughts, feelings, and knowledge of individuals—and the experience of the multitude of nations, of races, throughout all ages and periods of history, have not belonged only to individuals, to the multitude, to the nations, the races, but have always gone back until they came to that depth where they were assimilated with what is called the divine mind.

All different minds are the different leaves of one tree. Some minds are branches, some are boughs of the tree, and there is just the one source to which all are attached. Not one object or life can exist that has not one central point in which everything meets and joins together. And that meeting ground is called the divine mind.

The Brahmins therefore taught people to bathe at the point where rivers meet; the purification of life was by bathing at Sangam. Those who really understood it knew that this pictured the divine mind, and the purification in life lies in touching that depth of life's sea in which the myriads of forms and names all join. The activity of all beings is directed from that center. The Qurʾan says, "No single atom moves independently of the hand of God."[3] That is, no activity of any kind takes place either here or in the starry space without the impulse from within, and from that depth of life where all minds and the effects of all activity unite.

Coming now to the moral side of the subject, we ask, "In what way should we carry on our life? Should we be satisfied to depend on one power working?" No, that would be just like paralysis of a part of the body. The hand would not move. Just think, where have your thoughts and impulses come from? We may ask, "Should we then realize every impulse that comes? Should we not take action in every case, seeing they come from God?" No, for it is the realization of mind that makes things right or wrong, good or bad, spiritual or material. It is your own thought; not the action. It is as you make it. Although the impulse is from within, if it is wrong, you have made it wrong; if it is right, it is because you make it so. The law justifies you. There is no other law. It is your law.

Every mind whether stupid or wise, wicked or virtuous—every mind loves good and beauty. What is good? Good is that which is beautiful, what you admire, what you cannot help admiring. You admire the beauty of a person's kindness, beauty of action, feeling, and thought. Nobody tries to see ugliness or to follow the path of evil. Is there anyone who will say, "Please do not be kind to me; please deceive me?" No one likes to be fooled. Wickedness is to seek to gain and not to give; but the wicked person is still awake to beauty.

The mystic is guided by his or her own mind. That which we seek in life we must give to another; if kindness, give it; if goodness, give it; if service, give it. The whole secret of happiness

3. Qurʾan 10:61.

in life lies in this. When we seek happiness in the kindness of another, it means that we depend on the kindness of another person to make us happy; and as long as we look on another to make us happy, we keep expecting that which we ought ourselves to have given. Not till then do we know what justice is.

The world is a dome, where every action is the echo of another. Do good—it will come back; if not from one person, it will come from another. That is the echo. You do not know from which side it will come. It will come a hundredfold more than you give.

Give love; will you get coldness? Do good; can you get evil, if you do good? You cannot be a judge of the action of another until you yourself are selfless. Only then will justice come to you; only then will you understand the nature of justice. Self is the wall between you and justice. There is only one thing that is truly just, and that is to say, "I must not do this." But when you say this to another you may be wrong.

The mystic develops his or her mind in this manner, purifying it by pure thought, feeling, and action ("pure" means free from sense of separateness)—only following this one line of thought. Whatever difference in principles of right and wrong religious faith may show, no two individuals will ever differ in this one natural principle. Every soul seeks after beauty; and every virtue, righteousness, good action, is nothing but a glimpse of beauty.

Once having this moral, Sufis do not need to follow a particular belief or faith, to restrict themselves to a particular path. They can follow the Hindu way, the Muslim way, the way of any church or faith, provided they tread this royal road: that the whole universe is but an immanence of beauty. You are born with the tendency to admire it in every form, and you may not blind yourself by being dependent on one particular line of beauty. You will not get it from another. Give it. Make your action, your thought beautiful, and let others get your beauty.

How is the perfection of mind reached that we have to touch? It is reached through contemplation, through realization and understanding of the one current running through the whole of life. We begin to contemplate on that. The mind that we call in religious language the Almighty, and in mystical terms the divine mind, is the depth of life, the depth of activity with which all activity and every activity is connected.

Therein is the whole of religion. The mystics' prayer is to that beauty, and their work is to forget the self, to lose themselves like a bubble in the water.

The wave realizes, "I am the sea," and by falling into the sea prostrates itself before its God. "Be ye perfect, even as your Father which is in heaven is perfect."[4]

4. Matthew 5:48.

7

WILLPOWER

When the mind inquires into the nature of willpower, it becomes a question whether it is a power of the mind, a power of thought, or a power of the brain. Those who cannot see beyond the power of the brain call it brainpower; those who cannot see beyond the mind, call it a power of the mind. Those who cannot conceive of the existence in a person of anything above the feelings consider willpower to be a power of feeling. A Sufi understands it to be the divine power.

It is the divine will that is manifested throughout the whole universe, which has created the whole universe; and it is part of the divine will that manifests itself through us. Everything we do in life is governed and directed by that power. Were it not that there is but one power to govern and direct, how would it have been if one foot determined to go to the north, and the other to the south? Our two eyes might have turned in opposite directions, one to the west, the other to the east, had there not been one willpower behind them to direct their gaze toward one object. When lifting a certain thing, one hand might have gone up and the other down, had there not been one willpower to govern both, and cause them to join in the one movement. This shows that each individual has one willpower that governs several organs of our physical existence as well as our thoughts and imaginations; all are directed consciously or unconsciously by the one power. We could not have accomplished one thing in life had willpower not been at work.

But there are two ways in which the willpower works: first, when it is lighted with the light of intelligence; second, when it is not so lighted, but works by itself.

When it works by itself, we call it accidental. We do things accidentally that we have not intended to do. But when willpower works and makes our mind and body work consciously, at such a time the light of intelligence is followed, and the willpower is acting consciously. This is the difference between the happenings and occurrences. In the one we are conscious of what we are thinking, we are conscious of what we are speaking and of what we are doing—in proportion to our willpower and to the light that is thrown upon it from the light of our intelligence.

We have acted without willpower when we have to say, "I have done something I should not have done; I have said something I should not have said; I have thought something that I should not have thought." When a person says, "The action I did is terrible; I said something I should not have said"; during that time the person said or did it the willpower was there, but the strength and light of intelligence had not fallen upon it to the extent to which they should have fallen.

There are two parts in our being, the willpower or governing power, and the vehicles, the mind and the body. Both are governed and controlled by that one governing power. In one aspect of our being we are sovereign, in the other aspect we are minister, and in a third aspect we are servant. We are minister when our mind works, and we are servant when the body works. We are sovereign when the willpower works.

And when this power loses its control over the mind, then the thoughts become disordered; they dwell in any regions and on any lines, even on such as our moral standard has perhaps not drawn for them. And our body also works in a disorderly way when the power of the will is lost. Therefore all illnesses, all failures, all disappointments and faults in life are caused by just one thing: the weakness of willpower.

A person, not knowing this, sometimes considers the willpower to be a power of thought and mind. He or she does not know that behind mind there is something. When the will is behind it, the body is powerful too. Perhaps you have seen or heard of the Indian fakir who lifted an elephant. How can a man lift an elephant? However strong he may be, what comparison can there be between the two? What power is at work? It was his willpower that was greater than the elephant's.

The great things in this world that humans have done, and the wonderful things they have done in this wonderful world that we see all around us, are all the outcome of human will. Animals, with all their strength, have not that will. Therefore, puny human stands before the elephant and says, "Sit down," and the elephant sits down; "Stand up," and the elephant stands up. With all the strength in its body, still the elephant listens to the human. That is how the fakir lifted the elephant. Humans make tigers, lions, horses work; one can even make one's thought and will act through inanimate things. Even through objects one's willpower can be manifested. But when one does not realize its effect upon living creatures, how can one experience one's power over objects?

Jalal ad-Din Rumi, in his *Masnavi*, speaks of fire, air, water, earth, and ether as beings, while people call them things. To people they are things, to God they are beings, obedient servants. Whatever God wishes, they do. As the servant acts according to the master's desires, so these elements act as God desires.

Further, not only does the will of God work through elements, but the human will also, in proportion to the power of the will. A loaf of bread given with willpower can cure a person's disease more successfully than a medicine, if there be enough willpower with it.

In the East, there are superstitions that have a mystical meaning. When a person goes into a new business, or takes a journey, their relatives give them flour or rice in their hand, or some betel nuts, with the wish that they may meet with success. The thing itself is nothing. But behind it there is willpower, and the persons who have received it have believed; and therefore they have responded to the willpower that has been attached to the gift. There is the harmony. The one who wishes to have good luck receives it.

The lesson of Christ can be understood after understanding this: it is the willpower that does the work. "If ye have faith as a grain of mustard, ye can remove mountains."[1]

In referring to such things, it is not to be inferred that people should be prepared to believe in superstitions or become superstitious. It is to show that they must know the value of willpower, and use it in their profession, their business, their home, in all things. Would it not be a desirable thing to have willpower; would it not be desirable to have strength in the body? If we are satisfied with feebleness of body, it may be that we are also satisfied to be without willpower.

All light is for us, all inspiration is for us—why not use it, as long as we know how to use it, to make the best use of life? If one wishes to abuse power, one may abuse bodily power, fighting everybody, boxing and wrestling. But that is another part of life. Power is necessary and should be developed; and when one is anxious to develop power, either of body or of mind, one ought to remember that the willpower is behind it all; that if the will is developed, the physical and mental power can easily be obtained. The willpower governs the body and the mind.

Now coming to the question of the human will as opposed to the will of God: which is which? We understand the difference when we perceive that the nature of willpower differs only according to whether it is in its fullness, or whether it is only limited. The willpower in its fullness is divine power; the willpower in its limited state is the individual will. And if there

1. Matthew 17:20.

is anything that can be called the source of the whole creation, it is the divine will, it is the will of the absolute Being. If you do not desire to call it will, you may call it force, strength, or might. But force, strength, might, energy, are all dead words. Force can be without intelligence, energy without intelligence, mind without intelligence; but will means force, energy, might, with intelligence! Therefore it is called divine will instead of divine energy.

A person with a materialistic mind would call it energy. But why energy? Is your intelligence energy? It is beyond energy. Is your will only energy? It is energy with intelligence. Therefore divine will is energy, but with divine intelligence. In all there is intelligence.

If we observe nature keenly, we see how divine wisdom is working. The animals and birds of tropical countries have fur and feathers that differ from those one finds in the Himalayas and in cold places. They have suitable bodies, suitable skins; their life, their whole existence is harmonious in the place where they live.

A human's desire, the desire of the senses, is met by the possession of every sense, every organ of sense, each suited to gratify the desire of the being. The eye meets the requirement of the sense of sight. With all our intelligence and great research no one can make a new eye so adaptable and fitted for the purpose. This wisdom that makes us understand and believe that behind all this there is that intelligent God and intelligent Creator, not only a life or energy or force; it makes us ask why anyone should call God force or energy, and not God.

The light of the sun that we see, of the stars and planets, is not their own. It is the light of the sun that illuminates the planets and is reflected from them; it is the same light that they receive that they reflect. So it is with the human. It is the will of God that is reflected in the human. Although every star is not necessarily a sun, yet its light ultimately comes from a sun.

If people have divine light in them, why should they commit sin or do evil, or why should there be anything that we call wrong or a sin? If it is God's will, how can it be sin? We understand this when we consider the difference between wrong and right, sin and virtue, good and evil. These differ with different people. It depends on the standard of each one's evolution; it depends on the goal or ideal that each person has placed before them. That is why the Prophet said, "The religion of each person is peculiar to that person." It is a great fault on our part when we accuse others of an untrue or false belief, untrue or false religion. We do not know that perhaps they have a religion that is suited to them. Their evolution or attainment in life, their temperament, their standard of morals is different; therefore we ought, if we only could, to keep to our religion. The standard that we believe for our good is quite enough.

Our intelligence and experience of this life on earth creates within us a world of experiences; and these experiences teach us, by comparing one with the other, "This one is for our happiness; this one is not for our happiness." That which is for our happiness we call virtue, and that which does not contribute to our happiness we call vice. In this way the world that we make into our own is a world of personal experiences, either in our own lives or seen through the lives of others. Therefore it is quite natural that a person in Tibet should have a different religion from a person in France; and a person in Persia different from one in Colombo. Although humankind is the same everywhere, one's religion is one's experience in life, and therefore one's own evolution, one's own experience, added to the temperament of the people that one lives with. One can see what is good for one, and what is not; what is right and what is not right; what gives one happiness, and what keeps one from it. The world itself becomes a scripture or book to the soul. If one does not consult it, one is thoughtless. But one that consults with the world that one has created within oneself, that one is wise. Sometimes in one's world one has decided a certain thing is a sin or evil, and yet when it comes to an action, or thought, or speech, one cannot follow the directions one has already made in one's world—either because of the weakness of one's mind or body, or because of the weakness of one's will. One fails to fulfill the law of one's own world, of one's own scripture that one has written. Therefore one falls, and that is considered by one to be sin. It is the same with virtue. We have our own sins, our own virtues that we have made from our own experiences.

If a child throws a knife at anybody, it has not committed a crime, because it has not yet set that action down as a crime in its world of experiences; it has not gathered it into that world. It only becomes a crime when the child knows it to be criminal. After that it becomes responsible for its deed. "Judge not, that ye be not judged; for with what judgment ye judge, ye shall be judged."[2] You judge others according to your world of good and bad; the same world, the same scripture that is your religion judges you also, when you do wrong. And no persons would do wrong if their willpower helped them to do right, because how could they do wrong in a matter that the scripture of their own heart tells them to be wrong, had not their willpower failed them? Therefore those who repent after their crimes, faults, and failures show thereby that it is not that they have wanted to do them, but that their willpower has failed them. The willpower was not strong enough to help them to carry out their own standard of good, as it should help all through the journey of life.

How can willpower be developed? Are there any exercises by which it can be developed? Are there any rules to follow? Is there any knowledge to acquire? All three things are required.

What exercises would help the willpower to develop? The first exercise would be to check every act, word, and thought that we do not wish to occur; to avoid unintentional actions, speech, and thought. The other exercise that is necessary for

2. Matthew 7:1–2.

the development of the willpower is that of seeing that your mind does not rule you, that your body does not rule you, but that you rule your body and rule your mind. Desires such as appetite, thirst, sleep, even the desire of moving or standing or walking—all these desires must be under control. There should be a time in every day when every desire of the body is checked. See if you can do it; and then as long as you let the body go without listening to it, do so. It is a great trouble to rule the body, for it is not willing to be ruled.

Yogis, fakirs, Sufis may be seen sitting, standing in one posture for hours together. All the postures adopted are to control and govern every atom of the body, so that it may be in the control of the will. I do not mean that one should devote all one's time to these things, or even that one should have certain exercises for this. When one understands the matter, and carries it out in one's everyday life, then one's life becomes a continual progress.

Next, there is the control of the mind. The mind sometimes does not listen. We want to think of our business, and perhaps the mind thinks of the state of our health, or about a neighbor. It insists on thinking of something else. It may be as unruly as a wild horse that cannot be controlled. The next step to gain control of it is by concentration, by absorption, by meditation. Concentration should be in everyday life. It is necessary that our bodies and minds should act according to our will in our profession, in our office, in our ordinary life.

There is a tradition of the Brahmins that Rama had two sons, Lahu and Kusha. They went with their mother to a city, where they dwelt with a great hermit of the time. Lahu, a young lad, went out to wander through the town and look at its beauty. To his great surprise he found a beautiful horse running without a rider. And when he inquired whose horse it was, people said, "This horse is let loose with the intention that anyone who can catch him may be crowned as king of this country."

The lad, with the enthusiasm of growing strength and hope in life, thought, "What a good thing it would be if I could catch this horse." So he ran after it, and tried to catch it; but every time when he approached near the horse, it slipped away. Again he ran after it. And again when the horse was only a little distance away, he was just able to touch it, but again it slipped away. This went on for a long, long time. He was away so long that his mother became uneasy about him, not knowing whither he had gone. So she told Kusha that his young brother had gone out and not returned. Kusha went out and discovered that Lahu was after this horse. He was very glad to note his brother's ambition. He knew, however, that he would never catch the horse unless he were instructed what to do. Finally Lahu, knowing how to catch the animal, succeeded and was able to bring it before the authorities, who declared him a king.

This story tells us about willpower. The mind is just like a wild horse, and the will is the only thing that can catch it. The thoughts and imaginations are all so unruly that we cannot think or feel what we wish. If that were done by us, then neither could sorrow touch us again, nor could unhappiness come near, because it is the thoughts and imaginations that bring sorrow. If we could think what we wish to think, if we could feel what we wish to feel, life would be a heaven for us. When we do not feel what we wish to feel, when we do not think what we wish to think, it is just because of lack of willpower. That which is the governing power cannot hold it.

The elder brother of the story is the teacher who shows the path to his younger brothers, who are groping in darkness. He is sent with a message from God, the Father and Mother of children on earth, to guide his younger brethren.

Those who are seeking after the power to control this vehicle, and have the ambition or desire to obtain the crown of life, to them will be granted the inheritance of the kingdom of their country.

8

PERSONAL MAGNETISM

Everyone sees how great the influence of personal magnetism is upon success in everyday life, profession, business, family, and daily occupation.

Sometimes we notice that we go to a certain shop to buy a certain thing, and there is something about the manner of the salesperson that impels us to decide to visit the same shop the next time we need that kind of article. Even if it is a long way to the shop, we prefer not to go to one that is nearer. Similarly, it sometimes happens that a person goes to a hotel or boardinghouse or restaurant, and someone treats them in such a way that they decide to return to that place rather than visit another.

So with doctors, solicitors, barristers, scientists, professors, and teachers of all kinds. Doctors may be well versed in their knowledge, they may have a great many degrees, but if they lack this personal magnetism, instead of curing patients they may make them still worse. Sometimes doctors cure patients before giving them the prescription. Just by a word of kindness, by a manner, a tenderness, a sympathy they make the patient feel so much better that the disease, which before was too much to bear, appears to be curable after all. Half the pain has gone with just seeing the doctor, such a difference does personality make. It is a great healer.

Then there may be solicitors or barristers who antagonize their clients as soon as they see them, and so the latter do not wish to go to them next time. Another person will impart courage and hope; their personality, their speech, everything, will show that they are the person to follow, to go to for help.

In family life many times disagreement arises for the same reason, or agreement arises for the same reason. The father, mother, husband, wife, have personal magnetism that can hold. When this magnetism is lacking, a person finds it better to be among friends than to be with a relative; a person would rather go out than stay at home. The home becomes a strange place, because there is not that magnetism that the person lives for. It is as if in midwinter one comes to one's room and finds it cold, because there is no fire there; one wishes that one were somewhere else where there is a fire.

Personal magnetism can create beauty around one, can attract one, can make one attractive to others, serviceable to them. It is soothing; it is healing.

What is personal magnetism? Is it a development of psychic or occult power? Is it an education, or is it refinement?

The answer is that education helps personal magnetism, because knowledge is light, and light is beautiful, and it always helps. But this is not personal magnetism. People may be very educated and at the same time very disagreeable. Saʿdi says that an educated person without practice is like a donkey loaded with books; it is carrying them on its back, but it does not know it or act accordingly. It has a load of knowledge that serves no purpose. If one's education has not made a person human, what is the use of education? It is just learning, available for earning money with.

You may think, if it is not education, is it psychic power? It is not necessarily psychic or occult power; it is the natural psychic power, the natural occult power that we call personal magnetism. It is not necessary to attain psychic or occult power by a certain practice or study; one should already have that power; when used beautifully it is personal magnetism.

Then is magnetism politeness? Is it polish? As polish is the fashion of today, every person learns it when they mix among people. But this is not necessarily personal magnetism, though the person may think they have a winning manner.

If there can be any real explanation of personal magnetism, it is the making of one's own person into that which one expects from others. One usually makes the mistake of expecting something from others and not doing it oneself. For instance, a person is very pleased if they are well received in a friend's house, if spoken kindly of, if they are well attended, when their vanity is satisfied by the action of others. They are very glad if others have a good opinion of them and overlook their defects. But seldom do they pause to be thus themselves.

If we only tried to give to others all the things we demand from them; if we overlooked their bad points instead of expecting them to overlook ours; if we only thought, "How inconsiderate I was at that time when I spoke so rudely to so-and-so." If we only gave to others all that we would wish them to give us, all that we are pleased for them to give us, that would create a personal magnetism. If we did to them all the things that we expect from them!

The word *gentleperson* in the English language is a very good one in this respect. It has come to refer merely to dressing well; but the ideal behind it is good. It is the ideal of gentleness, and gentleness is the essence of personal magnetism. There cannot be a better lesson than that given in the Bible where it is said, "Blessed are the meek, blessed are the poor in spirit."[1] But the difficulty is that people give little attention to all these things; they think these things are too simple. And at the same time if you ask them the meaning of "poor in spirit," they will find it very difficult to answer. Not many will know what that means.

1. Matthew 5:3–5.

It is seen by comparing the spirit of a human with the spirit of an animal. If the tiger is lying in a place, and you want the tiger to get up, it will roar. If a person is lying there, and you say, "Will you please let me sit there," they will say, "Certainly," because their spirit is poorer than the spirit of the tiger. And such is the difference between a person and a gentleperson. Gentlepersons are those who show the poorness of spirit in themselves, a spirit of accommodating another; if they have a place, letting another sit in their place if that one wants. They feel "It does not matter if another person sits in my place; it is still better." There are those who, if you talk roughly to them, give back your words four times more heavily and coarsely than you have. There are others who, if you talk roughly to them, bear it and perhaps do not give an answer at all, or perhaps they understand and consequently avoid a fight or quarrel in their search for peace. As it is written, "Blessed are the peacemakers."[2] It is not merely the kind of peace that prevents fighting and bloodshed and strife; we may make this kind of peace many times from morning to night. There are a thousand matters about which we can quarrel and get annoyed with one another. So throughout our daily life, at all times, there are opportunities of making peace.

We always admire those who show gentleness in their movements, in sitting, walking, in their voice or words, in their thought; we admire it consciously or unconsciously. There is always a charm in gentleness, and yet a person neglects it when the time comes to practice it. That which should come first comes last. If only one thought, "How I like gentleness on the part of others." If a person has gentleness of voice or expression or word, it is so charming, so winning; we know this so well and yet we always forget it at the critical moment.

The poorness of spirit comes from meekness. Meekness is mildness, which is contrary to what we call roughness. Roughness of action or roughness of speech is contrary to mildness

2. Matthew 5:9.

or meekness. Our eyes naturally always enjoy mildness of color instead of striking colors, because of the aggressive power in the latter that our eyes cannot bear. We experience the same thing in the sun and moon. We do not like to look at the sun, but in India we enjoy the moonlight nights so much; one wishes the moon shone every night. Why? Because it is mild; it shows meekness. Our power is the power of light; our strength of speech, thought, and action is of the same kind, and the same nature as the light of the sun and moon, respectively. If the light be too strong, it irritates; if it be mild, it soothes.

If you treat everyone with gentleness, your personality is always welcome wherever you are. The same gentleness in your speech always gives you success, and always means friends for you. If we only had control of our words; if our words were always of that meek nature!

Among the musicians and poets of the East special attention is given to education in meekness and mildness. There is a Sanskrit saying: "Art becomes twice graceful when the art and mildness are together." How true it is. When you have admired the art of the artist and say, "How beautiful it is," and they say, "Oh, it is nothing, it is your kindness that causes you to admire it," their magnetism becomes great.

From a sovereign down to the most ordinary person, it is mildness that wins the whole world. People of all positions in life, and of all grades of evolution can do such a great work with this one little possession. Saʿdi says, "If your word is sweet, you conquer the world; wherever you go, you win men's hearts." Is it not the meaning of the words of Christ when he says to the fishermen: "Come with me; I will make you fishers of men";[3] that is, "I will teach you those manners of humanity by which you will win everyone you may come in contact with." Do you think a person can become a fisher of men by their cleverness, by their artificial polish? False is false; gold is gold. The true

3. Matthew 4:19.

gold will last; the false gold will lose its brilliance. Polish is just like false gold. A person may wish to win wife, husband, father, brother, all by their cleverness, by their polish, but they will prove to be false even on a very unimportant occasion. Polish may please the eyes, but it cannot please the heart. One can polish one's actions, but one cannot polish one's heart. The polish of the heart comes from the feeling. The action of the heart is not harmonious with the roughness of the feeling, for feeling will come out. All that is real will come out; the polish is only beautiful for a moment. It may prove a person to be very gentle and clever for a moment, but it does not last. The person's friends will leave him or her in a short time. The relatives will all know in time that it is just external, all cleverness, not that which will last forever. It is the truth that lasts for always. All the beautiful qualities should be true qualities, not false, because the value lies in the true and not in the false.

In ancient times, people of great descent, royal families, princes, people of educated and religious families used to go out into the world, and were not recognized as such because there was no international communication in those days; no nation knew its neighbor. Yet it happened that these persons were always recognized by their manner, recognized as belonging to such a family.

Evolution has made all humanity a family; and now is the time when every individual should consider that, as a member of the family of the whole humanity, they ought to show themselves as human in nature, and how superior they can be to the animals and the lower creatures. If we only did the things that animals do, if we also only ate, drank, slept, bit each other, got the better of one another, we should not do anything great. Their whole life goes in being ever in pursuit of their food. In the night, animals join together and make noises in the jungle. If we also enjoy ourselves in that way, then our amusements and joys and comforts are not greater than those of animals, unless we show some quality in our personality that animals do not possess.

A Hindustani poet, Amir, says, "It is much more precious than any wealth to collect the wealth of good manner."[4] Because by good manner we can make another person as kind as our own father and mother; as kind and sympathetic as our own brother and sister, as respectful as our own son and daughter, if we only have that manner. If we know how to be motherly, how to be fatherly to our youngers, if we know how to behave respectfully toward our elders, if we know how sympathetic and polite and good we ought to be to those who are poor or servants, or who depend on us, if our manner is beautiful, there is no heart we can fail to win. The children of the wealthiest people may, owing to the ill manner of the parents, want to sacrifice all their fortune, their father and mother, in order to go away from them; they would even sacrifice life itself. As with children, so with less near relatives. They cannot attract as long as they have no good manner; all the physical magnetism passes away. During youth, a person may be very magnetic, but when their youth passes away their attraction is lost. But the attraction of personal magnetism grows with years and can be used at all times. Even an old man or woman is attractive, so that people will say, "What a nice person. By going to them we can feel so filled with joy and comfort." Although the nearest and dearest will not always desire to spend time with an old person, they find themselves attracted to an aged one who has personal magnetism.

The Prophet said, "God is beautiful, and loves beauty."[5] What is beautiful in life? It is not only trees and plants and flowers and the external physical world; the higher beauty is the beauty of personality. By the beauty of personality our heart is filled with joy; by the beauty of nature only the eyes are

4. Amir Menai (1829–1900).
5. Hadith.

satisfied: the heart is not satisfied. It is the beauty of personality that fills our heart with joy; there is something imparted to us that we cannot explain. Animal magnetism passes away with the strength of the animal. The animal beauty all goes when the person is ill and their physical energy is lost; there is no longer any attraction.

Personal magnetism helps in all conditions. If a person is poor, it makes them rich, because their personality is such that they receive the attentions, the service, and all their life's demands with less trouble, even in spite of their humble position in life. Do you not see round you how a person of beautiful personality, however helpless, will always attract the good, the bad, and all around them? A person that lacks it, however rich, however educated, however great in position—perhaps their position will attract those who are forced into their society—will only attract such as are looking to get some of that person's wealth. That person's relatives, forced to go before him or her, only long for the time when that person is not, but his or her wealth is theirs.

Let us think about the prophets. There are so many followers of Christ in the world today, and perhaps it is true that not everyone understands his teachings and follows him because of his teaching. But if there is anything of him that is known to the world, if there is any of his fragrance left in the world, it is his personality. He was ready to forget and overlook the faults of others; he was ready to attend to the service of the poor, ready to play and be equal to little children. It was not, "I am a teacher from God, and people must come and bow before me."

That, then, is the attitude. The poorness of spirit; the harmony in life; the harmonious temperament.

From the highest to the lowest we always find people in a state of disharmony. In clubs, associations, meetings, institutions, parliaments, all will dispute and fight. This teaches us that, however evolved people may be in their education, their position, or their power or wealth, by that they have not mastered the law of harmony.

Whoever has mastered the law of harmony has developed humanity within themselves. They will harmonize equally with the wise and with the foolish. It is not because they are wise that they harmonize with the wise, or because they are foolish that they harmonize with the foolish. Foolish people gave their lives for Christ; wise people worshipped him for his wisdom. "They left their nets" and the fishing where they had spent all their lives because Christ harmonized with them. He answered their questions; he was tolerant.

So too with the story of Krishna. He is looked on as the incarnation of God, one of the greatest teachers the Hindus had. He was a child with little children, a cowherd with every cowherd, he was harmonious with everybody; he was wise among the learned, and was merry among the happy. He was not a king; he was not poor; he was one among all. The young and the old, everybody loved him. When he played the flute the cows and the deer and all the animals of the jungle would come to listen. It was not the mere skill of his music, because music is not attractive if the personality is not attractive; it was his personality that was attractive.

There were two friends speaking together, and one said, "That funeral that is passing is of a person who is going to heaven." Another funeral, passing later, caused this friend to remark, "This person, for him the place is hell." The younger of the two friends asked, "What do you know about it?" "Oh," said the other, "it is so simple: behind the first one were people walking with tears in their eyes, and they all looked so sad. So he must have won their hearts by his personality. His magnetism must have made such an impression that all the people appear sad and sorrowing. And the other funeral, with that there were few people; and they were laughing in their sleeves and winking, and everybody had a smile, which shows that they were very pleased to get rid of him."

Whatever possession, whatever power, whatever honor, whatever wealth, whatever belongings, whatever property we have, nothing is of any use in the end, for all is passing. But if there is any one thing that is worth gaining in life, because it lasts forever, it is humanity.

9

LOVE, HUMAN AND DIVINE

Love is considered to be sacred, whether it be human or divine, according to the view of the mystics, philosophers, and thinkers. That it is possible to regard it thus is shown by the fact that in its root it is beyond both the human and the divine. As it is written in the Bible, "God is love"[1]—three words that open up an unending realm for the thinker who desires to probe the depths of the secret of love.

In ordinary life we make the meaning of this word into affection for our surroundings, for our relatives, or our beloved, but when we think deeply about it we see that from start to finish it represents the power underlying the power of all activities and all intelligences.

When we study life from the material standpoint we see there are four different stages, the mineral kingdom, the vegetable kingdom, the animal, and the human. And of these four domains it is said by a dervish, "God slept in the mineral kingdom; God dreamed in the vegetable kingdom; God woke in the animal, and God realized God's self in the human." And this gradual progression shows to us that underlying it there is a sense of life that has expressed itself in every step toward the completed development of love.

1. 1 John 4:8, 16.

In the mineral kingdom we find no tendency toward love. But, as the intelligence develops—in the vegetable kingdom—we feel that sympathy is reflected from us into the flowers. The plants perceive and feel that which comes from us. A loving person may attend to plants and rear them and water them with love and sympathy; and they flourish so much. But in the hands of another it may not be so. If we only watched plants closely we should see how much they feel our presence and our love. They flourish according to our love; the more love we give, the more fragrance, the more sweetness. People are always working on farms and in gardens, thinking them material things, looking to see how plants can be helped by material means; if they could only believe it, there is a still higher means of helping them to grow, a spiritual means—the use of love and sympathy.

There is a story in the East of Puran Bhagat, who was once living in exile in the forest; and after a long time during which he had developed the true love in his thought and feeling and spirit, he returned to his country. The first thing he wished to do was to sit in his garden, which had gone to ruin during his absence. He went down to it in the guise of a sage, and began to water it with his little water bowl. The garden at once began to flourish, and in a short time it became such a miracle of beauty that everyone in the city began to talk about it and say, "This must be some spiritual man, since the garden begins to grow and flourish." The touch of the saints and sages and prophets makes things grow.

Every kind of power lies in this one thing that we call by the simple name: love. Charity, generosity, kindness, affection, endurance, tolerance, and patience—all these words are from one; they are different names of the different aspects of only one thing: love. Whether it is said, "God is love," or whatever name is given to it, all the names are the names of God; and yet every form of love, every name for love, has its own peculiar scope, has a peculiarity of its own. Love as kindness is one thing, love as tolerance is another, love as generosity is another, love as patience is another; and yet from beginning to end it is just love. It is love's different manifestations into different directions, which distinguish themselves differently and have different purposes.

According to Sufi metaphysics love has two different aspects, *jalal* and *jamal*; and each aspect of love has its peculiar sphere. The jalal of love is the power of love. You may call it psychic power, willpower, or power of mind; yet it is one power working through different channels. And this is the power of love; its power manifests and acts according to its force. Its force is greater when it is unlimited, and less when it is limited. That which is called imagination, thought, perception, conception, inspiration, and intuition, comes from the jamal aspect of love.

In the third stage of evolution, which is called the animal kingdom, love is still more manifest. The animal is more capable of perceiving and feeling our love and kindness, our pleasure and displeasure. When you enter a house the dog may be delighted, or he may recognize your displeasure and feel depressed; cats recognize our love, and so also do parrots and other pet animals of different kinds. Thus we see that the cat is vexed because another cat comes into the house, and we read how, when Joseph was in the well, it was a dog that brought him bread from a neighboring town, and fed him during the time that he was in the well. And in Arabian stories we hear the story of an Arab who was protected and guarded by his horse when he fell wounded on the battlefield; the horse became his protector.

In the human being, love can develop more, though sometimes a person proves to be not only worse than animals, but even more dead to love than a rock. You would wish to be with the rocks rather than with such persons. This is because they have developed selfishness with their evolution. They are more selfish than any other creature in the world, unless they wipe off the impression of selfishness from their heart.

It would be no exaggeration for me to say that why some cannot achieve occult and psychic power and the intuitional and inspirational faculty is because they have not developed the power of love; and the reason of this failure is that selfishness has kept them back from developing the power of love.

Humans do not differ from animals in their passions and emotions. Human beings differ from the animal by their human qualities; these are not eating, drinking, or seeking its kind. Human qualities can only be developed by the development of love. Humans have fought in all ages with their brothers and sisters on account of differences of religion, differences of faith, differences of belief, differences of church, differences of community, not knowing that each religion, each time it was given, has only brought a message of love, taking a different expression each time. It has been given in different ages and to different people; they have received it according to their evolution; and yet there has been really only the one teaching, that of developing love. "Love your neighbor; love your fellow humans; love your enemy"—there has always been the same lesson given.

Christ told the fishermen, "Come, and I will make you fishers of men,"[2] that is, "As fishes come into your net, so your heart full of love will become a net that will attract every person to it." Rumi says, "All who see me feel attracted to me, yet not knowing what it is in me that attracts them." Is it not the secret of the whole of life? If we could see to whom we are attracted in life—father, mother, sister, neighbor, or anybody that we feel drawn to—then it would seem to us to be the magnetic power, or psychic power. But there is no greater magnetic power than love. Its magnetic power is very great. It changes one's voice, one's heart, one's manner, one's form, one's movement, one's activity—everything becomes changed. What a difference between water and rock; that smoothness and that liquid state of being, the rise and fall of the surface of the water compared with the rigidity of the rock! The great teachers of humanity

2. Matthew 4:19.

become streams of love. It is the first sign of the sage or holy person that they become love themselves. Their voice, their feeling, their presence, everything makes you realize that there is something open in that that we do not find in everybody; this something is their deep love,

The development of love is many times hindered by different obstacles in life. The first obstacle is ourselves. We begin our life with selfishness, and all that we want is for self; and if there is a tendency to love, it is for one's own happiness, and one's own joy. When the question comes, "How much do you love me, and how much do I love you?" it has come to be a trading in love. "I love you, but you do not love me" is as much as to say, "I have bid so much, and I expect a return of love." This is trading in love. Trade cannot lead anywhere, because trade makes you think of the self, and love is beyond that. To love is to give; it is not to take at all. The true lover never speaks of what they have done for their beloved, because they love for love's sake, not for the sake of a return. If a person begins to love and makes it a love fed by the love of their beloved, then they seek an impossible thing. If a person keeps waiting for the love of the beloved, they are bound to find that nature cannot grant that desire, unless both are traders in love. Then each takes the best of the other; each may think they love, but neither truly loves. Love teaches the lover patience, forbearance, gentleness, because the lover thinks, "My beloved will be displeased; I will be as gentle as possible in my action and in my movements." These thoughts are a correction to the lover. With every such thought that passes in the life of the lovers they correct themselves. Hope is the only thing in life that keeps us alive, because it feeds on love. Patience is fed by love. We can never have patience with anybody without love. How valuable is patience! As it is said in the Qur'an, "Allah loves the patient."[3]

3. Sura 3:146.

Another hindrance to love is where it depends on the beauty of the ideal, be it physical beauty, beauty of thought, of character, or of personality. Whatever beauty it may be, whenever love depends for its continuance or for its existence upon the beauty of its object, it must some day fail. Therefore true love does not regard the body, the external object. Properly speaking, love prepares its own ideal. To take an instance, a person says, "Oh, I have loved you for your beauty." What will that one say when youth has gone and the beauty is lost? Where will the love be then? The love will change too. And if the love has gone with the passing of the beauty of the object of its love, what then? Another may say, "Oh, I love you for your personality," and yet perhaps within a month the beloved may not show the same personality, the same attractive goodness. What then? We think a flower is a fleeting thing, so soon does it change; and yet the human heart is liable to a quicker change than even the flower. A person may be very good one moment, very kind; and at another moment the contrary; calm at one moment, at another restless; at one time so affectionate, at another indifferent; all according to the state of mind in which the person happens to be at the time. So it cannot last if it is allowed to depend on the beauty of the ideal. Such love is dependent and would sooner or later die. That is why so many hearts cannot keep the flame of love alive in them. So often it happens that lovers grow cold just for the lack of understanding that love must not be for an external ideal, that lovers have to prepare the ideal in themselves; they have failed to make the self-sufficient love within themselves. Not so the sages, the holy ones, the wise ones. They know that a person who is kind today can be the contrary tomorrow. Therefore the wise lover expects both opposites in the external and inner beauty of the beloved.

Those who have developed the ideal love within themselves by the aid of an object to love transform their nature into a more and more loving one in time. Their love for a certain person is akin to learning the ABCs, for by learning the ABCs you come to be able to read not only the primer, but any book that comes to you. By learning to love one, you gain a light, a torch, by the light of which you can read all things in life; it is as if in your nature you have developed something that you can give to everyone.

In the East there is a saying, "A loving son is always a loving husband." This is a true philosophy. It teaches the fact that one who has known from the beginning of life what love means, has laid the foundation of a whole life of being truly loving. Those who are faithful and kind to one friend can be kind to all—acquaintances, servants, neighbors, and strangers alike—because they have developed in them that quality. But when people pretend to love they are kind to one and bitter to another. This shows that they are really not lovers. The real lovers will show their kindness, gentleness, sympathy—all aspects of love—to everyone they meet.

When we think about occult powers—knowing the condition of other people's minds, their pleasure and displeasure, also the joy and pain of another's heart, knowing what is going on at a distance, receiving news from far away in the world—all these are gained without study, just through the power of love. It is all so easy and simple to one who loves. The traders with love cannot know this. The real lover will know such things without special meditation or concentration, for what can exert a greater concentration than love? If one's thoughts are scattered over pianos, chairs, tables, jewels, dress, one cannot understand such power; but if one has an interest in an ideal, the power is there before you seek it.

Therefore all occult and psychic power is the power of love. But it is not only a matter of love for a living person. There is a love for art, for science, for music, for poetry, for all the different aspects of beauty. Love in every direction shows you the sublime vision of the beautiful. It is those that have loved the beauty of poetry that are able to enjoy its beauty and to express it to others; those that have love for music that are enabled to give their music to the world and attract the lovers of music, as well as being able to enjoy its beauty themselves. Love's power ever shows its magnetism afresh through all the ages.

But love in its higher sense teaches us that there is a love, an object, a beloved, that can last with you and prove satisfactory, to compare with which there is nothing else in life worthy of all our love; and that one object is God. But among those who say, "Oh yes, I love God," very few tell the truth; many times that is a false pretense. How can you love the formless and colorless? It is impossible to love one whom one cannot circumscribe within any particular beauty. It is only those who pretend to be spiritual because they are godly and pious toward one of their own sect that say, "We love God." It is as absurd to say this as to say to a beloved, "Oh beloved, I love you very much, but I do not like to look at your face." For God says, "I have made the human in my own image." When one person is prejudiced against another and still says, "I love God," how can God be pleased with that kind of love? How can that be true love for God that refuses to see the beauty that is before it? It would be as if God said, "If you wish to see me, see me in the human face. That is my own image." It would also be as if a person claiming to love an artist were to say to the artist, "I love you very much, but I cannot bear to look at your picture." What kind of love could that be? The artist has given all their soul and life to that art; their very self, so to speak, has become art, and their whole satisfaction lies in your appreciation of their art. How can those claim to love the Creator who do not love what has been created? For God could never have become known had there been no manifestation. So one cannot pretend to love God who does not find sufficient beauty to admire in God's manifestation.

So, too, if one limits one's love to a single object, saying, "I only love this and there is nothing else I need," surely that one has not a right kind of love either. True love is limitless. Though it begins by being limited in such a way, yet it progresses and some day breaks out. Such a thing is constantly happening in life, but people do not understand the psychic law that underlies it. Eastern people say, when someone loves another person intensely and does not care for anyone else, "There will be some mishap there some day." There is always some breakdown, some danger awaiting, some trouble in the future, when love is not allowed freedom of flow. It is limited. The Japanese and Chinese have called God jealous, because God does not allow two persons to be devoted to each other. God cannot tolerate this narrowing of love. If one tried to put the whole sea into a little jar, the sea would break it. The sea of love breaks its limited channel. To speak of the jealous God means that the unlimited force of love cannot allow its expression to be directed toward one limited object. That is how the love of God alone is the culmination of love, for love is as vast as God. Verily, love itself is God.

There is a beautiful story that has been dramatized and acted in India for hundreds of years; the people will never get tired of seeing it acted, so it is acted even today. It is called "The Court of Indra."[4] Indra is the god of heaven. His court is made up of devas and peris. The latter dance in the court, the devas are to attend the pleasure of Indra. No earthly creature is ever allowed to enter, nothing of the earth is ever seen or allowed in the court of Indra. Once a peri (the Green Peri) happened to fly on to the surface of the earth, and she saw a prince of that land over which she was flying whose beauty charmed her so much that she thought that if she could in some way or other take him to her high dwellings, she would be happy. She told one of the devas about it, and he carried away Gulfam, the prince, while he was asleep. He wakes up, and finds himself in a strange place, and breathing a different air. After great bewilderment he sees a peri, a creature much more beautiful than the creatures of the earth. He looks at her and asks her

4. See, for instance, *Indr Sabha* (1859), by Amanat Lakhnavi.

how he comes to be there. She tells him he is in Indra Loka, that she loves him and will be happy to keep him there. "I will do anything for your happiness," she says. Gulfam forgets all about his kingdom, and lives with the peri, most happy in her love. Every day she has to leave him to be at her duty, and every day she returns, never saying whither she goes. This arouses his curiosity, but still she will not tell where she goes and what she does. Finally she does tell him, that she has to dance before Indra every day. Then he wants to go and see. She expostulates, but at length consents to take him. She keeps him behind her, and hopes to conceal him with her wings as she dances before Indra. But one of the devas discerns him and tells Indra, who for a long time will not believe it possible that a human being could be in his court. Then he discovers him, and pronounces a curse upon him, while the peri is to be banished until she shall have undergone the successive stages of purification through earth, water, fire, air, and ether. Not till then can she be allowed to enter the heavens again.

The story shows that in the highest dwellings where love takes a person, which is Indra Loka, in that sphere the king is Indra, the perfection of beauty. The highest love must be for God; it belongs to God. In its development love should aim toward that idea. The peri is the human soul, Gulfam is the human body. The soul, which is heavenly, becomes interested in this earthly body; and when by the power of love it comes from the earthly body to the heavenly sphere, it brings to heaven an object that is only destined to be on earth. The love of a limited being is not allowed to remain in heaven, and will be condemned to be purified and uplifted until it can nevermore find satisfaction in a limited object, in the love for a human being. Homage must be paid to the sovereign of heaven. True love must have free flow; and for that free flow the teachers have taught us to learn to love from the limited, and thence to advance in love till we attain to the love of God, the Unlimited.

10

INTUITION

Intuition is a part of knowledge that is beyond one's personality, and above the knowledge of things and names that one has. It comes at times when one becomes passive, and one exposes oneself to that knowledge, consciously or unconsciously.

There are some who are more intuitive, and there are others who are less so; and if you study the nature of their character, you will know the nature of their intuition. Those who are confused, who are constantly hurried, who are changeable in their nature, who have the fear of death, of disease, of their own action, of their enemies, of their surroundings; those who have constant doubt, thinking, "Can I trust this person, or that?"—"That friend may or may not prove worthy," and so on—it is all these who have less possibility of possessing intuition. Those who can trust without troubling themselves much more, those who have few doubts, are usually clearer in their perception. Those who trust in the inner guidance, who understand the secret of the instinct that works through animals and all creatures, those who are pious, those who wish to walk in the light, who always prefer the right way of thinking and speaking and acting, it is these who experience intuition many times in life.

Intuition is the first step, inspiration is the second, and revelation is the third. When revelation begins, it has arisen from intuition; for intuition is the first stage.

What is its way of manifestation? How does intuition take expression? Intuition is of two kinds: it may come without intention, without being invited, or it may come when you ask yourself a question. In the first kind a person may be sitting down, and the thought comes to them that a danger is awaiting them; in what way it may occur they do not know, they just feel it. Next day they find that something was going to happen to them. Then they sometimes think that happiness is coming from a friend, that a person from whom they have been parted for a long time is coming to see them; sometimes they think an enemy is going to turn into a friend—and yet they have not been thinking of the subject previously. The thought comes to them suddenly. It proves real; it proves right. Without inquiry a thought comes to you that tells you of a coming event. People sometimes take this to be a spirit communication; sometimes they take it to be thought transference from someone else. Both things are possible, but intuition is a greater and higher thing than spirit communication or thought-reading, because it is pure; it is your own property; it belongs to you. In this you do not depend on a spirit, or upon another person sending a thought to you. In this you are perfectly independent; you receive the knowledge from within, which is far superior, and greater, and higher.

The second variety of intuition is that concerning which it is said in the Bible, "Knock, and it shall be opened unto you."[1] Knocking at the door is asking within one's own self, "What will become of this particular business, or aim, or object that I am thinking of?" As soon as you knock at the gate of God, which is your heart, from there the answer comes, and it is a truer answer than any other person can give. There is no one who can know about our life, affairs, objects, motives, as much as we do ourselves. And therefore nobody can advise us better than ourselves.

1. Matthew 7:7.

Humankind cannot understand this secret, and consequently begins by depending on the advice of another. This would be advantageous if it were possible to have the good fortune of having a better adviser. Sometimes the persons from whom advice is asked are foolish, sometimes they are an enemy, sometimes they themselves are in confusion and cannot advise. Therefore people keep themselves from their real and true adviser—the guiding faculty within.

Intuition begins in the form of impressions. As soon as you see a person you have an impression of that person. Their face, their features, their expression, their atmosphere have in a way made an impression on you as to their goodness or their righteousness, their wisdom or foolishness, their being useful or not, their being displeased with you or not, their being your friend or enemy; whatever condition there may be, you receive it without knowing from any other source that these are their feelings. According to your own openness of spirit you get your impressions. You may receive a kind of impression whether you will be successful in your business or not. All these impressions convey to one that one's intuition is beginning. That is the first step.

After having intuition about individuals in respect of their relation to yourself, the next step is intuition with respect to those activities in which another person is telling you of their projects. You have an impression of whether it will be successful or not. You cannot give a reason for it; or even if you say the reason, as you utter the reason you become aware that that is not the reason. For as soon as you begin to think it out, you at once descend from the higher pedestal, from the spiritual source of information. To try and prove the basis of the truth of its spiritual source by means of reason, that is to use the thing of earth to establish the thing of heaven. A proper reason for an intuition cannot be given.

The source from which this knowledge comes is not reason. People who are very good at reasoning can go on fighting all their lives, and yet nothing comes of it. Ultimately their reasoning turns into a play on words and terms; and as a word can be made to mean anything, they have a chance of easy escape from being caught by the person against whom they argue. It is just like wrestling; or just as in a court of law two barristers take up their points as truth, even though they may know for fact that they are not true. They fight with their reason and logic.

First of all, the necessary rule is that when you see that your impressions are right and your doubts cannot break them, and you have been right in ten impressions and wrong in only one, then you know that the wrong one was not the impression you thought it was. When that impression has evolved, then you are able to know things intuitively. The difference between imagination and intuition is sometimes puzzling to define. Both come in the same way. When a given imagination began to construct itself, we cannot say. The imagination came suddenly; but so also does intuition. That is why it is difficult to discriminate between them. The truth is that if imagination is with light, then it is certainly intuition. Every imagination is intuition until it has been corrupted by reason; when the intuition is corrupted by reason it becomes imagination. But every imagination and every thought with the light of intelligence open is always an intuition; and therefore to an illuminated person any thought and every imagination is intuition. To that one there is never a thought or imagination that is not an intuition.

But it is difficult to keep it from being corrupted by reason, because as soon as it is produced we doubt whether it is right or not right. We doubt it until we have killed all the truth of our intuition. Our doubts are always the enemies of our intuition; and therefore practice is required in everyday life to keep intuition from being corrupted and finally destroyed by our doubts. We ought to build a fence around intuitions as if they were delicate little plants, and protect them from being destroyed by reason and doubts. By doing so, in time we grow to be sure of our intuitions, and then we never fail to get things right. And when the intuitions become right, dreams become right. We see what is really going to happen in every thought that comes to us, the truth of life. Then our life becomes a miracle; there is no need to look for wonders in the world. Our own has become full of wonders. To the illuminated one every night's dream becomes a book that tells the past, the present, and future, both of oneself and of all those whom one cares for or wishes to know about.

The next step consists in inspiration. Inspiration is not only the coming of a single thought, a single idea, but of a flow of ideas. You may express them in poetry, in music, in philosophy, in speech, in writing, in thinking. The inspirations come as many ideas. Inspiration is a developed intuition. The expression of inspiration is according to one's particular ability. If one speaks a beautiful language, one can express one's ideas in that language. All prophets and messengers have received the message, but they have uttered it in different languages. Why should they receive it in different languages? Surely it is one idea, one knowledge from heaven, and it is expressed according to the language customary with the receiver, seeing that one has no other in which to express it.

The angels are not as great as humans, because though they are gifted with the higher knowledge and are in the higher spheres, they have no power of expression. Humans get their knowledge from the higher source, but express it through the means provided by the lower spheres.

The Qur᾽an says, "God said to the angels: 'I am going to create a human being, who will be the chief of creation.' They asked, 'Are we not a satisfactory army of servants who are always busy in Thy praise and admire Thy beauty and glorify Thy name? Why intendest Thou to create one who will do evil therein, and shed blood, as they do?' The answer was, 'Are you capable of appreciating all that I have made? Can you tell me what are the names of these things that I have made?'" God asks the human; the human tells God all the names of things, the things that are sweet or bitter, the names of all manner of things; the human knows and enjoys all these things in nature. Therefore God says, "We have created them that they may be the chief of all creation, and enjoy all that we have created."[2] Therefore those who think that the heavenly knowledge is sufficient are mystical; but the joy of the heavenly knowledge and the full understanding of it comes from being able to express it in this world's medium of expression. Therefore we can have knowledge both from within and from the external world. When the two are together, there is a perfect expression.

The last and most delicate degree of intuition is revelation. This comes to prophets and perfected beings. This is a full light thrown upon the human personality—full light from within. To their eyes, ears, sense of taste or touch, all things disclose their secret. Those who have received this knowledge even partly, have by receiving it come to understand the properties of this plant or that, that this bitter medicine is good for this purpose, this sweet one for that, this drug or that vegetable for another. The knowledge of the property of the names and forms of the world are understood by them to the extent that revelation has helped them. When they look into the mind, they know all about the mind. When they give time to know about the earth, they come to know it. Whatever it be that they try to know, that they obtain; that is revelation. Those who look in the higher spheres are prophets, those who look on the earth are scientists, musicians, soldiers, and so on. It is from the direction in which one has studied that one receives the revelation. In the higher spheres all things become clear to those who direct their attention to these spheres.

People even see their future in the teacup, with limited light; similarly they see it in cards, in the crystal, in the coals of the fire, in smoke. All these things have the future written in them;

2. Sura 2:30–33.

it is the same light that shines upon these things, and begins to reveal itself in them. It is not only the writing, but all things in nature that begin to reveal the secrets of nature to a person.

Saʿdi says, "When the eyes open and begin to see with the divine light and divine sight, even the leaves of the trees become as the pages of a bible to them."

11

FAITH

When the question of faith comes before the orthodox, they always think that it is their religion that is spoken of. To have faith in a religion, in the priests or clergy, in a certain dogma, or ceremony, or principle, or in a certain form of teaching, this is what is usually understood by the word *faith*. On the other hand, those who are intellectual and look at life from a different point of view say, "Faith is blind; why should we believe blindly?"

To mystics, faith is the only power that works through the whole creation. They do not mean by faith a belief in a certain religion or dogma or ceremony or book or teacher; they mean trust—a trust even in the absence of reason.

Many people possess this quality naturally, while others do not seem to possess it. We may think that one person has brought faith with them and another person not, because they have or have not that quality. But when we study life minutely we find that there is no soul that does not possess faith. How true it is when the Prophet says, "Every soul when born is a faithful follower (*muslim*, which means 'faithful'); it is afterward that he turns, when he turns to the contrary."[1] This really means that every soul is born on earth with a simple faith,

1. Hadith.

and it is afterward that it doubts. If it were not so, we should never have been able to learn the language we speak. Was it not learned by faith, from infancy? When the mother says, "This is a tree," the child says "tree"; when she says, "This is water," the child calls it "water." And there are many things that the parents speak of, apart from ordinary language, and the child believes them as they want the child to believe. Whether the name given to the things be right or wrong, the child takes them as its guardians wish it to take them, because that is the child's natural tendency.

In the beginning every soul is faithful. Then how is it that one loses this quality that nature has given? One loses it by the knowledge of names and forms. As one grows one covers one's faith with the knowledge of names and forms, calling that "learning." At every step in one's progress toward knowledge one compares things, and considers some things better than others, saying of one thing, "This is true," of another, "This is false"; "That is what I can believe and rely upon," and "This is what I cannot believe and rely upon." The one thing one calls true, the other false; but in reality neither is true nor false. It is only at the beginning of knowledge that one passes through this condition. Later, when one has raised oneself above ordinary knowledge, one arrives at a stage when one is able to say, "All that I have called true is not true, and all that I have called false is not false." One finds that, whatever difference there is, it is a difference of comparison. This point of view is difficult and vague, and everybody does not perceive it.

The course of human life involves so many disappointments, so many failures, so many heartaches, that no one can avoid doubting. There is a peasant saying, "He who once has burned his tongue with hot milk tries to cool buttermilk by blowing on it." When someone has been deceived by one person, they distrust ten people; when they have found one person unreliable, they may perhaps consider a hundred others are also unreliable. After failing in one thing they suspect they will fail in a thousand things. So many things take away that natural and powerful quality that was at first present, that faith that is the secret of the whole creation, the secret of all success that can ever be attained in life. This faith is broken by life's discouraging experiences. When confidence in others is lost, then confidence in self is lost also; and the more it is lost, the more failures one meets. Doubting persons consider themselves to be wise, and one of simple faith to be a fool. Whoever they see, they suspect; whatever they hear, they question whether it be right or wrong. They will doubt even their friend in business, waiting for the time to come when they can trust that friend. But that time never comes. Their very doubts create doubts in the mind of the suspected person; and often the doubts come true, as the effect of the doubter's thought; or at least it creates an illusion that for the moment shows the picture of their doubts.

How truly the story of Othello demonstrates this. The more he doubted Desdemona, the more proofs for his doubt life created. His doubt was fed more and more by the illusory proofs, until in the end he could not possibly believe the least thing contrary to his doubts. So it is with our own lives. We doubt; and that very doubt that which we fear happens, because it is created by us in the other person's heart. Whether the actions we see support our doubt or only seem to support it, yet our suspicion creates the desire in the doubted person.

We can experience the same thing with dogs. If we have the least fear of a dog barking or biting, he will bark and come up to bite us. If there is no fear in us, the dog will not come toward us. The fear that makes us suspect that the dog will bite is enough to give the dog the desire to bite, because we are looking for it to do so.

If we could only develop the quality that is called faith, about which so much is said in the scriptures, in the Bible, in the Qurʾan, we should find what power it would carry. It is the secret of all success.

We are here to fulfill the purpose of our life. What is that purpose? Our desire, our inclination that is constantly at work in our mind, that is the purpose of our life. If we are unable to fulfill that inclination, we go from this world without accomplishing our purpose. As Omar Khayyam says, "Heaven is the vision of fulfilled desire / Hell is the shadow of a soul on fire."[2] If the desires are not fulfilled, the soul is naturally on fire. But there is no reason why the desire should not be fulfilled; the very existence of a desire promises its fulfillment. In the heart of man is the desire of God. The Qur'an says that without the will of God not even a single atom can move.[3] This shows that every wave of thought and feeling, every motion and action is from God. Every thought that comes to our mind is God's thought, even if it appears to be a thought of everyday life in the world.

Once people realize that every activity and impulse that comes into their mind is really from God, from that time they feel that it must be fulfilled. If it is not fulfilled, it is their limitation that has become the cause of its hindrance; they have allowed their weakness to hinder its accomplishment. It is their lack of faith that generally meets with failures. In faith is the secret of fulfillment or nonfulfillment of every thought. There is no doubt about the fulfillment of a desire if one's faith works with it. But when one's own reason and doubt come and destroy the hope, one generally meets with failure.

What an important part faith plays in life! Can there be anything equal to it? In the Arabic language it is called *iman*. The whole of religion is faith, however much people have called the separate religions faiths. Faith itself is a religion.

Now the question arises, is one to believe and trust anyone blindly? Would that not be a blind faith? Would it not be covering the reason, the power of discrimination between

2. *Rubaiyat*, verse lxvii, trans. FitzGerald: "Heav'n but the Vision of fulfill'd Desire / And Hell the Shadow from a Soul on fire."
3. Sura 10:61.

right and wrong, between possible and impossible? Suppose a person says you are going to be a king, and you believe it, this would be a blind faith, since there is no possibility of its being realized; still more impossible would it be to believe if someone said, "You are a king," when you see no sign of kingship in your life, but the contrary.

The answer to this question is that the first lesson to be learned is to have faith in oneself. How many among us there are who have no faith in themselves! It is this very lack that makes them have no faith in others. Once one has faith in oneself, one can have faith in others also. For instance, if I esteem a person to be good and spiritual, what does it matter if the whole world should not think the same? But if a person says, "I do not know, perhaps the other person thinks right, and I do not," then that person has no faith. That person does not know what faith is. They may have faith in another, and yet as the days go on, the time comes when they will lose it. A person who disbelieves in themself cannot believe in anybody else, and is really an unbeliever. Faith must begin within. Belief in oneself should be so strong that even if a thousand people say no, one will say yes. To look to others for every opinion, not trusting oneself to say whether it is day or night, is to end by not only distrusting others, but by developing a kind of insanity.

Sometimes a person will say, "I had great faith once, but in the course of my life I have met with people one could never trust. They deceived me, and since then I have lost faith in everybody." That person is much to be pitied; that one has lost so much more than anybody else. The good quality that was in that person has been killed by bad experience. How important it is that the heart of the faithful should be kept unbroken!

In India there is a custom of making birds fight for amusement. It is called *baterbazi*. Two birds are brought together on a table, while all stand around to see the fun. As soon as the birds see one another they attack each other. The owner of each bird thinks, "My bird will win, the prize will be mine." But as soon as it appears as if one bird will be beaten, its owner takes it away, saying to the other, "You have won, we will not continue the fight." This is because he wants to save his bird from being disappointed. The bird would then be without faith.

Those who have no faith in themselves, those whose faith is broken, are like the bird who is allowed to be beaten. However strong it may become, there will always remain the impression on its mind of having been beaten; and this it cannot stand.

It is like this with the elephant, giant animal as it is. Once it is beaten, all its strength and power go. For years it will not forget it. With all that power that is within it, it will never attack another elephant. The faith that really gave it its power has all gone.

In the Hindustani language there is a saying, "Failure and victory are each in the mind." If there is failure, it is in the mind; if there is victory, it is also in the mind. As long as the mind has not failed, a seeming failure may be a victory. But if the mind has failed, a seeming victory becomes a failure. That great power that the mind has is nothing but the power of faith. People who have done great works have not done them in accordance with the number of things with which they were provided at first; for instances occur in which people began life without a penny, and yet have ended their lives the possessors of millions. They have had no help to encourage them in life, or to raise them in life; they have raised their position themselves.

So we see that reason has no part in faith. People may be called fanatics, because they work only by faith, thinking that faith only enables us to imagine things. But there are numberless people who are thinking and reasoning all their lives, asking themselves, "Shall I do this? How can I do that? How can I overcome these obstacles?" All the time they are thinking of the hindrances, waiting for suitable environments to come; and they never come. The whole life may be spent in the pursuit of something reason forbids them from attaining.

It is quite otherwise with faith. When there is faith there is no thought about whether there are any means of accomplishing the desire that has come to the person's mind, or whether there are no means. This does not matter when faith is there, to care for and to defend the thought, to rain upon the thought and make the plant grow and bear fruit, so that some day one sees one's thought fulfilled.

Ask those people who have had wonderful lives in the world. See what they have to say about it. What does Christ say? What does Muhammad say? Christ said to Peter, when he walked on the water, "O thou of little faith, wherefore didst thou doubt?"[4] If Peter had had faith, he could have conquered the waters.

In the different wars that the Prophet of Arabia had to face throughout his life, what do we find? From the beginning to the end there were wars. He was born an orphan, for his father was not living at the time of his birth and his mother died in giving him birth. There were no means, either of money or of power; and when the message was given, then the whole community rose against him; even his relatives were against him. What stayed by him? It was his faith. His call to his people was to have faith.

It once happened that when the army of the Prophet's enemies had success, one among them by chance caught the Prophet alone. He was sitting on his chest, and wanted to kill him. But before doing so, he said, "O Prophet, all your life you have taught the name of God. Now tell me where your God is. Where has he gone?" And the Prophet called on the name of God, on whom he called night and day; and as soon as that name came to his mind, the strength of the whole world came into the Prophet. With one bound he brought the man down, took his sword in his hand, saying, "Who will save thee now,

4. Matthew 14:31.

since thou art again in my hands?" And he answered, "Thou, Muhammad." And Muhammad said, "O man of little faith, till now thou hast not learned the lesson. Now thou hast seen that my faith in him saved me. He has just saved me. If thou takest the name, he will save thee too. Ask him."

The strength of that faith and the hope it imparts, the power it gives, the might that faith can give, is there anything like it?

One person may doubt and doubt. Things will come, and perhaps things will not come. Another person will trust, and he will be watching, and his trust will become bigger with every experience.

There is a story of a Sufi who was traveling with a caravan through Arabia. Among the travelers were some with provisions for their expenses. They came to a place where it was said, "This is a place where robbers are likely. Everybody must take care of his own purse. Since many caravans have been robbed about here, we should be prepared." This young Sufi also had some money, but he thought to himself, "I have no place to keep my money. I will find some man with whom I can leave it. To whom can I give it for safety?" He was wondering if there could be any village or habitation, but could only find a tent some distance away from where the caravan had come to a halt. So he went, and found a man sitting smoking his pipe in the tent. He went up to him and said, "I do not know you, sir, but I have heard there are robbers here and that many caravans have been robbed, and I am a poor man. I thought I must save my money, if I could only see someone to whom I could trust it; having found this tent, I feel I should entrust it to you." He left the purse, and returned to the caravan. When he arrived he found that the caravan had been robbed, and all had lost their money. He was very glad he had escaped. They were all moaning and lamenting about their losses. He thought that he at any rate was safe. Then they described the robbers, saying how many of them had come, how many were there.

Then he returned to the tent to fetch his money again. He found the same man smoking there, but he was surrounded by many men, for he proved to be the chief of the robbers. The others were all sitting there, fighting and disputing what share each should take, and the chief was helping them to divide their spoil. So the young man was afraid to go nearer; and at the same time could not help thinking how foolish he was not to have kept it, for while he was bringing it the robbers had come, and so he would have escaped anyway. They lost everything, but he himself had fooled himself. While he was thinking this, and was about to turn away, the chief called out for him to be fetched. He approached the chief trembling, because he believed that now even his life was in danger. The chief said, "Why did you come here; why are you trying to go away again?" The young man asked, "Are you not the head of the robbers? Then why should I not wish to go? What use can it be to come?" The chief answered, "Man, I received your money to keep; I did not rob you of it. You trusted me. The money is therefore your trust. Even if I am a robber, I am not dishonest. I gain through robbery, not by breaking trust. You trusted me with your money, and your money is safe. Here it is for you to take back again." So the young man was delighted, reflecting what a good thing trust is, inasmuch as one may have faith even in a robber, for he had proved himself trustworthy.

We can see this in our everyday life. A servant, a helper, an assistant, a coworker, a partner can be made either trustful or distrustful, trustworthy or unworthy of trust; this we do ourselves by our own faith. How true it is that when faith is beginning to fail, when doubts begin to come, the loss of faith goes on until one begins to doubt one's nearest and dearest friends. Husband can doubt wife; wife can doubt husband; brother can doubt sister; parents can doubt children. One can doubt one's nearest friend, and in the end one doubts oneself. There is the last limit; from then life can be nothing less than a torture.

The question arises: is it right to cover our reason, and act according to our faith? The answer is, "No, it is not right." Reason is the servant of faith, and faith is the sovereign of reason. But failure comes when reason becomes the sovereign, and faith the servant. Success comes when faith is sovereign and reason is the servant. Reason helps faith; reason is the servant of faith. If faith says, "I wish to open a factory," reason replies, "Yes, you can proceed with your factory in this way. There is your success." Reason is servant; faith is the first thing. Faith says, "I will succeed." Reason says, "These are the different paths you will have to take." This is how faith is helped by reason.

It is very different when reason is sovereign. When reason is sovereign, it says, "Open a factory? Why, just look at yourself, without a single penny in your pocket." Faith says, "Yes, you are right." Reason says, "You don't know anything about a factory; how can you pretend to carry on such work?" And faith answers, "Yes, I will not think about it any more." When reason is the leader of faith, the result is failure; it is when faith is the leader of reason that there is success.

In regard to the matter of trusting people a person may think, "Is it right to believe in anything a person says? Is it right to trust everybody? There are many people who are not worth trusting; shall we then trust everybody in order to develop our trust?" The answer is yes. Perhaps you will have failures, but you will only trust another person when you trust yourself; when you have faith yourself then you will have faith in another. Without faith in yourself you can never have faith in another; to have faith in another is to have faith in yourself. It does not matter if once or twice you are disappointed; but if you are afraid of being disappointed even once in your life, perhaps all your life you will doubt; and therefore there will never come a time when you will be able to trust anybody, even yourself. There are many things that can develop your trust. Sometimes an unworthy person can become worthy of trust.

The Hindus say that if you have faith in an idol god, that god will listen and grant your desires; and if you have no faith in the God of heaven, even God is helpless to do anything for you. The Bible says that faith like a grain of mustard can remove mountains.

There is a story that once a preacher was speaking in a little village in India. The peasants he was speaking to could not understand philosophy or mysticism, or about the great problems of life. What they taught was, "Have faith in God; faith is such a great virtue". Speaking about faith, the preacher said that if a person repeated the sacred word he would be able to walk on water. Everyone was delighted to hear this, saying, "What a great thing! He is always talking about this same thing." Next day an old man came and said, "Sir, I cannot understand the deep problems of life, but I was very delighted with your idea last evening." The preacher answered, "What was that?" He said, "I was very much surprised. Will you come and dine at my place? It will be such an honor." The preacher said, "Yes, with great pleasure." A day was appointed. When the day came, the man arrived to fetch the preacher, and they set off together. On their way there was a little river that had to be crossed. When they reached the bank, the preacher said, "Where is the boat?" "Why do you ask for a boat?" the peasant replied. "The other day you said that when you use that sacred word you can walk on the water. And I was very much astonished to find that it is so. Why take a boat when it is only necessary to say that word?" But the preacher could not do it; he was not a true teacher. So he said to the old man, "You are my teacher. I have spoken, but you have acted; and if I had had your faith I should also have been able to cross."

This shows to us that things sometimes seem obscured, as if in a mist, as through a glass darkly. We fear beforehand that a thing will never come, that there will always be disappointment, failure, sorrow. Depression comes on; we begin to think the times will never alter, and the conditions continue. The only remedy to clear these clouds away is to look for a better time, to hope for something better in life, to feel that every thought, desire, and impulse that comes to our heart is from God, and that it is to be accomplished with all power for some purpose. Not even circumstances in life, not even friends and advisers in life, not our reason or our doubt should be allowed to break the fulfillment of our thoughts. It is through that one thing, faith, that our thoughts are kept powerful and full of strength; it is by nothing but that one thing—faith.

12

THE EFFECT OF PRAYER

Keen study of life enables us to perceive that every individual is dependent upon every other. This is true of all aspects of life. The rich are dependent upon the poor, the strong upon the weak, the wise upon the foolish. When we see how limited people are even at their best, we see that it cannot be otherwise than that one must depend upon another in order to obtain the needs of life.

It is evident that servants are dependent upon the wages that are paid them, that workers are dependent on the money they receive. But there are needs that money cannot buy, and then they who receive repay by love or kindness or care. Times come when money is too poor, when influence is powerless to buy or take. When this is so, the natural thing is to pay respect and adoration to the one in life to whom money and influence cannot be given. It does not matter whether the respect and adoration is given with a selfish or an unselfish motive; in either case there is the same dependence. One is dependent upon one's beloved, or upon one's spouse, or upon one's neighbor, even upon one's servant. How troubles and difficulties begin if that servant happens not to be at home! Whether one pays money, or whether one can only show love and adoration, one is dependent just the same. From the time when one opens one's eyes as an infant, one's life is nothing but dependence all through.

Those who watch keenly will see what is real dependence, and how far-reaching that dependence is in our life. Those who need money, are they not dependent on persons who have money? Those who desire position, are they not dependent upon someone who has position, such as a secretary of state, a lord, a duchess, a high official? The more one reflects, the vaster does one see this web of dependence to be. More and more clear does it become that all the sources upon which people depend exist for the use of the different individuals. One individual desires or needs wealth; and therefore there are people who have it, and that person can be dependent upon them. Another may desire or need a rise of position; therefore there is someone who is in a high position, who can distinguish that person or place that person in a higher position. That person will bow to this one; they will respect this one; they will do anything to gain this one's favor and kindness.

When we discern that every individual has some different source of power before which they bow, to which they turn, on which they are dependent, the question comes, "Is there any one source that is supreme above all these other sources of power? These various sources depend on one another. Is there one that reigns over all?" The answer is, "Yes, there is one. There is a source that reigns over all other sources of power. This one source is that which we idealize, and name God."

Those who idealize this source call upon it, pay all their respect to it, turn to it in every difficulty, in every trouble, in every want. There is no one who will suffice to console them, there is no means of assistance, no help to be obtained, but this one ideal on which they fix their eyes, this ideal that is not known nor seen, yet idealized in the mind. How poor all other sources are compared with that one source! Whereas all the various sources to which people bow, on which people depend are so uncertain that today they are kind and tomorrow they are not, yet that one source is all-sufficient, never changing, and almighty. From that source all things can be obtained. All other sources are only apparent powers; for after all, even if they do succeed in giving anything, it is still really the one source that has given them the power to provide for our needs.

The nizam of Hyderabad, the last king of the Deccan, was a great mystic and a very good man.[1] He used to say to those who had obtained access to him and made a complaint of not having yet received help, "Have you got an order from There? If you have got one from There I will give you help, but if you have not got it from There, I will not give it to you."

In the Qur᾽an there is a sura that says, "God alone is rich, and all are poor."[2] The more we study life, the more we see the truth of this sura. People may live in palaces endowed with all manner of wealth and comfort, and yet they can still reflect, "If I had that, I would never be unhappy again." People may have their motorcars, their furs, their wealth of millions, and yet cannot truthfully say, "I am perfectly happy." Can they say, "I have all that I need in life?" Is there anyone who can say this? You are more likely to find such a one among those who are poor than among those who are wealthy.

This shows that God alone is rich. Whoever has need is poor. Poverty means need. As long as there is need there is poverty. Since one's life is full of needs, one must be in poverty. One is still in darkness if one does not realize that there is only One who is rich.

Undoubtedly we, all of us, have our needs through life. How many times do we experience disappointment regarding them. How many are disappointed in love, in money, in help, in service. How apt the heart is to be discouraged, disappointed, broken, feeling, "Oh, this is my brother, my only brother, and yet he has not helped me at this hour of need." Or "I

1. H.E.H. Mahbub Ali Khan, d. 1911.
2. Sura 47:38

looked on her as my sister, and yet she has failed me at this crucial time." So many disappointments do people meet in life. One depends, depends on limited sources, never reflecting that these sources can only sometimes be helpful, that many times they are quite unable to help, however much they may desire to do so.

There remains the one source that is always helpful, and can always help. It is only because one does not see God, does not realize God, that one doubts whether there is such a being as God or not. However religious or pious one is, one always looks to a material agent for help. However religious or pious, one cannot explain God; not even a mystic or philosopher can explain God. The ideal of God is the first lesson that must be learned; and it cannot be learned by analysis. Therefore the intellectual mind that seeks for an analysis of God is always sure to be disappointed. The philosopher spoke truly when he said, "To analyze God is to dethrone God." Analysis can never portray even the ideal of God. That is how it is that every messenger—Muhammad, Christ, Moses, Abraham—emphasized the one word: faith.

But it is not to be thought that these seers and holy ones and teachers who had such power and realization could have wanted the world to imagine that this faith should be blind. They themselves learned the first lesson that it is no use beginning with the idea, "If I analyze God, I shall believe in God." Such a one will never believe. The first step is faith, and not reasoning or intellectual perception. Can you explain to anyone why it is that a diamond is worth twenty thousand pounds? Is there any reason for this? "Yes, you say, it is because it is sold in the market for that price." There is no other explanation. You may answer, "It is a stone." And I may say, "Yes, it is a bright stone; no doubt it is better than glass. It is certainly brighter than a crystal. But why twenty thousand pounds?" The answer is just this, "It is twenty thousand pounds because your ideal has made it so." The ideal is only another way of saying, "There is no explanation." You have to take it that twenty thousand pounds is its value. It is the same with every ideal, even with the ideal of God. An ideal is beyond explanation.

We rise by treading the path of faith. Some day we shall realize what God is, but that only comes after the first lesson has been learned. Faith is the ABC of the revelation of God. This faith is begun by prayer.

There are three different kinds of prayer.

1. One prayer is thanksgiving to God for God's great goodness, for all that we receive in our life; asking God for God's mercy and favor and forgiveness; asking God to grant the desires and wishes that we have. That is the first prayer. This is the first lesson that one has to learn. The other kinds of prayer can only be used as one develops.

In thanking God for all that God has given us we develop that very thankfulness that a person so usually forgets. If we could only reflect upon how many things there are in our life for which we should be thankful and appreciative. But we scarcely ever think about them. We so often think about what we have not got; and therefore keep ourselves always unhappy, when we might be thankful to have a few pennies in our purse. Instead of that we think we should have a few shillings. The consequence is that one forgets to develop the thankful nature; one is unthankful to everyone; and therefore, whatever is done for one, one is still unthankful.

It is the same with all the trouble and struggle that there is in the world. It is one's neglect of all that is done for one, one's neglect of acknowledging one's appreciation of all that is done for one, that causes the spread of unthankfulness. Having forgotten the prayer of thanking God, how can one thank another? How that beautiful custom is disappearing, of saying grace before partaking of the meal! This custom is no longer to be found at fashionable tables; only at houses where there is no fashion, for when fashion comes, the things that are helpful, moral, and spiritual are forgotten. But what a beautiful thought it is to say grace even before a bread-and-butter tea, before a humble dinner. When thanks have been given to God, however simple the dinner may be, it becomes delicious, because of the feeling of thankfulness, the feeling that this is a gift that has been bestowed upon us.

Think, too, of Saʿdi who was traveling to Persia, sorely stricken because he had to walk with bare feet in the hot sun. It was so painful to walk that he thought, "There can be no one in the world who is so wretched and miserable as I." But two minutes did not pass before he came across a man whose feet were both useless, so that he was crawling along the ground, and only progressing with great difficulty. This caused a prayer to rise in Saʿdi's heart, and he became thankful he was not afflicted like that. He thought, "If I have no shoes, at least my feet are healthy and sound."

It is when we engage our whole attention in observing the misery and difficulties that are around us that we become discontented. It is when we are blind to the goodness and kindness and sympathy and service and help that our fellow men and women give us, that we become discontented. There is so much to look at in our lives to excite the feeling of thankfulness in us.

Then there is the mystical meaning of thankfulness. Those persons who are always grudging are so much the more in need of prayer. If they pray they will prepare influences that will remove the miseries and wretchedness in their minds, for all this misery is created by their minds during the act of grumbling and having a grudge. Those persons who are thankful and contented and appreciative of all that befalls them in life develop the sense of goodness in their life. The more appreciative they are, the more thankful they become, and the more do they receive. Thankfulness and appreciation inevitably attract more of their like to themselves. All that we give is also given to us. But grumbling and grudging also attract their like to ourselves. If those persons to whom we give a reward or gift receive it grudgingly and grumblingly, shall we give them more? Indeed, the fact that we do not give them more gives them still more to grumble about. But those who are glad and thankful and appreciative of what is done for them, you think they are so good. It gives you such a feeling and such happiness to see them happy and appreciative and contented, that they encourage you to do more, and it encourages others to do good also.

Besides thankfulness there is the request for forgiveness and mercy. The effects of this are also to be seen in our daily life. A servant, or child, or young person who is abrupt will push against you and never say, "I am sorry." But another person says, "I am sorry," and at once you have forgotten the harm that person has inadvertently done to you. That is the effect that the person's request for forgiveness has produced.

In some countries and among some people (for instance in France) there is a custom that when a person meets you at the door or on the stairs, he takes off his hat and says, "Pardon." There is no reason why he should do so except that he chanced to meet you, and he thinks that perhaps he should be forgiven. We find that the sensitiveness of a person's heart is so delicate that even the presence of a stranger causes a jar. But by saying "Pardon" that uncomfortable feeling is at once removed, and in the place of that the good feeling of friendship is introduced. However great a fault may be, if a person only comes and says, "I am very sorry; I will never do it again; pray forgive," the friendship at once comes back. On the other hand, however trivial and slight the fault may have been, if pride prevents the person from asking forgiveness and pardon, perhaps they will lose that friendship for the rest of their life. Their pride prevents them from asking pardon. The fault may have been very small, and they may say, "I do not care about it"; and yet the friendship is broken. How many there are who would be ready to forgive if only the other came and said, "I am sorry." But not everybody will do it, nor will admit they have been at fault.

To ask forgiveness of another produces a proper sense of justice in one's mind. One perceives the need for asking God to pardon one's faults. When one asks for forgiveness, that forgiveness develops in one's nature too, and one becomes ready to forgive others. Christ says in his prayer: Forgive us, because we have forgiven others. The virtue, the secret is in that. By asking forgiveness of God you give up the desire to demand forgiveness from your fellow men and women, and you desire to give forgiveness to them. We see this with the Arabs and Bedouins in Mecca and the deserts. They are so ready to fight one another and kill each other. They may be fighting, and actually have their knives drawn to kill one another; and yet if a third person comes along and says, "Forgive, for the sake of God and the Prophet," as soon as they hear these words they will both throw away their knives and shake hands. The handshake is the seal of friendship. Though the Bedouin has no education, yet he has such a devotion to God and his Prophet that no sooner does he hear these words than he at once offers his hand, and from that day there is no spite or evil thought in his heart.

If we only had that feeling! With all our education and learning, with all the claims of civilization that we make, we are not as good as these. We retain the bitterness in our hearts. We never reflect what a poison it is. The very people who would shudder at the idea of having something in their body that is decayed and offensive, something that should not be there, but should be taken off, or cut out, or removed, will tolerate that poison of bitterness in their mind, the real and higher self; they will not take it out, but will foster it. Did they not lack the sense of forgiveness, did they not neglect to cultivate the habit of asking forgiveness, they would become ready to forgive and forget.

Have you ever experienced the joy when two friends who have quarreled have mutually asked forgiveness of one another? It is as if there were no more possibility of ill feeling. It is the most delightful sensation. It feels as if the doors of heaven were open for both. When the bitterness has gone, it is as if a mountain had gone, and the heart were free again.

The third part of the first kind of prayer is our need. This is a delicate thing, and yet it is a great virtue. What a beautiful nature it is that will refrain from asking relief from trouble, from difficulty and suffering except from the one Friend! Such a one is too shy to ask anybody; such a one has that sense of honor that forbids one to intrude. This is a virtue, and not pride. The door of faith is kept open for that Friend upon whom one can call, and ask, and obtain ease. "There is one to whom I can go in my trouble and distress and despair. You are the one, the only one. You are the one before whom nothing is hid. If I desire to unburden myself of this trouble, You, O God, are the one to whom I will go."

What a great thing this is! What a sense of honor it is that causes one to refrain from telling one's suffering to anyone but God, believing that God will help more than any one can help. Perhaps another person could help, but it will not bring the satisfaction that comes when it is God that has given the help. What a great pleasure, what a great honor God has done to give one help. That is what comes when the problem has been solved that comes into the life of every noble person, everyone with tender feelings, with inherited good and religious sentiments, solved by deciding, "There is no one whom I will ask in my poverty and trouble and need, but only God."

These are three things that go to make up the first kind of prayer.

There is a story of the emir of Kabul. He was once traveling in the jungle on a shooting excursion. It happened that his bodyguards and people had remained behind, and he could not find them. Being hungry and thirsty, he thought he would go somewhere in the fields to see if there were not a house where he could obtain some food. At length he found the house of a peasant, and said, "I am hungry; can you give me some food?" Of course they did not know it was the emperor, and they were very glad to bring a bowl of buttermilk—the drink of the poor people there—and bread, with a few pickles and some butter. The emir was very glad for all these simple things; so hungry was he that he found the dish delicious; besides, the goodness and the kindness with which they welcomed him satisfied him still more; and how glad they were to serve him! All these things impressed his mind. He said, "How do you get on?" They expressed their contentment in saying, "Thanks to God, we get on very well. Sometimes famines come, but we have had no difficulties. The last one was twelve years ago." The emperor replied, "Whenever you have difficulties"—giving them his seal—"bring this to the city, and show it to any of the authorities and I will try my best to help you." They said, "Thank you, sir," and hesitated to accept the royal seal, since their hospitality and kindness was given without thought of reward, but only out of their desire to please, and out of love and goodness.

But a few years later a time of famine came round, and it was very severe. So hard was the famine that they had no animals left in their fields to work with; there was no food, and their children began to starve. They could not bear to see the starvation of their children. The wife said, "Will you go to the city, and take the seal, and find the man who gave it to us? Perhaps he will be able to help us. The trouble is nothing to us; but our children are starving, and it is great suffering for them." Saying yes, he took the seal and duly reached Kabul.

There he shows the seal to a policeman; and as soon as the latter sees it, he says, "It is the seal of the emir," and therefore takes him to the palace. The peasant had never seen a palace before, but he goes there and is told that the emperor cannot be seen till he is at liberty. The peasant must wait in the hall.

So he sits in the hall, where the emir is offering his prayers. The peasant stands and waits for the emir, trembling at the prospect of seeing him, for he did not know before that it was the emir himself who had been at his house. Then he begins to wonder what the emir is doing there, bowing and kneeling and prostrating himself, and performing all the proper ceremonies of prayer. After a time the prayer is finished, and he calls the man, saying, "I am at liberty. For what reason do you come? How is your family?" He replies, "The famine is very bad, and that is what has made me come. But please tell me what is it you have been doing all this time." The emperor answers, "Offering prayers to God." And the man says, "To whom? God? God? For what?" "It is to give me all that I seek, and to give my subjects all they need—God's support, God's protection." So the man says, "Is there anyone who can give you and your subjects what they wish?" "Yes, it is God who can do that." So the peasant replies, "If there a is person higher than you, why should not I also ask that person in my need?"

The king was moved to tears at the sight of the patience, the spirit of this man, whose family was left starving; he is here before the emir seeking for help, and yet as soon as he comes to know that there is a greater king, a king higher than all the kings of the world, he says, "Why should I not ask him too?"

The emir was much moved. He sent all that was needed, with the word that the King of kings had sent it, not he.

What honor, what spirit it brings when we fix our trust on the one who is called Almighty, who is almighty. Rumi says, "When fire, air, earth, and water all seem to us dead things, the elements, yet they are servants to God. They work for him, and they always obey him!" And he goes on to say, in another part of his *Masnavi*, "Man, when he becomes intelligent, begins to see causes. But it is the superman who sees the Cause of causes, the Source of causes."[3] God is the Cause of causes, the precedent Cause. One who looks at the precedent Cause sees the cause of all in time. People may study causes all their life, and yet never come to understand the Cause of causes. All causes, before that Cause, become effects. That Cause remains the Cause that is called the Word, and then became Light. The

3. *Masnavi* 1:838, 840–46.

Qur'an says that when the word was spoken, all things came to existence. And Saint John says, "Without him (the Word) was not any thing made that was made."[4]

What is this Cause? It is that inner divine impulse that has made itself active in every direction, and has accomplished whatever it purposed. It is that which has accomplished all things. The one Cause behind all things is the Cause that we call the power of God.

2. There are two more kinds of prayer.

When people have evolved, they begin to use still higher prayer. That prayer is the adoration of the immanence of God in the sublimity of nature. Read the lives of all the prophets and teachers from Krishna to Buddha, Moses to Muhammad, Abraham to Christ, and see how they dwelt in the jungles, and went into the forests, sat beneath trees, and there recognized the divine immanence in all around them. It is a prayer, not to a God in heaven, but to a God living both in heaven and on earth.

What praise of God, praise of God's creation, praise of God's nature will develop in one! It develops in one such an art that nothing can compare with it, a sense of music with which no music can be compared. One begins to see how natures are attracted to one another, and how they harmonize; one sees how inharmonies are produced. The causes of all such things become clear to one once one begins to see into nature, to admire the beauty of its construction, its life, its growth; as soon as one begins to study nature and its causes.

Those who have praised nature through their art appeal directly to one's heart. Those who praise nature in their music become artists in music, and those who have expressed their praise in poetry and verse are seen to be great poets. All of them appeal to the human heart because they have seen God. They have seen God in nature; and not alone in nature, but also on

4. Qur'an 36:82; John 1:3.

earth. They have turned earth into heaven. That is the next, the higher step.

Zoroaster has said, "Look at the sun when you pray; at the moon when you pray; at the fire when you pray." People therefore call them sun worshippers, fire worshippers, when all the time this worship was merely a way of directing one's attention to all the witnesses of God that express God's nature. The one who cannot see any traces of God anywhere can see God by looking at all these beautiful things, and observing the harmonious working of all these things.

From beginning to end, the Qur᾿an points to nature, showing by the sun that rises in the morning, and by the moon that comes in the evening, by the nature that is over all, that there is God. Why does the Qur᾿an always express it in this way: if you wish to have some proof of God, look at nature and see how wisely it is made? Or is it without wisdom? A Hindu poet says, "Mankind, with your wisdom you become so proud that you think there is nothing else worthy. You know not that there is a Perfection of Wisdom before which man is not as a drop to the ocean." People look at the surface of the ocean. Yet they are so small that they cannot even be compared to one of its drops, limited as they are in intellect and in their knowledge. They seek to find out the secret of the whole creation through their intellect, whereas those who have just touched it have bowed to God, forgetting their limited self. After that God remained, and spoke through them. Such are the only beings who have been able to give any truth to the world.

As Amir says, "He who has lost his limited self, he it is who has attained the High Presence." Do we not forget ourselves when we behold the vision of beauty? If we are blind to beauty, no doubt we cannot see it, and then we cannot forget ourselves in the beauty and sublimity of vision. When we perceive the beauty of nature we bow our head in love and admiration. "I cannot study you, for you are too great, you are too beautiful.

The only thing left for me to do is to bow my head in prostration at your feet."

If we could only see this perfect beauty around us, if we only had our eyes opened to it, we should at once bow the head in all humility before ever deeming to make a study of it. No pride could find a place in our heart. Without any doubt we should bow our head before this beauty and wisdom of the Creator, the art of the Creator and the Creator's skill in the flowers and plants and leaves; in the construction of human beings, their birth, and all other things in life.

It would suffice did we but once ask how all these things have come to be. But, as the poet says, "Where there are no teeth, milk is given; when the teeth come, the food suitable for teeth comes also." The eyes are so delicate, and a delicate eyelid is formed for them, to cover and protect them. How all the organs of the human body are fitted and suited to the purpose for which they are made. And with all that there is also the beauty of the art with which the things are made. And the height of beauty is attained in the skill shown in the making of humankind.

Whoever has seen beauty, has found that beauty cannot exist without wisdom. Wisdom is behind creation. The One Life, which has created the lakes and plants and birds and all things, is both One Life and One Wisdom. The flower, the leaf, and the fruit and branches all come from one root, even though they have different names. It is all one. It might be called he or she; yet it is both. When we see that life with wisdom is both he and she, we see that wisdom is behind all things that we see; and then we say that that which is behind all things is a person whom we call God.

3. The third way of prayer is still greater. It is the way followed by philosophers and mystics. Advancement in the spiritual path is gradual. One cannot use this third way without first having used the other two kinds of prayer.

The third kind of prayer is that of invocation of the names of God, of the truth of God's being. These are symbolic names. In their meaning there is a subtlety. God's nature is explained in this form of prayer; God is analyzed. The benefit of this prayer is perceived when one has arrived on this plane. And the benefit is that one has passed from being a human being, as in the first prayer, through being a holy being, as in the second prayer, to become a super-being. Why? Because this third prayer is given in order to bring one still closer to God. Not only does this prayer draw one closer to God, but it makes one forget one's limited self until it is entirely forgotten in the end, leaving only the self of God, the only ideal and aim of all teachers.

One has not arrived at one's ideal goal until one has used prayer to help one to this stage.

When we look at things from a mystical point of view, we shall find that there is one single straight line, which is called aim. That line represents the line of the life of any being. The upper end is God, the lower end is the human. The line is one. But though that line is one to the mystic, to the philosopher, to those who have realized the truth of God, yet the line is unlimited at the upper end, limited at the other. One end is in immortality, the other in mortality.

The innermost yearning of life is to see the ends brought together. It is the third prayer that draws the end closest to the human near to the end that is God. When one evokes the name of God, one forgets one's limitations and impresses one's soul with the thought of the Unlimited. This brings one to the ideal of unlimitedness. That is the secret of life's attainment.

Human beings are the picture or reflection of their imagination. They are as large as they think themselves, as great as they think themselves, as small as they think themselves. If they think they are incapable, they remain incapable; if they think themselves foolish, they will be foolish, and will remain foolish; if they think themselves wise, they will be wise, and become wiser every moment; if they think themselves mighty, they are mighty. Those who have proved themselves to be the greatest warriors, where did their might come from? It was from their thought, their feeling: "I am a mighty one." The idea of "mighty one" was impressed on their soul; and the soul became might. The poet had poetry impressed on his or her soul, and so the soul became a poet. Whatever is impressed on a person's soul, with that the soul becomes endowed, and that the soul will become. If the devil impresses itself on one's soul, one will become a devil; if God is impressed on one's soul, one will turn into God.

13

THE MYSTERY OF BREATH

To a mystic the subject of breath is the deepest of all the subjects with which mysticism or philosophy is concerned, because breath is the most important thing in life. The very life of a person is breath. One lives in the presence of breath, and in the absence of breath one is called a corpse. After death the organs of the body are just the same as before; the only thing that is lacking is breath.

Breath is that within ourselves that keeps all the parts of the body in connection with one another, working together, depending upon one another; it is that which enables one to move, to put one's muscles into action, to keep the whole mechanism of the body always at work. There is no other force or power concerned in all this than this power of breath.

Mystics know that it is regularity of breath that brings good health; that irregularity of breath is the cause of all illness. Many teachers and students of physical culture know that it is not the exercises and practices of this culture that cause the muscles to develop, that impart strength and vigor to the body; they know, as did the ancient mystics in India, that it is a matter of the breath. To practice for one moment with the help of the breath will do more than a whole day's exercises carried out without considering the help of the breath. In the last case the muscles cannot be developed, whereas in the first case the physical body is easily developed with very little physical practice. That this is true is easily shown by looking at the porters at the railway stations. If physical labor were the only thing needed to develop muscles, would they not all be veritable Sandows?[1]

It is especially in India that we can study how men work with heavy things. Sometimes a man will carry on his shoulder a burden that it would ordinarily be impossible for a man of his physique to carry. Yet such a man can not only lift it, but he will walk with it. And when you watch you will find that the secret lies just in the way of breathing. If he did not breathe correctly he could not possibly carry the weight the least distance. There is in India a man called Rama Muti. He can lift elephants and stop motorcars running in full force. When he was asked, "Whence did you get this gigantic strength? You look like an ordinary human being, not like a monster"—he was not extraordinary in size—he said, "You know, and yet you do not know. The secret lies in the breath, which is all power." As people cannot see it they do not believe the possibility of breath giving power. They attach all importance to the things they can see and hear and touch. They are so material that they cannot see anything beyond the matter that their physical eyes are able to see. They are as a blind person who can only feel and not see. They cannot see that strength is something greater than a rock.

How difficult it is for them to perceive the truth of which the Bible speaks: "Your faith will remove mountains."[2] They think mountains are stronger than faith. They say, "How can faith be stronger than the rocks and the mountains? A person cannot lift the mass of a mountain. Surely the mountain is stronger than faith!" The idea is too subtle, too fine for them to understand.

And it is the same with all other fine and subtle things in life. So much more importance is given to the study of the material

1. Eugene Sandow (1867–1925) was famous for his strength and was known as the "father of modern bodybuilding."
2. Matthew 17:20.

sciences, while the spiritual, the higher knowledge, is neglected. More importance is always given to the development of bodily strength. Therefore, when people go to the seaside, often the first thing they do is to weigh themselves, so that they can find out how many pounds they have gained during their holiday. They never think how little time it will take to lose all those pounds again. The weight they have gained at the seaside they will lose again. They do not understand that it is energy that makes a person move and feel active and in good health, not one's bodily weight. Is it not true that the addition of weight to the body makes one lazy and comfort-seeking, and often results in illness? And yet how pleased many people are when they have gained in weight.

Then when we consider the mind, we find that breath has to do with mind also. The mystic knows that the breath that we perceive by exhaling and inhaling through the nostrils is not the essential breath, but only the result of a current that runs not only through the body but also through all the planes of a person's existence. That which the nostrils feel is the result of the activity of breath. Were it not so we could not explain how mind, which is so much vaster and finer than the body, and is a separate element, can possibly exert an effect on the body, and the body on the mind.

Every passion, every emotion has its effect upon the mind; and every change of mind, however slight, has its effect upon the body. Physicians in all ages have realized that consumption is generally an outcome of constant worry.

What keeps mind and body connected? What keeps mind always active? What gives mind its vigor to create imaginations, to create thoughts, and not only to create them, but to retain them by the faculty we call memory; to keep the knowledge by the faculty we call reason; to possess emotions that can sometimes be felt and sometimes not felt? Where does mind keep all these things? What force can it be that is behind them all? Is it not the breath? That is why the mystic studies and realizes and masters the breath, in order to master not only the physical body but also the mind.

From the mystical point of view it is evident that there is some strength, some current, some affinity that runs through and binds together all the trees and plants in a forest, and causes the desert to be without them; that causes the coal mine to have coal all round it, the gold mine to have gold all round it, the sulfur mine to have sulfur all round it. This strength, or force, draws all these elements together.

So it is also with the tides of the sea. That accounts for the waters running in the same direction, whether at first they tended to the south, the east, the west, or the north; it accounts for the surface of the waves keeping a rhythm. Wherever we look, be it the changes of the seasons, the changes of the weather, and even the constant circles that the earth makes in its journey, all these show the same underlying current beneath them, the current of the whole nature, which is the real breath.

The whole universe is going on with a certain rhythm; there is a current that keeps the whole universe going. It is one breath, and yet it is many breaths.

There is a tide that has a cycle of forty days, and a tide that has a cycle of seven days, and another of thirty days, and yet at every moment waves are rising and falling. There is a wave under the wave, and a wave over the wave. There is a tide that turns twice a day, and a tide that turns once a month. So is it with breath: one breath, and yet many breaths.

Then consider how the trees keep together. One tree, and yet its branches and its fruits and its flowers all take different directions. Every branch has a different direction, and yet all keep together. What is it that directs the vigor and the strength of one branch, and not the others in that direction, for they are all attached to the same tree-stem? Is it not that life current that runs through it that directs their ways? As long as it runs through a tree it produces fruits and flowers.

So it is with animals and birds and humans. The same current of life runs through all. The human is the ideal being, as the scripture says. Humans are ideal because intelligence is given to them to perceive the secret of this breath, whereas from animals and birds it is hidden. The life of all creatures is mysterious and full of wonder, but the human being alone is blessed with the intelligence that conveys the power of understanding the secret of the breath. If there is anything more lasting than our transitory life, it is this, the secret of our being. It is by this that one is able to master life both here and in the hereafter.

Having understood this truth, mystics have been able to teach that the religion of all religions is the knowledge of self, for the knowledge of self brings the knowledge of life. This life current that runs through the center of a person's being, attaching mind to body and to all other planes of existence as well, it is this that is all-important. It passes from one's innermost being out to the body, which is the instrument whereby one is able to experience life on the surface. When one has knowledge of this, one begins to realize: "I am not so small as I had thought, not so weak as I had thought; I am much stronger in other planes. I can live much longer than I could on the physical plane. I can see myself in all the different planes by means of that inner knowledge of the breath."

Therefore to the mystics breath is as a lift—a lift in which they sit and rise up to the first floor, and then to the second, and then to the third floor, in fact wherever they wish to go.

The mystery of the Sphinx, and the mystery of Buraq, which is mentioned in the life of the Prophet Muhammad, has to do with this. When the Prophet reached the court, or gate, of God, the Buraq was sent. The Buraq was an animal with wings, and the Prophet rode upon it in order to reach the gate of the highest heaven. He passed gate after gate as he passed the seven heavens. In the end he arrived at the gate of the highest.

What does this allegory mean? The body of the Buraq is this physical body. The wings represent the capability of the breath reaching far and yet retaining its connection with the physical body. The Prophet mounting upon his back represents any soul who treads the spiritual path. Whoever has courage, whoever has faith, whoever has confidence, whoever has trust, whoever has patience and hope and perseverance can tread this path and make use of the vehicle the breath.

If we read the history of Buddha, who was a yogi, we shall find that without yoga and without spiritual meditation—which is accomplished by breath—no one in this world has ever attained spiritual perfection. The healing power of Christ, the magnetism of Muhammad, the miraculous power of Moses, the charm of Krishna, and the inspiration of Buddha—all these were attained by breath. And how did they attain it if there were not a current passing between us on the earth and the source of energy, the source of power and magnetism?

Is it not plain that breath conveys even the words that go out from our lips to the ears of the hearer? The voice is breath. The word is breath. Without breath speech cannot be produced. And yet people may easily accept this, and say, "Yes, it is true that it is breath that does this," but they will not willingly believe that thought is breath also. They can see the movement of the air that arises from speech, and they wonder if it is meant that thought is also a movement of the air. This is because they do not understand that it is all a life current, that is, breath. It is easily seen when it manifests itself upon the physical plane, but on the higher planes it is not seen; yet it extends higher than the planes. If there is anything that connects the human with God, if there is anything that connects the mortal with the immortal, it is nothing but this bridge that we call breath. It is a bridge whereby to pass from the world of mortality to the world of immortality; it is the bridge whereby immortality passes down to mortality. That life that seems mortal is but the ray of immortal life. That which seems mortal is the globe or shell. It is not life that is mortal, it is the cover that makes it seem mortal.

From the time when people perceived that there is a secret in breath, they have thought that they would use their understanding of the secret in order to be able to perform wonders and reach the spirits, master the elements, read thoughts, convey thoughts, and perform any psychic or occult phenomena. But to seek to do these things is to give pearls to buy pebbles. How wasteful to spend life in gaining these powers when breath is the rope that takes us from this mortal plane to immortality, saves us from the struggles and worries of this transitory life, and leads us to the happiness and joy and peace for which every soul longs! If breath can accomplish these pearls, will it not also accomplish the small things, the pebbles, the worldly needs? Yes, it will. To have performed a few wonders is nothing after all.

Some are perhaps striving all day to obtain their bread in a comfortable manner; others are always worrying about how to maintain themselves and their children. Another is thinking, "What can I do to save my fellow humans from their trouble?" If we compare these people, in order to see who is the greater, we notice that the one is greater whose ideal is greater. Whenever we consider the great heroes of the past and present, those whom we admire and to whom we look with hope for right guidance, we shall find that what has made them great has been the greatness of their ideal. The lower the ideal, the less the efforts; the higher the ideal, the greater the life. If we direct all our intelligence and strength and wisdom to accomplish some little thing, it is only a waste of life. To consider what great things one can accomplish, to seek to do those things that will be most useful and valuable to others, that is the ideal life. Those who have earned money just to keep themselves comfortable, what have they accomplished with their life? If they have just gratified their wish to roam about in a motorcar, to set up a comfortable home, to have people waiting upon them, they cannot be happy, because they have not accomplished anything with their life. They may possess many houses, they may possess so much in the bank, they may make a great name; but it will amount to nothing in comparison with the one whose power is greater than all wealth, position, and fame. Such a one will be much happier with the small things of the earth; that person has gained that peace to which the pleasures and transitory joys of this earth offer no comparison. The one life is like the lips touching a cup of delicious wine; the other life is like drinking the whole cup full of heavenly wine. What a difference between just touching the wine with the lips, and drinking it! The pleasures of life are like touching the wine. The experience of these pleasures is only like a dream, a passing joy; it comes and goes again. One longs for the joy of that little pleasure to stay; but how can it stay? If you try for thousands of years, you cannot keep the happiness that is external. The only way to obtain the eternal bliss is to do as the mystics do, and rise by the aid of the breath from plane to plane, finding the greater joy and the greater happiness.

It resembles the taking of a drug. A person may sit in meditation, and dream and imagine they are very happy. A materially minded person may easily say that meditative persons hypnotize themselves into thinking they are full of joy; but is it not hypnotism when a little word of flattery pleases one, when a little silver and gold produces such a change of expression in one's countenance? But the materialist, not understanding this, will laugh at the mystics and call them dreamers. If the mystic is a dreamer, what is the worldly person? Is that one not a dreamer too? What produces the joy in these things that are of no importance? If it is good to be hypnotized by silver and gold, is it not better when the mystic is hypnotized by his or her divine ideal of perfection? The silver and gold will certainly be snatched away; at least the mystic's ideal of God will last.

When we consider how this life and our environment can cramp and restrict us, we understand how it is that with all our hopes we still seek solitude, try to be by ourselves, and close our eyes to all the passing things. The life and activity that are directed to experiencing the pleasures of life, the transitory sources of joy and pleasure, all fade away before that which we seek in solitude, where we strive to reach the inner and enduring things. Even if our bed is comfortable, if our house contains all the comforts that the heart can desire, the mind still goes through all manner of torments, and sleep will not come. We may take a little rest, and sit still in order to obtain peace; but the real trouble never goes. It is to drown this trouble that people take drugs and intoxicants, and lose themselves in the pursuit of common things, however undesirable. Every soul strives to obtain some remedy that will enable one to realize the joy and pleasure and peace that one's inner life unconsciously seeks; but one cannot get it. If one tries to obtain it through drugs, one only becomes a slave to the drugs; if one tries to obtain it through intoxicants, one only becomes a slave to them. If, failing these, one still seeks to gain one's desire through other vices one still fails to obtain contentment.

Come to the mystics, then, and sit with them when you are tired of all these other remedies that you have employed in vain; come and have a glass of wine with them. The mystic wine is the absorption within, which removes all the worries and anxieties and troubles and cares of the physical and mental plane. All these are now done away with forever. It is they who are at rest; it is they who experience that happiness that no others experience; it is they who teach the way to attain that peace and happiness that are the original heritage of one's soul.

14

CHARACTER AND FATE

When people hear that an influence is exerted on fate by character, they at once wonder how far this can be true with regard to the people whom they see as being well off and favorably circumstanced. They cannot dare to think that others' degree of rank and wealth could be attained by good character and its effects.

This is the first stumbling block that one meets with. When one begins to idealize or admire a character, one has one's own practical benefit before one. And when one thinks, "Am I practically benefited?" the heavenly bliss is disregarded. The first thing one thinks about is one's fate—"If only I could meet with a good fate! If only I could attain to good fortune!" If one gets all one wants by having a good character, at once one is disturbed by the disappointment of finding that the actual facts do not agree. If it is in business, for instance, surely it is constant application that makes the success, and not the personal character.

If we question whether good fortune lies in the achievement of worldly power, or in the gain of wealth or position—if that is all good fortune—then it is very poor; it is the poorest fortune. However high people are raised in rank, and however great the wealth they possess, whatever position in life they occupy, that has nothing to do with their happiness and satisfaction of mind. It is fate that has to do with happiness and satisfaction.

Even if someone is living in a palace, their heart my still be in torment from morning to night. Is that enjoying a good fate? They have a thousand difficulties; their own longings are their enemies. Is that good fortune?

Happiness may exist in a cottage. Yet one who suffers from lack of money says, "What good fortune the rich person has!" But the rich person says to him- or herself, "All they want is to get what they can out of me. They wait till I close my eyes in order that they may inherit what I possess. Many minds are constantly working against me."

Is it health? Is health good luck? Is such a one the possessor of a mind at rest? Is such a one's heart satisfied?

If not, then are not these things desirable? Surely they are desirable; but can you say they are the only good fortune that one can attain? Can you say that they are the only things that can satisfy our need in life? It is only when we lack wealth or health that we say good fortune lies in them. And when we attain them we still find we are not satisfied. Therefore it must be something else that constitutes good fortune. It is not being very religious or pious. It consists in the attainment of what we wish, what we desire, and what we would choose to have.

What do we desire? All things that seem to us best according to our evolution; these we think we desire, and wish to have, and consider to be good fortune. But when it is a case of giving these things, we are not willing to do so. The whole secret lies there. If we could only grasp the fact that it is for us to give to others that which we expect them to give to us. For instance, suppose we like to be in the company of a righteous or calm person. Our desire is to deal with such a one. In a profession or in business we always think, "If only I could have a righteous and just and reliable person to deal with." But when it comes to pass that we are put to the test, when it comes to be a case of "Are we righteous?" we fail to meet it. When others expect us to treat them righteously, nicely, kindly, and to be stable and reliable, we forget that it is for us to show these characteristics. We think so much of our own aims that we forget what it is that we ought to do for others.

The seer, therefore, teaches that all things that we desire and think beautiful—instead of desiring them from others, we ought to produce them within ourselves. What a task that is! What a great self-sufficiency it would be if every country always produced that which it seeks from others, what an independent life it would be to produce within ourselves what we expect to obtain from others! Instead of depending on them for something that we ourselves can give them, we should experience the joy of giving, the joy of being kind to others. What joy and freedom we should ourselves find in being kind to another. However natural it may be to have another love and admire us, are we not dependent? The wife and husband are dependent on each other's love; the friend is dependent on the friend's love. But in the other case we would be free and independent; because our joy would lie in the love itself, and not in the person. One enjoys life by doing kindness to others. Receiving kindness from others only makes the recipient expect more. One keeps saying, "They are doing this for their benefit; they are not considering me; they are blaming me; they did not help me; they did not deal nicely with me." One's life becomes full of grudges because one expects from everybody all the good that one wishes, and yet one does not know that one ought to have it all in oneself; that one should become independent. Therein lies the secret of character.

It is a wonderful thing that all that we possess in the way of character we transfer not only to our surroundings, but also to the animals and birds that may be pets in the house. If we could see exactly to what extent our character itself acts on our surroundings we should be surprised; the effect is so great. According to science we see that the law of attraction is such that it always attracts the same elements. When we emit goodness, we cannot have anything else but goodness; and even those who have not that element know it to be of God. All attributes and all goodness that are in the original spirit of God are also in the human spirit. However wicked a person may be, however lawless, however degenerate, if we are quite the opposite our power will be greater than theirs; their power will not have any influence on us. The power of goodness conquers badness. Badness is weakness; goodness is strength.

Those who have the habit of losing their temper cannot control others with the same temperament when near to them, because they have that weakness themselves. Therefore the others lose control also. Those who have control of themselves, it is they who will smile and say yes even if exposed to rages a thousand times. They will just wait. Those who have spiritual control have great control; but those who have it not can control neither spiritual nor physical events. They cannot control their sons and daughters, for they never listen to themselves first. If they listened to themselves, not only persons but even objects would listen to them. The self will never guide unless we allow it to do so. We always go astray when we are not guided by the intuitive self. Confusion always follows when we have disappointed our intuition, and failure always comes when the control has been lost.

A person's weakness spoils their affairs, for all the different places in which their affairs lie—family, life, business, profession, industry, and so on—are affected by every degradation of character. Do not think that someone of high position is always an ideal character; that one would come to a ten-times higher position if their character helped them.

It is the character that is our teacher. We do not need to speak to people about being virtuous, kind, righteous, for our own righteousness is enough to make them so; our goodness is sufficient to make our surroundings good. People are ever seeking psychic power and control, and it is all the time within themselves. Our self is the greatest enemy we have. The horse wants to go where its rider does not; it is the self that will not listen to us and does not act according to our wish. It is not what another person says, or what a priest says, or what a church says; the great teacher is both within and without. If we are willing to be guided, everything can teach us a lesson. If we wish to see the advantage of sobriety, we shall see it among sober people; if we wish to see the disadvantages of lack of sobriety, we shall see it among unsober people; if we wish to see the advantage of guidance, we shall see it among those who are guided. It is all a matter of experience and study; and our own guide to our true ideal will never fail to guide us aright.

We should do all that we wish others to do to us; and should not do that which we alone wish to do to others, although others do not wish it done. All that we expect from the world we desire for ourselves. But if we acted otherwise, we should become such great personalities in the world; instead of being examples of selfishness we should find our best in our nearest relatives, children, and friends.

Life in general is like a plant with thorns. Wherever we wish to take hold, there we find a thorn. The more our eyes are opened, wherever we wish to put our hand, there we get thorns—selfishness, because every ego wishes what is best for itself, and is not ready to give. And if we tried, out of curiosity, to become a rose instead of a thorn, we would make our life worthwhile.

When we begin to see our own faults, we then see how much more we should deserve the name of human beings. Ghalib said, “Even for man to become man is the most difficult thing of all the other difficulties that are in life.” One day a *majzub*, coming from one side of the marketplace, met another coming from the opposite side. (A majzub is one who has devoted their entire life to spiritual observation, living always far from the crowd, who think them crazy.) They made a little bow to one another. And it surprised a bystander to see two crazy people greet one another thus. “What brotherhood there is between crazy people," he thought. He then went to the place where the one majzub lived, and sat there waiting a long time until it should please the majzub to explain himself. After a long time the mood of the majzub became such that he would speak to him; and he placed his spiritual hand upon the head of this man, saying, "My child, go into the bazaar, and look at it; and come back and tell me what you see." So the man went back to the city, and looked at the crowd, and saw all things, and returned full of surprise. He was bewildered beyond expression, and said, "Every face that I see has the appearance of some animal; not a man's face can I see throughout the whole city, except the person to whom you bowed, and your holy self—these two!"

It does not mean that the faces are changed; it does not mean that the visage is different. It means that the garb of humanity, the appearance of the human beings, is not enough. If we can distinguish ourselves from other beings, it is only in the things that animals do not do that a human can be different from them. When it comes to eating, do not both eat? Both sleep; both seek comfort. Humans do all the things that animals do; humans can only be greater than animals in things that they do not do. And what are those things? Building houses? Birds can do this. Ability to fight? Animals and birds fight. The showing of art and skill? Animals can show these things—think of the spider, and how it weaves its web; it is wonderful.

Human beings were created in order that they might overcome that which animals have not overcome. And what is that? It is the ego. It is the ego that makes them selfish, that makes them get the best of their neighbor. This is the only real cause of all the disturbances of life, of all unrest, of all that we suffer, of all the harm that comes to us. The great enemy is the ego, the selfishness, manifested in husband, wife, son, daughter, friend, neighbor, servant.

Seeing how human selfishness is torturing the world, there is no greater need than to understand that no one is better than anyone else; that none can rightly think or imagine he or she can be better than anyone else, or helpful to children or family or surroundings, until this one thing is achieved, the suppression of ego, of selfishness. Do we not fight with one another unjustly, all because of vanity: "That is my thought; that is mine." "Me" is such a thing that everything but "me" is wrong. What I have, no one shall touch. This is the one thing against which all religious teachers preach.

Many think there is a great necessity of holding to self and self-interest. Yet even if humans do differ from animals, they resemble them in this, that where there are two dogs, and one has a bone before it, it does not want the other dog to touch its bone. Even though the dog is satisfied and does not require the bone itself, still it does not wish the other dog to come and touch it. "This is my bone," it thinks; "I will have it." And as long as the other dog is afraid, it is all right. But if the other dog is bigger, it will come and take the bone, and bite the first dog too. That is the picture of life.

Yet, when we observe the same sort of thing in humans, we say, "Oh, they were so good. I went to them at lunchtime and they were so kind as to ask me to take lunch with them." This is a human's feast; the other was a dog's feast. This is where a human should be different from an animal. An animal will not recognize its mother, or father, or its birthplace, but a human will. After humans have grown up they will consider, "My mother has taken care of me when I was an infant, and was so kind to me; and now she is aged, so I will do everything in my power for her." They dwell on all the respect they can show her, and how worthy she is of it. At once they show themselves to be human; the animal does not act in this way. Hence in the case where a human does the same as an animal, and does not care for those who did all they could for them in their youth, they show their lack of humanity. Forgetfulness and lack of appreciation of the care bestowed during childhood is characteristic of the animal.

Even angels bow to Christ, and Christ is the ideal human. Angels bow to the ideal human. Even when standing on the depths of the earth, such humans are higher than the angels and heaven, if they can only be human, if only they exhibit humanity. Christ said, "Ye are the salt of the earth, and if the salt have lost its savor, wherewith shall it be salted?"[1] This explains that the human is the ideal manifestation, higher than mineral, vegetable, animal, and other kingdoms, and even higher than the angels. If humans lose the sense of humanity, who is to come and teach them? The human is the one who is able to teach.

The human is the parent of humanity. If the father and mother lose their way, where shall the children go? How much depends on the preceding generation; it is to this that we always look for prosperity, for success, for the future of the nation, country, race, or family.

The real welfare to be sought is not the keeping of so much money in the bank, so many houses built, such and such an education at the university; it is the benefit to the future that is the guide. Parents should think of the welfare of the child even before it is born. The child will show what it has inherited; but how few parents think of that.

Our rest, our peace, our harmony, our tendency to all good and beautiful actions and things are the wealth that we can reserve for the child. The parent should know what psychic influences he and she can transmit to their children. You are the father, you are the mother; you are just like the planet that controls the souls and the spirits of that planet. You are the living planet; your influence is much greater upon your children.

The father and mother think that if they do such a thing, the child will do the same. "I must make my child follow my footsteps," they think. This is fate. Is it not the fate of nation, race, family, or the individual? To have their generation as ideal as they wish, that is the best fate.

1. Matthew 5:13.

People give their lives for the new generation, for the new hope. Should not one see that what matters is that the lives of the children should become better? The leaders of a town, the leaders of a city are looked to for the picture that these people are to follow. How can we prove ourselves fit for all these positions? The position that has leadership can only be filled after training oneself, and not someone else.

What an atmosphere one can create by one's character; what control one person can have on another's character! "Where are you going?" says one; "I am going to the library," says the other. The answer expresses truth and strength. But another who is going where they know their parents do not want them to go replies with hesitation, and they falter out the same words, "I am going to the library." The same words are used, but there is no strength in them, no effect.

What power character gives; what power truthfulness gives; what power is lost when the character of the prospective act is dubious! What fear the murderer goes through! He is himself half murdered before he commits the act, and after committing the act he is in a worse condition than the one he has murdered. His fear, his conscience, his kindness, his justice, his reason, all are in conflict; and he is himself half killed before he kills the other.

The power of character is the power of an army. With Christ there was an army of angels. With Muhammad there was also an army of angels. He stood, and thousands of people were running. When an enemy came near to the great Khalif to behead him, the enemy was afraid. But this fear was simply the power of control. Personality shows what has been sown in it. One cannot pretend to be righteous and good unless one's spirit has practiced it and that strength has really come. One's appearance and one's atmosphere can tell what one is, because one is the picture of one's thoughts. Whatever one thinks, whatever one is about, that speaks in one's atmosphere, in one's voice, in one's movements. In everything one expresses oneself as one is—how far one has evolved, and how far one has not evolved. Whatever one is, one shows.

How great the influence is! There is the story of a boy who was sent to Baghdad across a desert, after his mother had sewn a few gold coins in his blanket, telling him to keep it safe and not open it till he reached the city. This was a precaution against robbers, for there were no trains or ships or caravans; it was necessary to travel alone and on foot. When this lad arrived in the forest, the robbers met him. But he was trained to tell the truth, and so when they said, thinking he would not have money, being only a little boy, "Have you any coins, any gold, any silver?" He answered, "Yes, I have." His conscience would never permit him to answer no. "Where are they?" they asked. "They are sewn in this blanket," he said. But the very fact of his showing they were sewn in the blanket won the robbers' hearts, and made them righteous themselves. They said, "We would have stolen them had you not told the truth," and let him go free.

If a person thinks that God is all, but the whole world is vile, that one does not worship God, because God is all and God is beautiful. "God is beautiful and loves beauty,"[2] the Prophet said. And as God's being is in us, we are supposed to love beauty also.

What is beauty? Not only the external beauty, but the beauty of personality, the beauty of character, that is the real beauty. If we did not worship it, we should not admire it in other people. We cannot appreciate anything without beauty of character.

All gains, whether material, spiritual, moral or mystical, are all gains in answer to one's own character; and if we have no gains, we are deprived of them only by reason of our own character.

Truth comes to a person's soul, and yet truth is not the exclusive property of creed, caste, or race. We are all the children

2. Hadith.

of God, the Father-Mother Spirit of the whole Being. And we ought to be in such a feeling of kinship as to exchange helpful thoughts with one another all the time. We can take love and guidance from one another. Speech is not as great a help as contact. The privilege of meeting one another is great. When souls meet one another, what truth they can exchange! It is uttered in silence, yet always surely reaches its goal.

When God wants to destroy a thing, God gives it into unworthy hands.

15

GAIN AND LOSS

To the view of a mystic neither is gain a gain nor loss a loss; for that which appears to be a loss at one time, at another may appear to be a gain. The more deeply we think about it, the more we see that in every gain there is a loss, and in every loss there is a gain. That which seems to be a gain yesterday may prove to be a loss tomorrow, and that which is a loss at one time proves to yield a gain at another. Consequently mystics realize the joy of the gain and the sorrow of the loss in their right aspect; they discern what it is that turns a gain to a loss, or converts a loss to a gain. The more deeply we consider the subject, the more do we discern that there are certain gains that are only momentary, because material; that to attain them we may have sacrificed a greater gain. Of course if we do not see that greater gain, we do not mind the loss. We can only see what we have lost or what we have gained after we have discovered whether the gain we have sacrificed really was a greater one or not.

Every experience in life has three aspects: (1) that in which it is in the state of a motive; (2) that in which it is in the process of achievement; and (3) that in which the experience is an accomplished fact.

In the first form, where the experience is as yet only in the form of a motive, we can have no clear conception as to whether it is a gain or a loss. We start out, for instance, with the thought, "I desire to start a business; in this business I shall be profited." That represents the initial motive. The next step will be the actual building up of the business. It is now that the gain or the loss becomes more clearly perceptible. But the gain or loss is most clear after the business is accomplished. The experience is now realized. Hitherto one has not realized the benefit or otherwise, but in the final stage one is able to form a true estimate as to whether the idea of one's life has led to gain or loss.

In life we discriminate between two things: the real and the false. We think more of the real, and less of the false. We discriminate between imitation gold and real gold. We pay more for the real gold because it is more lasting. The two samples of gold may be equally bright; hence it is evident that the value we attach to things is in proportion to their lasting power. Similarly, if we could see what things in life are lasting or passing, we should discriminate between real loss and false loss, real gain and false gain. The gain or loss that is momentary is not real. So, too, joy or sorrow is a momentary state; the joy over a gain today may tomorrow prove to be a sorrow. If we knew the realities, we should never grieve over the loss of things that experience shows to be only of a transient character.

On the one hand we are working for our own individual benefit and interest; but on the other hand there is a universal power that is more mighty than ourselves, and more just in its working. When these two powers, the *qaza*, or universal, the *qadr,* or individual, are working harmoniously, things come right. But when they clash, that which is thought right by qaza will happen without regard to what qadr may think right or wrong. Those who know this, and harmonize their will with qaza, the universal will, begin to experience divine impulses, and they begin to feel every time what is and what is not harmonious in the qadr also. To such as these there come fewer failures in life. Life is easier because they swim with and not against the tides.

Our sense of justice is partial because it is obscured or shadowed by our likes and dislikes, by our personal interest and lack of interest in people and things.

In the Bible it is written, "Where your treasure is, there will your heart be also."[1] If our gain is all in objects of a momentary nature, our heart will find no gain in this life or in the hereafter. Those who trust in momentary gain must accept the inevitable disappointment, both here and in the hereafter. Everybody in this world is selfish; for is it not true that the sages who renounce that which is valued by worldly people, after all only take up that which they understand to be really the greater gain? The only difference between their action and that which seems entirely selfish in those who are not sages, is that they sacrifice what they perceive to be a false gain. For anyone to do otherwise is to be like the dog that was running after its own shadow.

The privilege of having life on earth in this delicate human vehicle is too great to risk wasting on something that will leave one the loser in the end, however rich and ample the false gain may appear. What gain is it to have the object we have gained snatched from our hands at the last? What gain is it to have an object that has to be constantly guarded and watched against the rapacity of others? Everyone is on the watch to take your gain away and make it theirs; and this they can do with every transient gain. We always desire dependable objects and friends. It is our nature to long for something we can depend on for life. Our own nature teaches us that if we realize our life's desire, which we consider important, we realize only transient things. Has not this war shown us how artists lose their art, poets their poetry, kings their thrones, and many a person falls from heaven to the earth—all in a moment's time? What, then, is there in this world that can be depended upon? Have we not seen how parents have even sacrificed their lives in order

1. Matthew 6:21.

to give the desired happiness to sons and daughters? Have we not seen that friends that one relies on, in their turn depend on someone else and are disappointed? When we really think upon these things we are bound to see that after all we are only like children in understanding. We think ourselves clever and wise, and yet we do not really think deeply of life after all. Some day we begin to think, and then we see ourselves as parents see their children's acts. The child thinks its sand and toys are such important things—things that we grown-ups attach no importance to. And we too begin to see how childish our own life is when we assess at their true value these actions and desires that seemed so important to us yesterday. We think little things so important—dignity, ill-treatment, insults, reputation—and what do they matter in the end? Do we not see people praised and raised up high in vanity and greatness one day, and next day all about them is forgotten? Before the war every shop in Moscow had the picture of the czar in one window, and of Jesus with the Virgin in the other. Within three years, what a change! Even a whole race will change its attitude in a moment's time.

Praise, honor, love, kindness—are they lasting, are they dependable? Are we not seeking after wealth, or fame, or love, or kindness, or some help from morning until evening? However evolved we are with our education and experience, yet what are we really seeking? Things from which we cannot derive any lasting gain. From these false things we gain the experience that the things to which we have hitherto attached importance and valued are things that do not last. We learn at length that it would be wise to remember that all these objects and ideals and aspirations that we have in life should be judged according to whether they are dependable or not, lasting or not. After we have perceived the truth that this or that is not to be depended upon, we find that it is not necessary to renounce them all, to give up all things in life. You can be in the crowd just as well as in seclusion in the wilderness. You can have all good things—wealth, friends, kindness, love to give and love to take—once you have learned not to be blinded by them, learned to escape from disappointment, learned to escape from repugnance at the idea that the things are not as you would want them to be. You still undertake your business, you attain your wealth, you follow out all those things, but now your eyes are wide open; before, they were blind. This is the teaching of life. Thus it is that when you study life in the East, you will find that a Sufi may be a king or queen, or may be a fakir. The word *sufi* means "seer." A Sufi may still be a king or a queen. It is not the actual literal renunciation that counts, it is the personal abandonment of belief in the importance of transient things.

A person who pretends to be unselfish is generally foolish-selfish. It is the wise-selfish who are right, and still they bless themselves all the same. They are selfish, it is true, but they are selfish with true wisdom. They think out what it is in life that will benefit them most. The foolish-selfish person never puts money by, and thus never has any to give. The wise-selfish person will obtain money in order that they can express their generosity with what they have collected. Those who remain paupers all their life have never achieved anything for anyone. Therefore a person is wise who not only understands what is real gain and what is false, but also understands the price there is to pay for the gain. What determines our success is the thought whether one's gain is of more value than the price one has to pay for it, or whether the price one has to pay is greater than the gain one can obtain. One who perceives this clearly has learned the true business of life very well.

For every gain, then, there is a need for sacrifice. To gain anything you have to sacrifice something. To pursue two gains is to lose both. Therefore it is necessary to decide once and for all what is false. Follow the real; leave the false.

If there is such a thing as saintly renunciation, it is that of renouncing small gains for better gains; not for no gains, but with open eyes to see what is better and what is worse. Even if the choice has to lie between two momentary gains, one would always be found to be more real and lasting; that you should follow for the time. Take the torch of wisdom to show you your path through life, and you will end by realizing what is really profitable in life and what is not.

16

STILLING THE MIND

Before one can understand the use of stilling the mind one must consider the discrepancy between advising that the mind be stilled and advising that the body be not stilled. Life is nothing but an activity in all things. Inactivity of the body takes away its vigor and strength; the muscles do not have a chance to develop; the lazy, inactive person is always suffering from indigestion or some such ailment. How, then, can it be that when the mind is made "still," it will not suffer loss in vigor and strength? Would not stilling the mind stupefy a person? If the voice is to develop, it must be used in singing exercises and in carrying out certain practices; if the muscles are to develop, they must be used. How then can stilling the mind create power of mind?

There is great truth in this objection. Stilling the mind would stupefy and render it powerless, did the person not understand life's secret, life's law. It is true that in life on the physical plane our exercises and activity of the day must give place to rest, comfort, and sleep during the night. If our body does not receive that rest, it can never flourish. We need more rest than activity; we need more comfort than toil. And if it is not given, our health becomes unbalanced. And it follows that as much as it is necessary for the body to have comfort and rest after toil, so much is it necessary for the mind to have rest and peace after thinking and working.

Indeed, the mind is composed of finer elements, whereas the body is made of grosser elements, and that makes a great difference in activity. The higher the plane of existence, the more one is active; the lower the plane, the less are the activities. That is why the mind is naturally more active than the body. Therefore, if after toil rest is necessary, how much more does it apply to mind than to body? We usually rest our body at will whenever circumstances allow us to—we recline on a couch or in an armchair after coming from the office or work, and at night we rest and go to sleep—but when do we give a rest to the mind? The mind's rest is as necessary as the rest for the body, and yet we always keep it in action. It is constantly at work even if our body is resting. Even if the body is sleeping, the mind is producing dreams, and is constantly at work. How many people stand at their work for a whole day, during which the mind is no less busy with the work on the physical planes than is the body, for mind works with body; and yet they work with the mind the whole night long. The body is having rest and comfort, but not the mind. Even in an armchair they are still imagining, still working with the mind. The mind has no leisure; it is perhaps worrying, or planning, or thinking over the struggles and anxieties of which life is so full. And even if the body is asleep, there is still the constant working of the mind going on. There is hardly ever a time when the mind is at rest, except when nature gives it a rest by its being too exhausted to work anymore. The mind says, "I will have a good sleep." And if it has two hours' sleep only, still one wakes up with such joy and strength that all the world seems new. If there have been dreams, one can only say, "Yes, I have been to sleep, but I do not feel rested," because that part of the being has not rested.

All this goes to show the great practical need for the mind to be at rest, for the mind to be stilled. Those who make it a principle that work is always an advisable thing are one-sided.

Balance lies in perceiving that work and rest are equal needs to good health, both physical and mental.

The work of the body is sometimes kept under one's control, but one does not keep the work of the mind under one's control. This is not because one cannot do so; it is because one never thinks about it. Does one ever stop to ask oneself, "Why was I thinking? Was there any purpose in those anxious, worried thoughts? Was it not that the mind was just allowed to go wherever it wanted? While sitting quietly in a chair, were not the thoughts active with things that have nothing to do with my life, with things that do not matter in the least either to myself or to anyone else's life? It was just a waste of energy."

The more the mind is allowed to go without purpose, the more likely it is to become a vehicle, or machine, which all manner of influences around it—spiritual influences, spirit obsessions, other human beings—will employ instead of the owner. If the user of that mind is a proper person, then it may perhaps act properly, but if it is an improper person who uses it, then the work of the mind is wasted. In any case it would not be a fulfillment of the purpose of one's life. This purpose is to learn mastery, not to be a vehicle for others to use. One who does not direct one's own mind lacks mastery.

All this shows that the very first lesson that the mystic learns in life is the training of mind. It is not stilling the mind; stilling comes afterward. The first thing is to train, to check the activities. This is illustrated in the words *imagination* and *thought*. Sometimes we use the word *thought* when we should use the word *imagination*; sometimes *imagination* when we should use the word *thought*. Both are different forms of activity of mind. In the first case the imagination, the activity of mind, is uncontrolled, without our intention, and is not directed toward a certain purpose. People may be imaginative, and their imaginations may come out like beautiful flowers. But if there is no purpose, the flowers are of no use to the plant; that beautiful things have been produced is no credit, because no one knows from what source the imaginations have come. But in the case of thought, this is directed imagination; it is a controlled activity of mind. That is why we cannot call a thoughtful person imaginative, nor can we call an imaginative person thoughtful. One is thoughtful whose mind is directed by one's will, whose mind fulfills one's intentions, whose mind is under the control of one's intention.

Imagination may be very beautiful, or not; it may be right, or it may be wrong. Many persons who are praised as being imaginative may really be in the first stage of insanity. Those who have given deep thoughts to the world are only those who have controlled the activity of their minds. Those whose minds are working mechanically like a machine, or just reflecting the activity of those around them, may appear to be living beings, but the mystic would say differently; because it is not till one has gained mastery over one's mind, till one is above this activity, that one is a ruling power—a true "person."

When we think about it, we find that all the things that are accomplished in this world are accomplished by the power of mind. As it is written in the Vedanta. "The world is the creation of the mind of Brahma." That is, it is the thought of the Creator that has created the world. And if it is the Creator's thought that has created this world, we ourselves are not far from that Creator. The human soul is the spirit of the Creator, and therefore has within it the same power of creating by the power of mind as the Creator has. Whatever humans create in science, in art, in phenomena or wonder-making, in poetry, in music, in pictures, in everything that they bring into being, it is all achieved by the power of mind.

What is a human? Is not a human soul divine substance? The very word *man* is from the Sanskrit *manu*, which means "mind." Humans are what their minds are, what they think. "For as he thinketh in his heart, so he is."[1] Even the future, as

1. Proverbs 23:7.

well as the past, is what one thinks, because one becomes the image of one's thoughts. God created the human in the image of God's thoughts. If there is any self of which one can say, "This is [hu]man," it is the mind. The three words *mana*, *manu*, *manusha* in Sanskrit show that one is one's mind, is from one's mind, is the controller of the activity of mind. Should one not control one's mind, one is not a master but a slave. It lies in one's own mind whether one shall be master, or whether one shall be slave. One is slave when one neglects to be master; one is master if one cares to be master.

Mastery lies, not merely in stilling the mind, but in directing it toward whatever point you desire, in allowing it to be active as far as you wish, in using it to fulfill your purpose, in causing it to be still when you want to still it. One who has come to this has created one's heaven within oneself; one has no need to wait for a heaven in the hereafter, for one has produced it within one's own mind now.

There is a story of a murshid and a murid. The murid said, "O Teacher, I should like to see heaven." The teacher said, "Yes, this is the way you should meditate in order to see heaven." So the murid went and did so; but the vision of heaven that he had was not as described in the scriptures—that it is a place where one enjoys nothing but comfort and luxury, milk and honey, marble halls and white robes, beautiful gems and garlands of jewels, wreaths of flowers, and the waving of palms. But he could not see any of these. So he asked himself, "Has the murshid perhaps shown me a wrong heaven, or have the prophets given a wrong message in the scriptures?"

So he went back to the murshid, saying, "Now I should like to see hell." The murshid said, "Yes, this is the way you should meditate in order to see hell." And then the murid did this, and he saw in a trance that there was certainly a place, but there was no fire or snakes or serpents or thorns or tortures or imps or flames such as have been told to people for ages. So he could not understand whether his vision was right or wrong; and he went back to the teacher, and said, "I have seen in this way: I have not seen in heaven the things that are promised, nor have I seen in hell the things that are foretold as being there." "Oh," the teacher said, "all the things promised for hell you will have to take there from here. They are not kept ready for you; you will have to bring them with you. If you take sorrows with you, you will find them there; if you take hatred, you will find it there. Your mind is like a gramophone record, and if you use a harsh voice, the instrument produces a harsh note; if beautiful words and things, it will sing beautiful words and things. It will produce the same record that you have experienced in life. Indeed you have not to wait till after death in order to experience it; you are experiencing it even now."

Everything is reproduced before us now, if we would only listen to it and perceive it. Every good or bad word or deed is reproduced before us, though it seems as in a dream.

Did we watch life keenly, we should see how true this is. Joy, sorrow, love, all depend on our thought, on the activity of our mind. If we are depressed, if we are in despair, it is still the work of our mind; our mind has prepared that for us. So, too, if we are joyful and happy, and all things are pleasant, that also has been prepared for us by our mind. It is only when our mind works without control that unhappiness, sorrow, trouble, pain, or whatever we experience comes without our intention. No one could wish to create hell for him- or herself; all would create heaven for themselves if they could; and yet how many allow their minds to create these things for them, regardless of their own intention.

The control of the activity of mind is called concentration in the language of the mystics. The meaning of this word is often not rightly understood. People are apt to think that concentration means closing the eyes. But you may close the eyes for hours, and still the thoughts keep coming like a moving picture. You are never at rest, never at peace; the anxiety and sorrow do not disappear just because you close your eyes. It is concentration that does that. Concentration is activity of mind in the direction desired; our desire directs in which way the mind is to be active; the mind acts according to our wishes.

How difficult it is to do this is best known by those who have tried. As soon as the mind is still and inactive it begins to jump and run away from control. It runs in every direction but that in which you wish. You hold it; it slips away. Not till one begins to try and concentrate does one see how uncontrollable and unruly the mind is.

This truth is pictured very well in the story from the Ramayana, the great Hindu scripture, which tells about Rama's two children Lahu and Kusha.[2] The myth explains the condition of the human mind as being like that of an unruly horse. Is it not always running hither and thither; is it not like a wild horse running from place to place, further away every time you think you are able to touch it? When a person thinks, "I will not think of anything," do not a thousand thoughts come? That shows that it's nature is like that of the unruly horse, for the control of which skill is required.

The key to the problem of controlling the mind, the key of concentration, is given to us by our elder siblings, the murshid among the Sufis, the guru among the Vedantists, who is a teacher with experience of the horse, having trained it and mastered it. They say, "If you are without a proper friend, you will perhaps succeed in catching the horse, and perhaps you will not. But if you know the proper way in which to go about catching it, you will not be long in doing so." That is why it is so necessary to have a method of concentration. Mystics, yogis, fakirs, ascetics, have a method; and by learning that method the concentration is easily obtained. When the mind is controlled and made into a vehicle, absolutely in our hand, working as we desire, then we can still it also.

2. See chapter 7, p. 63.

The benefit of stilling is so much greater. If one only grasped the benefit of perfect stillness, even of only the body. You have seen a symbol of that stillness in the statues of Buddha, or of Krishna, or in the idols of the Hindus. What an effect that has! Compare it with the effect of people who come into your presence, but are always active, rubbing their hands, moving about, raising their shoulders, making grimaces, tapping on the table, scratching, fidgeting in some way or another. Do they not make you fidget? The whole atmosphere becomes disturbed. Why? Because there is an intense activity of mind making its effect on the body. The body and mind are both in an unrestful state, which passes on to everyone who is in the place, for it produces unrest in the whole atmosphere. We may not be conscious that this is so, but unconsciously we feel disturbed.

The great comfort that one finds after waking from a deep sleep cannot be compared with anything in the world; but more than that, the mystic sees in sleep the symbol of a great mystical state. Rumi, the Sufi teacher of Persia, says, "O sleep, in thee I find the divine bliss. Thou makest patients forget their illness; thou makest kings forget for the moment that they are in a palace; thou makest the prisoners forget for a moment that they are in captivity. What bliss, what joy of bliss when the soul is freed from its limited presence, from the presence of those different aspects of life that are keeping it captive!"[3]

Sleep is the time when the soul is free. That is why deep sleep is so great a state to the mystic. In the East they say: when people are asleep do not wake them; it is a great sin to do so. Of course in the West they cannot say this, because if you do not go to your work in the morning, what then? It would be a great sin if you did not wake them.

If there is such comfort and joy and so great a secret of heavenly peace during sound sleep, so there is a greater joy and peace and inspiration when the mind is stilled. The mind is so

3. See *Masnavi* 3:3541.

like water that our poets always call it the sea, the ocean. The nature of water is that, as you look in it, you see a face reflected there, your own image. If the water is not still, the face is not clear; when the water is still everything reflected in it is clear. So it is with the mind.

When the mind is stilled, it hears what another person says, it can think upon any subject that it sees; and when the person is developed the mind can hear even what is said from the other side; yes, even what God says from heaven.

Therefore those persons the ears of whose heart have listened to the Word of God have first accomplished stillness in their life. And what an atmosphere such persons can produce, what effect their presence has! It is more than healing, more than medicine. A person with a perfectly stilled, comforted, and rested mind will at once raise up another who is going through distress, or restlessness, or pain, or ill temper, or worry, or anxiety. The very presence of one whose mind is stilled gives such hope, such inspiration, such sympathy, such power and life. All the heavenly properties run so smoothly and freely from those whose minds are stilled that their words, their voice, their presence all react upon the minds of others; and as they still their mind, so their very presence becomes healing.

17

MENTAL CREATION

So absorbed are persons in this visible creation that they very seldom think of the value of that other creation that exists within themselves. Those things that tempt, that attract attention, that are of interest, all these are pursued by so many persons, who therefore become limited and unaware of that other creation that goes on unconsciously within.

In reality, every person is a world within him- or herself. But how little do people reflect about it. They are always conscious of being just like a drop in the ocean, whereas they do not know of the other state of being, in which they are the ocean and everything else a drop.

There is a passage in one of the sacred books relating how God created the earth, and then created the heavens. What does this mean? Was heaven created after the earth? The meaning is that this creation that is around us is first impressed upon the mind, and then the mind creates its own world, its own heaven. It is the creation of mind, a higher world, yet within ourselves; and this world may be heaven, or it may be the opposite. As Omar Khayyam writes, "Man's heaven is the vision of fulfilled desire, and hell the shadow of a soul on fire,"[1] which shows that the desire is the source of heaven, and its

1. See *Rubaiyat*, verse lxvii.

fulfillment. At the same time it is mental fire and disappointment, or worry, or anxiety, or torture that is the shadow of the soul on fire.

Centuries ago Zoroaster taught that there are three kinds of sin, and three kinds of virtue: those of thought, speech, and action.

A person always takes virtue in action as virtue, sin in action as sin; never thinking about virtue and sin also in speech or thought. Sometimes one's thought is stronger than one's speech or action. It is the experience of every mystic and every person who has trodden the path that the power of thought is much greater than that of speech or action. In our everyday life we find that if we think of a person bringing a certain book or flower we desire, we often find that person comes to see us, bringing this book or flower with them. You had not expressed the desire, and yet it has been done. Such is the power of thought, the creation of mind. "Thoughts are things," it has been said. But they are more; thoughts are beings. They are as much living beings as we are; they work as we work; they have life in them. "The words that I speak unto you, they are spirit, and they are life," says Saint John.[2] The spirit is the real life. A person is spirit; the body is matter. The body can generate, but cannot mind generate? It is the generation of mind that we call thought or imagination. Thought is controlled; the other is not controlled.

There is a saying in Sanskrit: "There are numberless gods, and yet there is one God." This means that as every planet is a world, every mind is a world; it is a living world.

The question is, if we make our world and mold our life, why should we have unhappiness, why have troubles in life, why have failures in life? The answer is, "It is the fault neither of the Creator nor of the world; it is the fault of our ignorance; it is the lack of knowledge." Buddha pictures this lack of

2. John 6:63.

knowledge in this way: it is as if you are clinging to the branch of a tree in the thick darkness of night so that you cannot see what is beneath you, whether it is land or sea; so you are always afraid of falling. You keep on clinging to the tree, and are suffering with the fear of how long it will be before you have to let go, thinking, "How long can I cling to this branch?" Yet under your feet there is nothing. Such is life until light comes. Then it is like the coming of the sun. When the sun rises you find there is no water, there is not even space; for the land is just beneath your feet.

The land of immortality is so far from us. But when the sun of knowledge arises we see that it is near, so near. Once one knows that, one need not be taught morals or virtue; one knows what is best for one, whither to go; one knows one's own creation. One knows that if one creates hideous spirits in one's thoughts, they will become monsters, and will work against one, and will ruin one's own life. But if one creates the spirit of love and kindness, others will help one in one's want, and one is always surrounded by love and kindness.

Once people realize this their life becomes different; they become the healers of others; they sympathize with the trouble of another; they serve in the difficulty of another; they seek to know if they cannot do something, cannot help in some way. A word may help; a thought of kindness and of sympathy will help. Whatever they do to others they do to themselves, because every thought of kindness or goodness or sympathy has generated a world of sympathy around it; and such persons cannot be without it. If they go to a land where no one knows them or understands them, they can draw sympathy and love, if they have created that within themselves.

This shows how important it is to be careful of what we say. Act under the spell of anger, say such things as, "I don't wish to see his face," or any evil words, and those who speak thus wish they had not said or done such things after the spell has gone; not even about an enemy do they wish to have said these things. But at the time they did not know that what they created lives. That which they have created they will be afraid of, and it will become their own enemy as well as the enemy of the person against whom their wrongful thought was directed. Not only that, but they will generate many more of the same kind. Once one bad thought is created in the spirit of anger or annoyance, a thousand other spirits are created out of it. A world may be created by giving an outlet to one single weakness.

All that we collect and gather in the external world for our happiness and comfort (for example, an estate) is limited. Not even a thousandth part of this world that we possess can we really call our own kingdom, our world. But our mind can create and can collect numberless thoughts and impressions, which all make up its real world. All our possessions, all that we collect in life, all these things that we have to leave one day are momentary; but that which we have created from our thought, from our mind—that lives.

A person thinks, "Oh, some day I should like to build a factory." At this time that person has no money, no knowledge, no capability; but a thought has come, "Some day I should like to build a factory." Then that person thinks of something else. Perhaps years pass, but that thought has been working constantly through a thousand minds, and a thousand sources prepare for that person that which they once desired. If a person can look back in their life at what they had thought of in different times, they will find that the line of fate (which in the East we call kismet, destiny) is formed by our thought. Thoughts have prepared for us that happiness or unhappiness that we experience. The whole of mysticism is founded on this.

If thoughts can accomplish this, so can love or imagination, or even a dream can accomplish it according to the impression that it makes. Some thoughts are as things, as objects; other thoughts are as beings. Some thoughts are as angels by our side, and some are as devils. They are all around us, either helping us toward the accomplishment of the objects before us, or drawing us back from those things we wish to accomplish.

One person thinks, and perhaps the result of the thought is very feeble; another has a thought today, and tomorrow the desire is fulfilled. Why is this? It is because of the power of thought. In the thought of one person there is more life, in that of another there is less life. The difference between an object and a living thing is that there is more or less life in them. But we call something life in which is consciousness and activity; we call that which lacks intelligence and consciousness an object. Yet, in reality, both are alive. People with a weak will have no strength in their thought. If they think a thousand times, it has no effect, because they have not that vitality or energy that is necessary for thought to live.

What is the vitality that gives life to the thought? It is the same in the human as in the vegetable or in the mineral kingdom. In the one case the life is on the surface, in the other it is covered. That is why we call them things in the one case, and beings in the other. So there are dead thoughts, and there are living thoughts. To which class a thought is to belong depends on the power called willpower. When there is willpower, the word is both spoken and done. This idea is expressed by the words *kalpa vraksha*, the tree of desire. The story is that whoever happens to sit down under this tree for a moment will have whatever wish he or she may desire fulfilled. Yet nobody knows where this tree is to be found. The tree is the mind; its root is the heart. That which gives power to thought, gives spirit or life to thought, is feeling. A person without feeling is as dead; with feeling that person is living, and so is their thought. Thought with feeling is a much greater power than thought without feeling. Merely to say, "I like your art so much" will have no effect when there is no feeling behind it. It is just a string of words. There is no life in it. But when those words are uttered with feeling, they go through your heart also; the thought becomes living.

There have been great people whose living thoughts could make anyone live; they could impart life, and heal. They have left their thoughts behind them, and people have treasured them as scriptures, as holy books; they have taken them for a religion. Such thoughts can never vanish nor die, such a long life has been given to them. Whatever form their thoughts have taken—music, prose, poetry, aphorisms, groups of words that will never die—they will live forever. There are others who have not known the value of this creation, who have not known the immortal character of this creation by the mind; they pass through life without knowing the value of the creation by mind. Such persons are foolish, stupid, grumbling all the time about people, and criticizing others.

There is a Hindustani poet who says, "Beware before you speak a word; you do not know that this world is a dome, and that in a dome there is an echo." So, in this world, whatever one utters is re-echoed. If a good thought is sent to a person, they may not know of it; yet you have sent a good thought, a thought of kindness, sincere sympathy, and love. You may not tell them; you may not see them; but even after ten years you will find something was prepared for them; something has made the friendship closer. That person will know that you have thought about them. The secret of this is that life is one. In it all these phantoms live and move; and we think that everybody is a different life, and yet there is only one life, which the mystic calls God, who cannot be divided.

The Sufi says that a human is not a part of God, for how can God be divided? Can you divide space? Since space cannot be divided, how can God be? How can this one life be divided? There is no division. There is no wall between any two people in this world.

Whether the thought be of bitterness, or sympathy, or love, or kindness, it reaches the other person. When the thought has feeling behind it, it has life, whether the feeling be of bitterness or of kindness. If it be bitterness it will destroy. But the consequence of such a thought will be that it will return to the giver; it will surely rebound; it will surely return to the one who sent it. Whether it was bitterness, or whether it was kindness it will equally return. But more than that: this thought generates as surely as do germs and worms. One thought of love makes a thousand beings of love and kindness come around one.

There is a prophecy in the Bible that when the next teacher comes, that teacher will bring ten thousand holy ones in their army. What does this mean? Does it mean ten thousand visible people? No, there will be numberless thoughts of goodwill and service to humankind, which will become their army.

Externally we are a single being, but internally we are a world. As vast as is the world around us, so vast is the world within. Asif says, "The limitation of the sky and land cannot be compared with man's heart. If man's heart be wide, there is nothing wider than this."[3] All can be accommodated in it; heaven, earth, sun, moon—all are reflected in it. It becomes itself the whole. This world becomes as one chooses to make it. If one only knew that! But since one does not know that, the world is not heaven, but has become its opposite. We blame others for our sorrows and misfortunes, not perceiving that we ourselves are the creators of our world; that our world has an influence upon our life within as well as upon our life without. For instance, if the self within is blaming a person, that person is blamed by everybody else; if it is admiring a person, that person is admired by everybody; if the self within feels guilty toward a person in the external world, that person will feel guilty; if it feels doubt about the right path, it goes through the world in that spirit of doubt.

We read in the scripture how Moses had a word with God on Mount Sinai. The angel Gabriel brought a message to the Prophet. What was the angel? What was Mount Sinai? Mount

3. From a ghazal of Asif (H.E.H Maheboob Ali Khan); see the version translated in *Minqar-i Musiqar* (New Lebanon, NY: Sulūk Press, 2016), 271.

Sinai is the human mind; God is within it; it is human feeling that builds a bridge from the human mind to the mount of God.

Rumi says so beautifully, "There is a flute, one end of which is in the lips of God, and the other end of the flute is in the human heart." What a beautiful simile! When the human heart is awakened, when the thoughts have become living beings, then where this feeling comes, its current runs from infinite to finite, from the objective world back to the world unseen, from God to human. A current is established. It is a human's thought that is the bridge to heaven.

Whatever the thought of a person has built, it becomes that one's heaven, with the singers, the *upsaras*, and fair ones. This is the true heaven. Those with an army of beautiful thoughts are in the Garden of Eden. They have produced a garden within themselves. There is a verse of Bedil: "These beautiful gardens and flowerbeds, if you wish to have them round you, you need not go and see them in the external world. You need only open the gate of your heart to see them there, and you will enjoy them."

People think such a world is only imagination, only exists in thought; but really this world is the only one that will remain in the hereafter. There will not be any other world, for this physical world will not remain. Every soul is creating a world. However vast a planet may seem in comparison to the mind of a human, yet the mind of the human is really the vaster. There is a world in this planet. As the Hindus have said, "Our planet has a god, and man is the god of his planet."

First, you must know what you should have, and you must become the master of yourself and of your thoughts and of your life. Then it will become agreeable and smooth to others, and you will become a blessing to all you meet in this world.

18

THE ATTAINMENT OF POWER

The possession of power brings with it the desire to attain more. We can attain everything that we desire, if we only know how. No one attains a higher position unless he or she follows something hidden. The tendency to arrive at some perfection is that which causes one to attain a greater perfection. Even if one attains wealth, the person is tending toward perfection. Napoleon attained something hidden that was great and wonderful, if we could only understand it. So a merchant has begun perhaps by selling empty bottles, and ultimately becomes so wealthy as to be able to found colleges, libraries, hospitals, and so forth—which proves there was an inclination to a certain perfection. Even though the ideal may not be so very high, the very inclination to attain power is great.

There is a spiritual or psychic or occult or telepathic power. How are we to attain to that?

What is at the back of the soul? Is it not that it must needs say, "I am a king, but in this mortal casket I have become a pauper." "I was created free, but in this flesh I am in captivity and have become weak," said Rumi. From an almighty state of being you have become a helpless being. When you become conscious of spirit, you become conscious of a mighty power hidden; and your spirit is the expression of the Almighty Power. The power is in unity, but is lost in variety.

Thus, for instance, if you hold a thing in your hand, you can hold it with strength, because all five fingers have united to hold the object. But if you wish to let it be lifted by one finger, this one finger may drop it, even though the finger belongs to the same hand. In all aspects of life unity is power. All religions show that power is in unity. This is the secret of philosophy.

There are two aspects of unity: first, the unity of variety; second, unity realizing itself. One is heavenly, the other is earthly. You cannot serve two masters. Unity is the only source of happiness. Unity in realization is far greater than unity in variety.

'When two hearts unite, they can break even mountains." As two fuse in love, the more does intuition grow, the more does one understand whether the other is happy, or pleased, or displeased, whatever distance may separate them. This is nothing but just the unity of the one person with the other. It is clairvoyance. The mother knows the condition of her son at the battlefront. She can see him in her dreams. The hearts that are united in love perceive the state of mind of the loved ones. They do not have to study mysticism or concentration, for they have natural concentration. The mother does not pretend to meditate; love teaches her meditation to a greater extent than a person attains who pretends to study it. You cannot hold an object in mind, however, when the heart has nothing to do with the object. Pebbles are not made to eat, and therefore you cannot eat them. The mind is never so satisfied with either an object or a being that it does not desire; therefore it is no use to concentrate specially on what the heart does not desire. The heart that does desire needs no special concentration.

Nothing gives greater power of confidence than love. If you love a person, you have confidence in that person. Hence the mother is as a god to her child. The hen is the most timid of birds until she has chicks; at that time she is under the spell of love, and would not hesitate to fight even an elephant if it were endangering her brood. That shows the power of love. Can any charm, or amulet, be more powerful than this? The one with a loving heart will travel the furthest.

Power can be attained artificially, by magic, or by the different laws of the power of sound, or of words, or of concentration. Such power can make a person ill, can make a person run away from the country, can make two hearts separate; many wonders can be performed by the power of concentration.

We do not exist only as body; we exist as heart, as soul. If the heart is kept dead all our life, and we give the body all the things it wants—soft cushions, comforts—is this all we need? The heart is still hungering. The heart wants to see that it is living. The heart longs to be alive. It has been created to love, and it is not loved; it wants to melt. But as it wants all the love and kindness to come to it, it withholds giving when the time comes for it to give. We take the love all the time during which the love is to be taken, but when the time comes to give, we do not give. Is love to give? Is love trade? Until this is known, it is impossible to understand love.

To love is to be the possessor of a heart, but not as a demon possesses a person. When a person comes to be "alive," this means that person has become the possessor of a "heart." Whose heart? Heart is that factor of our being, that factor of our thinking, that feels within itself a longing to express love; it is an awakening to love and to a feeling of love. This is the factor that produces thought; this is the factor that produces feeling; in this lies the creative power. All power that one can possibly wish to attain throughout life is reached by this means.

How can power develop in the absence of unity? Suppose everyone had magnetic power. They would make all the money they could from their clients. Would it be just for some to possess the power of making money, and for others to be perpetually their victims? No. Hence mysticism was kept hidden in the interest of the safety of others. Those who are not worthy of the hidden knowledge would use their power for selfish purposes—for themselves and for those who belong to them. If ordinary persons had this power, you could not even compare them with the devil. Rishis, saints, and sages have experienced the selfishness of humans. They know it would be bad for the world if this hidden knowledge were revealed. And who deserves to be illuminated with this knowledge? They deserve it who develop their soul in the thought of unity; and they alone receive it.

The progressive steps of enlightenment in power are shown when people transfer their ambitions to their family and then from their family to their city, from their city to their nation, from their nation to the whole world, and from the whole world to the whole universe.

When the joy of each person one sees is one's joy, when the pain of every person is one's pain, then one becomes a conqueror, attains power.

A majzub was wandering in the street at night, and a policeman asked him if he was a thief. He said "Yes," whereupon the policeman took him to the police station, and put him in a cell for the night. The majzub was as happy there as ever. Every seer has the same point of view.

19

WHAT THE POWER OF BREATH CAN DO

Breath, being the secret of all being, is the most important of all things. Whether you have a fine body or not has nothing to do with it. If you gain in weight, you are only getting your coat heavier; but our true being is the breath. If you put away your coat, there is nothing; if we put away our body we are nothing. When the breath has left the body, the body is useless. Therefore the importance of our being lies in the breath.

Breath is God. If God is manifest in anything, it is in breath. The activity of our physical being depends on our breath. This keeps up the rhythm of the pulse and the rhythm of the beats of the brain. The centers are kept up by the rhythm. If the rhythm stops, the centers stop. As the tick of the watch, so the swing of the breath. According to the rhythm, so is the condition of the body. Disorder in breath means illness.

In anger the rhythm of breathing is much quicker, even so much as to make speech impossible. "Speechless with anger" is proverbial. Therefore the breath acts on the mind as well. The lion, the leopard, and other fierce creatures have a very irregular breath; there is no rhythm; they are short-lived. The cobra never becomes excited; it breathes slowly, and attracts its food from any distance by mere concentration of will. It is very long-lived.

Breathing is the effect of breath. It is really a vibration rising and falling. There is a vibration in all things, in life and birth. In all things there is rhythm. It is the activity of God, and nothing else. There are different rhythms for the day, the hour, the minute, the forty days. There is a connection between this rhythm and the life of the universe—like so many candles and lamps.

Word—light—creation! The breath is the word. You cannot utter a word without breath. But a word is double, and breath is not; it is double because the sense comes before the sound.

Athletic exercises are really at bottom exercises of breathing. A porter does not become developed because he does not use his breathing for that purpose. He has had exercise without benefit. If the breath did not manifest through the voice, it would manifest in some other way, as the absent sound of thought. Wherever it is directed, it will go. If you do not speak, and yet think the same thought, the breath will travel silently. People think they cannot hear except with their ears, so much are they attached to their physical body. As soon as you are convinced that you can hear without ears, you will do so without speech. You can tell people are angry without their speaking, because they reveal it in their whole vibration. The very way a person says "Yes" tells you whether a person is willing or not willing; that is, it depends on the character of the breath at that moment.

People who live a material life, reveal it because the breath becomes material and makes a noise. It has become so dense that it actually makes a noise. In refined persons the breath is also fine. Cows and camels and buffaloes make a noise when they breathe. This at once shows the fineness or coarseness of the individual. Those who perceive these things can see them clearly.

All the different moods that we are in—inclination to laughter or crying, or heaviness, or exaltation, or meditation—all result from the breath. It changes in activity so many times during the day and night. It expresses a certain element (earth, water, fire, air, ether) as it changes. It makes one feel inclined to do certain things in accordance with the element.

All the different desires originate in breath; even the character of a person, even a person's luck, all depend on the breath. Those who know the mystery of breath can read the soul. Breath is a link from God to the human. Breath is purified by prayer. Fire worshippers keep fire before them in order to keep their breath in rhythm.

The science of breath is only transmitted by word of voice from the teacher when that one sees someone worthy to learn. There are three words that depict the stages of ability—*jalal*, force of breath; *jamal*, the gentleness of breath; *kamal*, perfection of breath. The latter stage culminates in "miracles."

A book is a dead teacher. People continually send their breath into undesirable centers. It is essential to have a living guide, and not try and study from books. A pure and good life is far better for the breathing. Do not let tranquility be disturbed, and the rhythm of the breath will keep regular; the mind will keep in good condition, and the body healthy.

Do not be so attached to anything in the world; do not be a slave to anything. Be beyond all desires. The law of cleanliness, the law of balance, being good to others, having good wishes, good thoughts, keeping a high ideal, and always wishing to attain the ideal. By doing these things, the breath itself will become fixed in the same mold.

20

THE KNOWLEDGE OF PAST, PRESENT, AND FUTURE

"What need is there of effort in life, if the future is already settled?" says one. Says another, "There is no predestination, for all things that happen are done by ourselves."

A person may be trying to do good, and nevertheless always finds it turning bad. Such a one asks, "Is there any hindrance by spirits?"

The Sufi studies what darkness is, in order to understand the light. That is Sufism.

The artist paints a picture in three stages: preparatory; stage of action; stage of completion—past, present, and future. The first stage is the design of the picture—that is predestination. We all do this. You are the manifestation of the eternal Sun, and therefore all the attributes of the Creator must be in the creature. Is it not so, that before doing anything we plan it? In our mind we have created. The Creator acted so, and so do we. We do it with a pen; the Creator does it with "nature." The Creator's art is nature. The Qurʾan says, "We have taught man by the pen of our nature."[1] It is our nature to create and by creating our art in nature we can see the skill of our painting.

1. Sura 96:3–5.

The art that we draw is according to the nature of ourselves, the creator.

Second, the picture comes on the paper; this is the present stage. Third, the picture itself inspires the painter. As it progresses the painter sees that in this place there ought to be a different color—this is not right, that is not right, and so on. And as the painter looks at the picture, he or she sees its faults, and so alters it here and there. So it is with each life. One stage of our life is predestined, the other part is that which we perform, and a third part of our life is that which is the effect of our actions. "As we sow, so we reap." All that we do, we see it in its reaction, and the reaction changes our life. The painter sees he or she must finish the picture differently—"so-and-so is not complete." So our actions tell us whether we ought to act differently.

People always want to know things they do not know. This dates from infancy. Children break things to see what is within them. But people do not know how to know. They expect too much. When they know how to know, then heaven and earth are both revealed to them.

If we want to see what is on the seventh floor, we must leave the bottom floor. If we are on the first floor and cannot get to the higher floors, it means, as mysticism shows, that we certainly do wish to go up, but are a captive on the first floor. That is the captivity.

Rumi said, "The bamboo-flute what is it that the flute says that makes you like it so much? Why does it mourn? Why does it win your attention so much? What is it that appeals to you? It moans for the separation that it suffers; because it has departed from its home, and has lost its original plant, the bamboo. It was cut off from its proper place. It mourns for the day that it was one with the whole bamboo-tree, it moans for the joy and the peace that it has enjoyed, but never receives again. It is the parting for which it mourns, and by which it appeals to you."[2]

So has it been with people. They wish to know about God, about heaven, about the things unknown, and about the world unseen, and they think they can see it from the first floor. They are not ready to believe there is anything on the seventh floor; they think there is no such thing as a seventh floor, nothing but the first. If they were released from this delusion, and if they were allowed to go to the other floors, then they would be able to see what the fourth, fifth, sixth, and seventh floors contain. And then they would know there is something through which one can obtain a knowledge of past, present, and future.

Suppose on the third floor there was a mechanism that produced instruments, one would know that on the first floor there must be a gathering of materials, and on the second floor an arranging into groups; on the third floor they come to be tangible appliances, and one can guess what is likely to be on the fourth floor.

Thus it is said in the Qurʾan that he sent his servant the Prophet in the midst of the night to the sphere of heaven, where he showed him signs such as he desired to show him.[3] In other words, God wants the one who wishes to realize God, God wants that one to know life; it is God's desire that one may see the signs that God previously makes and arranges, and the things that can be seen by rising to the third and fourth floors.

The floors represent planes of existence. We do not exist on the earthly or physical plane only. Being absorbed in this plane makes us awake to this but blind to the others. Language fails to explain the things of heaven. Those who have the experience of such things are bound to be silent, because there is no language for them.

2. A rendering of the opening of the *Masnawi*.
3. Qurʾan 17:1.

As a matter of fact, all the floors are really here. But as long as we are not open to seeing these floors, we are only on the first. Then, too, this mortal part must die; but we can die in this respect now, and pass on now to a perception that is beyond. The several floors are nothing but clothing. In this life, the light is hid under a bushel; the bushel is the physical body. It cannot be disclosed until the mortal part is removed.

If we depend on our eyes for sight, and our ears for hearing, and our mouth for speech, we are still dead. But we experience in life sometimes that which we see without eyes, and hear without ears, and speak without speech. If we have once seen without eyes, does it not show that we can see without eyes? Can you not see in a dream without eyes? Therefore the faculty of seeing and hearing is in us; but as we always depend on the physical body, physical eyes, and so forth, we become helpless and subject to death.

The teaching of immortality is to awaken. We must leave physical and material conditions if we are to live at all. One must aim at being independent of physical sight and hearing, and so forth. We know that if we really want to understand a thing, we close our eyes because we can see it better. If we are thinking in this manner, it means that we are listening to some thought coming from some other plane. At such a time we want to cut off and stop outward sound or sight. All the meditations and concentrations of the mystics, and their dreams, are their journeys to the inner planes. It is necessary, if the soul has the desire to know the past, the present, and the future, that it must satisfy its desire by a contemplative life. The more tired and exhausted the mind, the more meditation is needed.

Sages such as Saint Francis have spoken with rocks, birds, and animals, not as we talk, but by means of an insight into things; and every object expressed itself to them, speaking to them about its past, its present, and its future.

What a wonder that the animals and birds also know the future. Horses, dogs, cats know when someone is going to die.

They begin to cry. And yet people do not know it. Why should they not know it? Because their soul is so absorbed on the earth plane and in earthly things that the birds and beasts and animals are freed from—for they sit quiet, and meditate, and concentrate. People never sit quiet; and therefore the animals and birds, through their silence, are capable of knowing what the human does not know. All human activity brings death and decay much sooner; intuition is stifled.

There is the tendency in the soul to look forward to what is going to be, or at what has been in the past. It is the light of our soul, the intelligence, that does this. Intelligence working through physical means is no greater than intellect, but intelligence working free and independently from physical means is wisdom.

Wisdom is not cleverness, but infinitely superior to it. Wisdom works independently of the physical means, and therefore requires intuition. The clever person works by means of the physical body, but the wise person works independently of it.

Palmistry, astrology, and such like—are they the best means of knowing the future? All these means are right, none is wrong. There is always truth everywhere. The eye must look, and to whatever it looks, the seer will see. It is not necessary for the view to be in a certain symbol or teacup; it is as open as a book wherever the seer looks.

The head of a factory knows all things that go on there, but the workers only know that which goes on just where they are working. The head sees all. One person sees a square, another a street, another a house, another something less still. But the one at the top of the tower will see all of these. Seers will see all in their consciousness; wherever they cast their glance they will see still more clearly. As Saʿdi says, "Each leaf of a tree becomes a book of revelation to the one who sees; and that one reads the whole nature as a book."

21

SPIRITS AND SPIRITISM

Spirit in its true sense is the essence. The spirit of anything means its essence. And when we consider the true essence, there is only one. When we consider the true spirit, there is only one spirit.

But of course, in the world of variety, one life is many lives, one thing has many manifestations. This manifestation makes us see many forms, many names of a one and only Being; and when we begin to overlook the oneness of that Being and begin to direct our attention to the variety of manifestation, we see that the spirit of each thing is its essence. The spirit of jasmine, the spirit of a rose, and so on; each has its own individuality, its own essence.

Spirit, as understood by everybody, is the remainder of a human's existence. After one has gone into the grave, what remains of one is considered spirit. And it has a very beautiful name in Sanskrit: *bhut*, that is, the one who has been; the being that has once been.

The spirit world distinguishes itself as different and distinct from the spirit experiencing the world through the body. The spirit of camphor is not the color or form of the substance, but that odor of camphor has existed in its spirit. The spirit of cinnamon is the fragrance and the effect that it has. The effect is still left after its form and substance have gone.

Every object in this world, after its vanishing, leaves a mark of its essence just like the flower. When the essence is taken from the flower its external form is ruined, but it has left something that is its own.

Both body and spirit are human. The human is a double spirit. The human in its cloak, its physical body, is more complete than a spirit alone. When the flower is living and its spirit has not been taken away from it, both the flower and its spirit are joined. A person whose sense of discrimination and feeling is rather developed can find that visitors coming into the house bring with them a certain influence—good feeling or bad feeling, irritable feeling or a blissful feeling. There is something with them besides their knowledge, besides their beauty; and when they leave the house their body leaves as well as that strength and beauty and material part; but there is something left in that room for a certain time. The whole atmosphere is charged after they have gone, and we feel that there is something left. The more directly you watch life, the more wonderful it is. All the miracles and phenomena are before us. Our everyday life is a miracle. If we are only absorbed in things that are material and not in things of a delicate character, we do not see because we do not make ourselves sensitive. It is then that we think that what we do not see or perceive does not exist.

Consider, for instance, how infectious yawning is. From this we can never say there is nothing beyond what the eyes and flesh can see.

Influence goes out of a living person and affects others in the vicinity. If the influence is so strong during life, shall it not exist after the person is dead? Only the influence remaining is left, yet how much greater its influence must be. The light of the moon is the light of the sun.

There are two actions of sense, and two actions of the whole being: expressiveness and responsiveness. The whole universe works on these two principles. As soon as the expressing spirit expresses itself, the responsive spirit may receive its impression, just like a person whose picture is taken in the camera yields their impression when the camera is properly adjusted. If the camera is not rightly placed, there will be no image on the plate. If a spirit had a fondness for someone or something, and desires to be in the thought of this beloved one all the time, always surrounding the person, so, just like the camera taking the photograph of the person, this unconscious spirit of a person naturally takes the impression falling from that spirit.

People think a person has gone mad when they find he or she wants to be alone. Child prodigies may be the result of influence; under this influence they work, speak, write poems, dispute, and so on. If people die with the thought of revenge that they could not accomplish, or have not had the courage to accomplish, they may find someone else, such as a youth or child, who executes the act for the spirit without knowing why. Murders may even arise in this way.

The brain may be deficient in thinking power; the body may work on thought, and sometimes the thought may work on the body. Could not the mind produce decay in the brain, or is it true that it is always strain of the body that brings strain on the mind? Or does anger bring a strain on the body? The trouble usually comes from within.

Hallucinations sometimes arise from thought and from mind, either in the same person or in some other person. We call it obsession when it comes from without.

Sometimes the living person can express and the spirit re spond. We cover our spirit under our body. We cover our light under a bushel. We never allow the spirit to become conscious of itself.

We are not doing spirits any good by calling them back when they have no body; we have a body. Why not let them forget the experiences of this world of illusion rather than attract them? What good will it do them? One should only trouble others when one needs them very much. We should use ourselves as the vehicle of all experiences. We can communicate much better with another person who is clothed like us than we can with a spirit.

Is not God enough for our souls and sufficient to inspire us and to illuminate our wills? Is God not sufficient to guide our souls? Is God any less than a friend here or in the spirit life? God is the great well-wisher. In God mercy is complete. God is Soul of all souls. When we devote ourselves to the thought of God, all illumination and revelation is ours. God-communication is the best communication that true spiritualism can teach us.

If we give all our wealth to the universe as a whole, we bring it about that no one person receives much. But it is a great accomplishment actually to realize God; it means that a very high degree of spiritualism has been attained. It is most difficult to attain such a conviction of God that there is not the slightest doubt, but when this is so the mere thinking of the friend is enough to secure the friend's blessing; it becomes a privilege to be the friend of such a person. It is a privilege because that one is the friend of God.

People possess the knowledge that they have attained as they possess the wealth that they have acquired. And so when the soul is illuminated it will have the desire to find some other soul illuminated in like manner, and will find a great joy and bliss in its society. The soul will surely find others who are on the verge of illumination. Even a drunkard will find others to drink with; and so it is mystically. A very little light can be turned into a flame; and that flame into a very big flame.

Why is it better to become a mystic than to remain a drunkard? As a matter of fact, a drunkard will never be satisfied. The mystic will look for what Omar Khayyam calls wine, the wine of the Christ, after drinking which no one will ever thirst. The mystic will always seek the wine whose intoxication never dies off. It is the only wine—the intoxication of the love divine.

22

THE MASTERMIND

In the first place there is a question, "What is mind?" Is it the intelligence of the brain, or is it the activity of the brain, or is it something else? When people limit the word *mind* to brain, they certainly draw cause down to the position of effect.

There are two ways of looking at things: one, from the cause to the effect; the other, from the effect to the cause. The first is as looking from the top of the mountain to the bottom; the other is as looking from the bottom of the mountain to the top. The one who looks from the bottom fails many times to see what is going on at the top. Therefore mystics follow the other way. They perceive that those who investigate a higher truth by standing at the bottom of the mountain may sometimes succeed in seeing what is at the top, and sometimes they will not; and even when they do see, they do not see fully. It is different when a person looks from the top of the mountain to the bottom; and that is why the mystic goes to the cause, and sees from the cause to the effect.

But the great thing is to get to the cause. It is easy to agree with the teaching of Jesus Christ, where he says, "Seek ye first the kingdom of God, and all things shall be added."[1] This teaching may be applied even in the investigation of the knowledge

1. Matthew 6:33.

of human life, because as soon as one reaches the root of the cause, one has the light, and the light guides one. But the thing that is difficult is to get in when one is on the outside.

Humanity has striven after truth for ages; and yet there is no period in the history of the world in which humankind has not realized truth. The only difference is that one says, "I have discovered something," and the other says, "There is nothing new under the sun."

The mystic's view is, "What I have known today has been known before, and will be known after." It has never been known by all, and will never be known by all; but as the sight becomes keen, so a person will be able to see.

In the first place, what the mastermind is, is really explained by the power of spirit on matter. When we see that mountains are pierced through by the effort of humans, and that humans have crossed the seas, that they fly in the air—that itself shows that humankind is the master of creation.

But what is a human? Is a human a physical being, or is there something else called human? If the physical being is the human, then what of the elephant, who is twenty times bigger? The elephant would never have listened for one moment to what a human says, and yet when the human says, "Sit down," the elephant sits down; "Stand," and it stands; "Walk," and it walks. At the same time the elephant is conscious of its heavy body and the strength that it has. Then not only the elephant, but the tiger and the lion, the kings of the forest as they call them in the East—we can see them mastered in the circus by one human, although these most brutal animals keep killing other animals, and live by the terror they evoke, so conscious are they of their strength. The human has mastered them.

Evidently there is something hidden in the human. What is it? In Sanskrit, the word *mana* means "mind"; the words *manu*, *manushu*, *mana*, "man," "mind" all belong to the same root. The word *man* means "mind."

The physical being developed as long as the animal developed; but when the time came for mind to develop there came into being man, mind.

At the same time there is the question as to whether every person can really claim to be human, or as to what a human mind should be. This is shown by the story that one day Diogenes went seeking in the marketplace with a lighted lantern at midday, and when they asked him what he sought, he answered, "A man."

Ghalib, a Hindustani poet of Delhi, has said in his verse, "There seems to be a difficulty in all things; it seems difficult even for a man to claim to be a man."

The question is, What is the difference between human and animal? Is it not in the form of the human? But if the form only is human, we have the fact that, strictly speaking, all forms in this world gradually change into the human. The more we study the life of birds, insects, creatures, or even the vegetable kingdom, the more plainly we shall see how the human face has appeared, step-by-step, from the primitive preparatory stages, through all the different manifestations, until it has appeared as the human. So if it were the form that makes a human human, it would never have been named mind. So it is something beyond form that makes the human.

The whole matter is as Rumi of Persia explains in his *Masnavi*: "Our life on earth is as a captivity, an imprisonment."[2] An imprisonment in what? In a physical body that covers the light of the soul. And the mind is also helplessly attached to the body. It is the bodily desires—passion, anger, appetite, all the different desires and needs—that make the mind helpless and make the human hold on to them. All the worries, anxieties, depressions, and despairs arise from them. There is not a single moment in which the mind is able to stand aloof so as to reflect the light within, the light of the soul, so limited has it been

2. *Masnavi* 1:525.

made by the limited existence on earth. In reality, this is the whole tragedy of human life.

The one thing that hinders a person from advancing spiritually, or at least from advancing toward the goal that they have come for and are longing to attain, is the only thing, and it is everything: that the mind is so absorbed by the demands and wants of the physical body that it has hardly a moment to give itself solely to the reflection of the light of the soul.

A person may say, "I do not believe even in such a thing as soul, since there is no evidence of such a thing; I do not believe in a hereafter; I do not believe in a spiritual or a higher thing, only in what I see or enjoy in this worldly life."

What then? The answer is, "You believe at least in being happy; you believe in happiness being something worth attaining in life; you also believe in living; you do not wish to die. Not only do you believe these two things, but you believe in being left alone when you are tired, being left in peace, in having rest. You believe in understanding things you cannot yet understand." So people believe in four things. They may not believe in inspiration, revelation, or some higher spirit coming and telling them, but yet they believe in trying to understand things that puzzle them, in seeking to remove that cloud of confusion that hinders the light from coming that will guide them to the understanding of the things that at present confuse them. So there is a longing in them to find out something they do not know about.

In every person, therefore, whether spiritual or material, whatever view they have, there are these four inclinations, four desires: to live, to save their life even to the extent of risking it in order to defend themselves against being killed; to be happy, enjoying theatre, music, dancing, singing, a play, sport, something that pleases; a desire to know; and a desire to have peace, to rest, to be left alone. Whether they believe in God, in spirit, in heaven, in scripture, in a hereafter or not, they certainly believe in those four things. They develop gradually. As one studies more and more the nature of acquiring these things, that study itself becomes a form of religion; and attainment of the root of the four things is spiritual perfection. It is only that one goes on a religious path, another in the path of wisdom, another in the path of devotion, and another in the path of the form or ceremonial of worship. Whichever way it be, the constant pursuit after these four things brings the attainment of the same goal in the end, the goal for every soul. Some paths lead there sooner than others, that is all.

If we think more about the desire for happiness, for instance, we see that although every soul seeks after pleasure, or wealth, or position, or power to become happy, one finds that everything in life is changeable. That which one obtains, in the satisfaction of the desire for pleasure, or success, or achievement (which are all forms of desire for happiness) can only be held like air. How long can you hold that? Is it not always slipping from the hands, be it wealth or position? The most difficult thing in life is to hold it when you have it. It is true it is difficult to acquire, but how much more difficult to keep. Thousands of people are after it. "How can we get it from that person?" they ask. Relatives, friends, enemies, burglars, thieves, robbers, everybody contemplating that person's wealth; while that person holds it tight, more and more worried about it every day. So, on the one side there is the happiness of holding something that is not one's own, and on the other the strain of keeping safe that which does not really belong to one, and is changeable and momentary. This takes away one's happiness.

All the things that give happiness, however much pleasure and comfort they may give, seem so great a prize beforehand; but when it comes to paying the cost of having them, one begins to understand that there is no comfort or pleasure that is really worthwhile. As Omar Khayyam says, "When I am seeking for happiness, all pleasures and comforts seem to be blessing for that moment; but in the end everything is dust."[3]

There is a beautiful story illustrating this idea. In the palace of a Mughal king there was a housemaid, and when making the bed she was once overpowered by the sense of the beauty of the king's room, the fragrance all round, the windows open allowing the cool breeze to come in—so grateful when the summers are as hot as in the East. She felt she would like to sit in the bed a moment, and see how it felt. "How very soft, and nice, and very fragrant," she thought. And she sat there, and then felt she would like to lean on the cushions. But unfortunately she fell asleep. Then the king and queen happened to come in. He said, "What impertinence"; the queen was very displeased too.

In a moment a whip fell on her back, and she got up with a great horror, and looked hither and thither and then smiled. And the king and queen were amused to see her smile on receiving the whip. Said the queen, "Why do you smile?" She said, "Oh, it was a thought." The king said, "Tell me the thought." "The thought was, that it is so fragrant in this room, and the cool breeze so balmy, and this bed so soft and comfortable—I thought I should like to see how it felt, and I slept; and perhaps I did not sleep for more than a few minutes, or perhaps half an hour; and you came, and I received the whip. Now, by sleeping there half an hour I receive the whip, so I do not know what you will receive. You have been sleeping here for years together."

This is a lesson. There is no pleasure to be gained without a cost; it may be the cost of wealth or of time; it may be even the cost of life. People, absorbed as they are in the pleasures and comforts of life, think very little of this, and go on until the time comes when it is too late to think of it. Life has been nothing but a captivity to this constant longing for happiness

3. See *Rubaiyat*, verse xxiii.

and pleasure, which, when it comes, one finds oneself unable to enjoy.

So this teaches that the source of real happiness lies somewhere else. It is not in a building of sand that comfort can be got. It is in oneself that lies the building in which one can get comfort. Having discovered the nature of pleasures one may think, "After all, these pleasures were just like lips touching the wine and not drinking it. The wine is somewhere else." But in the end even the pleasure-seeker comes to the same goal, that of the truth.

The third thing is the constant desire to live. Every bird, animal, and beast, even the smallest insect in the world—as soon as you wish to touch it, it wishes to save its life; it runs away, it wants to live; even if it lives in the dirt its desire is to live. How dear life is to every creature. How much everybody wishes to live. And yet at the same time there is this force of destruction in the form of diseases and in the form of death, which sweep away so many. And still the desire in every heart is to live. This thought teaches that it is not the believing in God, in spirit, in religion, that is the secret; it is the desire in every heart for life. This too one can find by searching within oneself. The life is hidden within one, and when one begins to find it then one feels one is safe.

Then, if we think about the desire for understanding, we notice how everyone wishes to learn, to read, to study, to learn about things in every possible way. But the desire cannot be satisfied until the light within is brought to it, so that one may understand by this.

We come, then, to the truth that all things can be accomplished by the mastery of mind. And so the question comes, "How can mind be mastered?" The answer is that mind cannot be mastered until one is master of the body. The difference between a mastermind and a person without mastery is the difference between a person sitting on a horse with a saddle and holding the reins in their hand, and a person sitting on a horse while the latter is jumping and running wherever it likes, and there is fear that at any moment the horse will throw them; they are not able to control it.

People may realize all the different weaknesses in themselves, and be very sorry about them, and would like to give them up if they could; but they find the difficulty that whether they like some little weakness or not, they cannot hold themselves back from doing things, whether it be weakness of mind or weakness of action. This shows that though the desire of the soul is always to direct one on the right path, on the path of virtue, on the good path, yet at the same time one has lost one's control, and one is led away by some force one cannot control. The weakness of character is shown when a person says, "I do not wish to be angry; after being angry I am very sorry, but at the same time I cannot help it. I do not wish to hurt others, but at the same time when the moment comes, I cannot help it, I am abrupt." Then, even in vices such as drink, or thieving, or any weakness, it is all because of weakness of mind. When the mind has no control over its thoughts and feelings, when it is not mastered, all these things come to pass.

From all this it is plain that a person has two aspects of being: the servant aspect and the master aspect. When the servant aspect is fed alone and the master aspect is not, then the master aspect of the being longs to be master, and cannot be; and the whole conflict in life depends on that. When one looks at the master aspect and wishes to be master, then one becomes master of oneself; and one becomes not only master of one's thoughts, feelings, and actions, but one becomes master of one's affairs.

Then the key to what we call fate comes into a person's hand; one becomes the king of the kingdom that has been given to one from God; and when one has arrived at that stage, then comes a still greater and exalted stage that may be understood in this way.

In a small way we say, "That person is guided by that one, or listens to that one, or gives in to that one." Why does the person give in? The answer is this, that the ones who do not give in are those with the master aspect alive in them. The ones who give in have the servant aspect alive in them. To understand this secret is to understand the secret of the spiritual hierarchy. It is the secret of the coming of the prophets and of the mastermind, of what is called the superman. The symbolic picture of this is shown in Hindu symbology, where the devatas have four hands—two hands for the body, and two for the mind. The four make a perfect human. When there are only two external hands, material hands, and the other hands are not yet attached to the mind, the mind is not active and cannot control. There are these four different forces—the two physical arms and the two arms of mind, which set life on its feet—the four arms that make the perfect human, the mastermind.

Having these, one becomes responsible for one's affairs as well as the affairs of others; and the people who have been in the world as leaders of nations, leaders of humanity, and have led humanity to the spiritual, the right, the religious path, have not done so just through their intellect. No, there was some power behind.

There are many intellectual people going round from morning till evening; every moment of theirs is spent in their cleverness and polish of mind. But this is only an activity; it is not the power of mind. The power of mind is such that without speaking words the mind speaks. Without suggestion in words, the mind reflects what is in this mind or that. Things that the outer arms cannot accomplish the arms of mind can. Means are procured for the accomplishment of every object. In the fairy tales of old about the jinns it is said that one day a village teacher was teaching a class. Among them was a jinn, and he was in the form of a boy. But the village teacher did not know that he was a jinn. One day he wanted something at a distance, and he asked the boy to bring it. This boy, instead of getting up, just stretched his hand and got it. And the teacher was so frightened that next day he would not allow him to come into the school.

This story tells us of the mastermind. It is not necessary to be of a certain age to have the mastery. Sometimes a child may have greater mastery than a grown-up, and greater will. Therefore it is not dependent on age. "Where there is a will, there is a way."

For a person to say, "Take care of me, I cannot hold the secret, I must speak it out; I cannot hold myself back, I must give it; I cannot manage this; I cannot remember this"—all these weaknesses denote the lack of mastery of mind. The mastermind shows mastery in everything: in speech, in listening, in understanding, in doing all things.

Is this to be attained by contemplation, by concentration, by meditation? No, in reality it is in your everyday life, in your simple everyday actions that you develop the power of mind by this simple law: when you are doing some work and the desire comes, "No, I must go and rest and sleep," and you go and rest, you give in to your desire. You go and rest, but the work is not accomplished! Then a person says, "I must not be abrupt, inconsiderate; I must have consideration from now on." Next day something happens in which the person should be considerate and gentle, but thinks, "In this case it does not matter; it is a small thing; it is a very small thing." The person thinks, "Today it does not matter," and gives in. The excuse comes to the rescue: "With this person it does not matter; today it does not matter; at this moment it does not matter." As soon as one gives in to a slight weakness, next time one falls down again because the weakness wins every time. So all those seeking to attain mastery will find some weakness waiting for them; if it is not one weakness, there will come another.

One is neglectful who does not think of this law. One may think it does not matter; it is only a little finger. But if the finger fails, next time one's hand will fail; and in time one's mouth will be in the mouth of weakness until one is swallowed up by it. Then it has become too late. And when one's power has gone, there is no strength.

So what is the religion of the sages? Every religion is their religion, and yet no religion is their religion. Their religion is that of wisdom. They master the mind not only by all these things, but at the same time by the way of contemplation, by learning how to concentrate, by learning how to live life; in all they practice the mastery of mind; for if they do not master the mind, concentration will not help them. If the small things are not managed, how can they manage contemplation? How many people say, "When we sit for a concentration our minds go to a thousand things; we seem to be sitting in a chair, but our mind seems to be jumping all about." Where is the concentration?

Therefore it is helpful to concentrate, and it is helpful to be guided by someone who knows the path of concentration; but at the same time if people will not practice the law of mastery in their everyday life and in every thing, they will not be able to accomplish this great work.

23

THE DESIRE OF NATIONS

In the works of a great Sufi teacher, we find that he said, "In order to know God, know yourself." It follows that in order to know the desire of nations or of people, we should first know our own desire. Until we know ourselves, we cannot know about others. As long as we are ignorant of our own life's needs and wants, and of the secret of our own nature, we can never understand the needs and wants and the secret of another person's nature.

In reality, we ourselves are a nation within ourselves. More than that, we are not merely a nation within ourselves, we are a whole universe within ourselves. Therefore, if we study self, we shall find we can study not only a nation, but this whole world, and even all other worlds. To study ourselves also means the study of the primitive human condition, and the study of the primitive human condition is to study life in all its forms. We must learn about the inclination of life in all forms as well.

What is the inclination of life in all forms? There is a verse in the Bible that explains this, indirectly giving a hint of the secret: "For in him we live and move and have our being."[1] We live to move, and we move to make our being in God. Without moving we are not living; without making our being, we do

1. Acts 17:28.

not move, nor do we live. Therefore it is the condition of life that if we live we should move and progress, and attain that state of being for which we are purposed.

We can see that inclination in every being. A little plant, a tree—if we suppress its growth, if we build a fence around it, if we cover it with glass, it will not flourish, it will not bring out flowers; in time it will die. Why is this? It is because its life cannot express itself when it is covered, cannot express itself when there is a fence around it. It is not enough that it be alive, because life does not want only to live; to realize itself, life must be able to make progress, and progress is only made when there is free movement.

We find the same inclination even in little worms and germs. A little ant has the same desire. You wish to touch it, but it does not want you to touch it. You wish to keep it in a certain place, but it does not want to stay there. However much we say we will take great care of the parrots and the sparrows and the beautiful birds, saying we love them so much—it is no pleasure to them. Of course they will eat in their captivity, if they are hungry; they will drink water in their captivity when they are thirsty; but this is no sign that they enjoy themselves or that they are happy.

Why should they not be happy? It is because it is not their life's inclination to be restricted. Life did not give a bird wings in order to stay in a cage. Wings were given as the means whereby to enjoy life, to make a nest where the birds can live, to make the acquaintance of other birds, to enjoy the life of the jungle, and to find water and food for the comfort and ease of their family. It is in that way that they make their being.

So it is the same case with the animals and birds as it is with plants. For them also, life means to have a being, to move. Life demands to be allowed to move and have its being.

When we come to human life, do we not find it the same? However much we love our little child and suggest, "Sit here, I like you here so much," it will stay there for a moment, and then it will say, "No, let me play." You say to it, "Your life is to sit here." It answers, "No, I don't like to sit here." Then you give the child a beautiful toy, and say, "Sit here." Yes, for the sake of the toy it will sit for a moment; but in another it will take the toy with it and go away. "Let me have my freedom," it says. Does not this show that the purpose of life is freedom?

As long as people are ignorant of that they are ignorant of the secret of their own nature, and of the secret of any other. Neither they nor any other can be happy, however much wealth, or property, grandeur of position, or palaces they may possess.

Interdependence is a law of nature. We make our life by sharing the joys and pleasures and sorrows of another, but it takes us a very long time to understand this one thing. Our observation and study of human nature shows that life demands freedom; and yet on the other hand we find that nature develops selfishness in the human being, more than in any other creature. The demands of its life are so much greater, and it becomes so absorbed in satisfying these demands, and possessing and enjoying them when it has them, that it really forgets the secret of nature, really forgets the secret of its own happiness as well as that of others.

Not only does the individual person seek freedom, but also the nations and races and peoples throughout the whole world have been absorbed in the pursuit of freedom. Whenever wars have taken place, whenever there is bloodshed in the world, whenever there have been revolutions and various troubles in life, all the different disasters that have occurred are due to this same reason: on the one side human selfishness, and on the other the human lack of understanding the law of nature and the law of happiness.

Ignorance of this law exists in the human soul from childhood. Whatever a child sees that is attractive and beautiful, at once it wants to have it, never thinking whose it is at the moment. "No one shall touch it; that shall belong to me," it says. "I shall be happy only when I have what that other child has." Even if it already has a beautiful toy, it still wants to have what the other one has. It is this human nature that goes on developing regardless of the secret of happiness that can only be disclosed when the veil of ignorance has fallen off from before a person's eyes.

A person never understands what justice is, even though he or she may speak of it. Real justice cannot be perceived until the veil of selfishness has been removed from the eyes. The least spark of selfishness will prevent one from being just; one will continue to have a partial interest, because one will be looking after one's own interest; one will call something one's right and one's justice that furthers the means of accomplishing one's own interest.

The prophets and holy ones have all recognized the justice of God as the only real justice. What is the nature of the justice of God? It cannot be read in a scripture; it cannot be learned from a book; it can only be learned from the self within after selfishness has been removed. Our limited self is as a wall separating us from the Self of God. God is as far away from us as that wall is thick. The wisdom and justice of God are within us, and yet they are far away under the covering of the veil of the limited self. Whoever has arrived at that realization of the nature of God's justice is able to see all things in a different way from anyone else. That person's whole outlook on life becomes different.

From the most ancient times teachers have come as messengers, one after the other, in order to instruct humankind in this law of God's justice, the law of cooperation, the law of love amongst people. That which Christ taught, they taught; for that has always been their work. But it is the way in which education and new reforms have worked out in modern civilization that has covered the real spirit of religion; the nations gradually unlearned what true religion was, and became more and more depraved. Christ came to reawaken the ancient truth. And then Muhammad formed not only a nation with his spiritual message, but also formed a school in which love, cooperation, equality, and democracy should be learned—that the dependence of people on one another is what the happiness of humanity depends on. Hence it is written, "Every Muslim is a brother of another Muslim."[2] If there were a king and a prime minister offering prayer, a poor man can stand beside them and make his prayers with them.

How was the original spirit changed? For at first Islam taught the world directly and indirectly—directly to the followers of Islam, indirectly to humanity at large. Before the spirit changed the religion was sent by the Prophet, but afterward the religion was used as the instrument for forming a nation. Instead of a nation being the protector of religion, the religion became the protector of a nation. The desire to attain a God-ideal was degraded into a desire to attain a national ideal, in order to satisfy a selfish motive. No sooner did that spirit enter Islam than the whole building tumbled down.

In the history of the world this lesson has been taught not once, but a thousand times. As long as a nation works for the interest of God and humanity it will be always prosperous, but as soon as it uses religion in order to exalt the national ideal, then all falls down like a house of cards. We can see this in the history of Hinduism, in the history of Islam, in the history of the European religious sects. If there is the wish to rise, the ideal must be high; if there is the desire to fall, let the ideal be low. It is the love of the earth that will attract humans to the earth; but it is the love of heaven that will attract them thither. It is as the Bible says, "Where your treasure is, there will your heart be also."[3] When the whole of a person's ideal in life is their degree of education, their success in trade (all toward exalting the self, the individuality), then they are descending and not

2. Qur᾿an 49:10.
3. Matthew 6:21.

ascending. They are selfish as individuals, they become selfish as a nation, then as a race, and at last there is warfare; the racial ideal expresses its selfishness in great wars. Even people of the same nation will fight one another.

The same thing develops further when it appears between classes and parties, between labor and capital, the higher against the lower. All of them have a wrong ideal; selfishness is allowed to rule instead of the higher ideal.

And even that is not the end. The next thing that develops is disharmony of sex. Families become inharmonious because of the selfish ideal; the husband wants his own way; the wife wants her own way. The husband thinks, "As long as I am happy, that is all that is necessary." In whatever direction you may journey in life you will meet this tendency. Selfishness may begin with the thought, "As long as my country is benefited, that is my benefit"; and then it will narrow to, "If my family is benefited, if we become wealthy and have that desirable thing, that is sufficient for the day." And then it narrows down from, "For my father, or mother, or wife, or children," until it ends in "Nothing matters as long as I am happy myself." That one has now become cold, ignorant, and blind to the law that life depends on the happiness of those with whom we live. The whole life is one. In all these different names and manifestations life is all one. The true thought is, "If my spouse is not happy, if my children, my neighbors, my servants are not happy, how can I ever be happy?' An insult given to one will one day return.

How simple it is; yet how difficult for one to understand! It is simple to one who observes life keenly; it is difficult to one who is absorbed in oneself. Life is nothing but this. Life is not a particular philosophy, not a particular faith, not a particular religion, not a particular code of morals. Life is that dependence upon our surroundings, upon the life of our neighbors, upon the life of the nation, upon the life of the whole world. That is what keen observation and a wide outlook on life teaches one.

How the peace of the world has suffered during the past few years! Do not think that the effect of this suffering has not been felt by all the other nations, even though they were not actually engaged in the war. The effect has spread both directly and indirectly throughout the whole world. The whole of humanity has gone through the pain. Even the fishes of the sea have suffered with humanity in the catastrophe. The invisible beings have suffered. It is all one life. How could it be otherwise?

If the wound in the foot has an effect on the arm, even though the arm is not wounded, if the pain has its effect upon the whole body, how can it be otherwise between nation and nation?

We can see the operation of this law even in our own circle. When there is someone among our own acquaintances who is poor, someone among our servants, someone among our relatives depending on us, helpless or in distress, suppose we cause that one trouble, or do some injury, even though we may not know it at the time, some day afterward we shall discover it; it will return to us. It may return through some other channel. We may be too blind to see that it has originally come from that source. We may not see if we are in Africa that the harm has come from someone in China. But life is nevertheless all one.

Similarly when we bring joy and pleasure and happiness, it is never lost any more than is anything that is done harmfully or injuriously, or of a troublesome nature. Good deeds, kindnesses, forgivenesses, tolerance, acts of love—none of these are ever lost, and some day they will return to us. Even if the recipient appear faithless or heedless it is all the same. There is no need to be disappointed even if someone proves to be unworthy of our kindness or our love. When we realize that all life is one life, we realize that it is to that life that we give our love and kindness and mercy. Then it is bound to return to us. If not today, it may be next week; if not next week, it may be next year; if not here, then somewhere where we never expected it could even possibly come. "Thou shalt find it after many days."[4]

Though there may still be time to awaken to a true understanding of these things, it is often too late by the time that sufferings, troubles, and misery have come to the individual or to the multitude. If the person has so far failed to understand them before they actually came, perhaps they will never understand. When there is some little pain or bad feeling in them, they may think they have some illness, but if they do not think about it, if they take no notice of it, something worse may come. And so it has been with the world. The worst evil that has ever been should show humanity that it is time now to awaken and understand that it is not a study of national or social questions, not a study of religious questions that will bring an everlasting peace; but it is the insight into life that is the real religion and that alone can help people to understand life.

What is that religion? It is nature's religion of freedom, the religion that will liberate humanity. When people see that the ideal of every soul is freedom, and that they cannot enjoy their own freedom unless they have shared their freedom with others, then and only then can it be that troubles and unhappiness will cease.

A Hindustani poet says, "It is for sympathy that we have created man, not that he should worship God." There are so many angels in heaven who constantly worship God. Therefore, humankind, being the final manifestation, is supposed to do something different from the angelic world. God says, "We have made man to sympathize with his fellows, to be serviceable to others, to give joy and peace to others." Until one does that one is not really human.

The animals are all selfish; they all seek their own life's demands, and the satisfaction of their passions is their life. Their understanding of happiness is that it is just this gratification.

4. Ecclesiastes 11:1

Birds make their nests; animals have their holes. Therefore, if the only ideal necessary for humans was that they should attain comfort and wealth and position, they would be no different from the lower creation. The great difference is that the human has the power of sympathizing. The human it is who can say, "My mother has taken care of me; now she is old; I must listen to her; I must tolerate her hard words; perhaps she has only misunderstood. I was very disagreeable once, and yet my mother was always patient and kind and attentive through it all." If one's father has become old, if our friends are in difficulty, in every case we must have sympathy. Not as the animals who bite their aged ones, and forget their mothers and fathers when their own needs are satisfied, but as one who thinks gratefully of one's aged mother, of the spouse to whom one is united to share in sorrows and joys, in whatever way they are able to serve one another.

One is a human who thinks, "Though in business we have to make money and profit, yet by proving ourselves sincere and true in heart, by proving ourselves honest and in earnest, the business will increase still more and remain safe." One is a human in national ideals, in social ideals, in racial ideals, in the ideals of the whole humanity, who looks at nature with widely open eyes, and can perceive that the whole life is one, that all individuals are one embodiment of life.

One who perceives this realizes, "What I have taken from another, I have lost; what I have given to another, that I have gained. Whatever good I have done to another is my gain, and whatever good another has done to me is my loss." The kindness, the service, the love and sympathy that another has given is all lost when the person is gone. It could only be there so long as the person was there. But deeds of goodness done to another, of kindness to another, of consideration to another, all these deeds will last with the one who does them both here and hereafter.

24

DEMOCRACY

There is nothing new under the sun, said Solomon the Wise. People think democracy is something that has been developed in the human spirit and which was never known before. They think the democratic way is not only right, but new. But when we consider deeply, we see that life is the same, the ideals are the same, nature's laws are the same in all ages. And therefore these two aspects—the spirit of dependence and independence—have always existed, and have always manifested in their time. For instance, every soul knows that in its own experience the very first aspect to be experienced was the aspect of dependence. The infant is dependent on its mother and father; in whatever way they direct it, it acts and works. Then comes the age in which the child is old enough to understand its own affairs, and it says, "Yes, Father, that which I think I will do. I *will* do." The father and mother say, "Yes, our child has grown up, and it understands its own way; we should not interfere with him or her very much."

We see, then, that in everybody's life there have been the two phases: the phase of dependence and the phase of independence.

It is exactly the same in the lives of peoples, of multitudes, and of nations. It is always the same. At first dependence; then independence; at first autocracy, then democracy. The life and evolution of the individual and of the multitude are alike.

As freedom is the nature of every soul, so the child, the little child, seeks freedom. You want the child to sit in your arms, but it says, "Oh no, let me go and play." An animal, a dog, or a cat, which depends so much on the sympathy of humankind, at the same time does not wish to be deprived of freedom. That shows that at every stage of development life is trying to become free. That is why it is true to say that the spirit of democracy is not a thing just of today; it has existed in all ages. Sometimes it has appeared timely, and sometimes it has arisen untimely.

When we trace the cause, the reason for the spirit, we find that it lies in idealism. The human race first developed a thought of idealism in itself—religions, learning, education have emerged from this one human tendency. And what is this idealism? It is the silent consideration, that recognition of affection and attachment that we even see in beasts and birds. We see that deer recognize their mates, pigeons and doves have a kind of attachment for them. Sparrows and other birds have a tendency to share their responsibilities for their young ones with their mates. This all shows to us that the ideal has only culminated in the human being. Call it religion, wisdom, learning, whatnot, the only real human thing is idealism. As soon as a person begins to think, "These are my parents, and I would like to serve them, so that they may not have the cares and tiredness and struggles of life," that person shows idealism. Then the ideal extends to the neighbors: "When I was young, I could not help them; now I can help them, and I will care for the home of my neighbor, and protect them from robbery." Here the idealism has extended to the neighbor. Then comes the consideration of one's life partner—the co-ruler of the home. As one then sees the beauty of life, one begins to develop one's thoughts and imagination, making beautiful forms that shape themselves into beautiful ideals. One expands the ideal and becomes capable of higher ideals. Motherhood is regarded by everybody with veneration, fatherhood is regarded by everybody with respect. Neighborhood is looked upon with friendly feelings. The elders, or chiefs, or kings in the village or town, who have given all their thoughts to the welfare of that town or village—how are they regarded? "Here," they say, "is the father or mother of the village or town, who has looked after us all when we were helpless or not learned enough." In this way the idea of a ruler or rajah came, from the development of a certain kind of ideal. The civilization of whatever age or time always started to develop from idealism. The whole source of civilization is idealism and nothing else.

Why is the diamond worth millions of pounds, and a pebble nothing? Both are stones. Why pay more for one? It is just the ideal. Seven hundred dollars for a chair of Napoleon's, and who knows whether he ever sat in it at all! This only shows how everything is based on an ideal. Without it, nobody can exist.

In the ancient times the religion and the nation both went hand in hand; and there is no doubt that there is a great advantage in this, when we compare it with the other scheme—for no nation without religion or spiritual ideal, but only based on material lines, can suffice the needs of a world that seeks constant peace.

However greatly people are developed or learned, and yet are not in touch with the spiritual point of view, they remain selfish. Their outlook on life is partial; their justice is self-made. How can they claim to be a just ruler?

The two things began together from the beginning. The history of Khusrau, the old king of Persia, who was a prophet and king at the same time, shows this. He thought, "My subjects are my children—more than my children, nearer and closer than my children; their interest is my interest; for them I live, for them I am born. My whole life is for them." The whole life of the country was based on that model, that king's ideal. He was the instructor, the preacher, the ruler; he ruled according to the spiritual law.

Solomon was prophet and king at the same time. Rama, the Hindu king, was a prophet and ruler at the same time. Think of the impression they have left; to do this so many centuries ago, and yet, however many kings have come and gone since, the impression made by Rama still remains in the Hindu race. There are temples and shrines, and in them an image of the kings whose whole life was spent for the welfare of the subjects. A figurehead or leader is always the ideal whom all follow at each age, and is it not so today? When the president shaves his beard, everyone does the same. People keep saying, "I will get rid of this idol," but they can never get rid of it; it is human nature. From infancy, people wish to imitate somebody's walk, or movement, or expression, or way of talking.

"God is beautiful, and loves beauty."[1] God loves beauty through every soul, in the way of movement, word, expression—in whatever way the beauty comes. God cannot help following beauty, whether it be in democracy or aristocracy.

There is a story of a Persian king and a dervish who was standing in the street. Now, dervishes are self-educated people, who know and understand things; they are freethinkers. They do not abide by the law of society; they touch the depth of the truth, and all the superficial and artificial rules and laws of society and religion do not matter to them; they lead their lives free in thought and action; they are so happy in their philosophy that if they be clothed in rags and tatters it matters nothing to them.

This dervish was standing in a place where the king was about to pass. In the front of the procession were the pages, and they called out to him, "Get out of the way, the procession of the king is coming." He said, "That is why." He went back a few steps, and when the pages had gone past he came forward

1. Hadith.

again, and sat down in the same place. Again came the cry, this time from the courtiers, riding on beautiful horses: "Away, away, the king is coming." He said, "That is why," and went a few steps back and then, when they had passed, he returned to the same place. Then came the chariot of the king. When the king saw him standing in the middle of the street, he gently bowed his head to the dervish; and the latter smiled and said, "That is why."

A young man who was watching this could not help laughing. He was curious about it too and asked the dervish, "Why do you say to everybody, 'That is why?'" He answered, "It is plain. The gentleness of the king was why he acted so toward me, the dullness of the courtiers was why they were curt to me, the rudeness and crudeness of the pages and the bodyguard was why they were rude to me." For in the East, they pay respect to holy persons, even to a dervish.

Nobody in the world will deny this fact that the culture and the education and thought that have been cultivated for centuries among families, communities, and people must manifest its effect.

A thinker has asked, "Is one person's mind equal to another, or different? Why should there be a system of voting?" The answer is, it is never equal; there is an immeasurable difference between minds. One mind may be developed more than two, another more than ten, another more than a hundred, another more than a thousand persons. One person whom you meet and talk to and sit with makes you feel as if you had been in heaven, so full is that one of gentleness, knowledge, response, and goodness. Some other person, however free-minded you may be, you find that person's manner, point of view, everything is repulsive, and you cannot help it.

This shows that the root of civilization is idealism. The seedling was in aristocracy, the plant of civilization grows in aristocracy, and the climax comes in autocracy; for it is comfort and power that have always blinded people. You will always see people who are without money more thoughtful and considerate than those who have wealth; blinded with wealth they have no time to think of another person. Even helpless people will have sympathy and share your pain, while those who have the power to help do not.

This aristocracy on one side, and on the other side the authority of a church with temporal power, both reach a climax when they are blinded by the power of wealth. The aristocracy that was the virtue and climax of civilization turns into autocracy; and once that autocracy begins—ruler, president, elder, or chief of a family—there arises a bureaucracy; what the ruler does the officer does, what that one does the police, the constable, everybody does. As it is said in Sanskrit, "As the king is, so becomes the subject." Everybody values the leader. An autocratic leader produces an effect on every person, making those persons autocrats themselves. If the king is fond of luxury, the one whose duty it is to wait on the king also becomes fond of ease and comfort. That one is too lazy to get up in the morning, because the king is lazy also.

When this is so, it means that the time has come for another form of life to appear. That is why there come wars, revolutions, floods, strikes, rebellions. These are all signs that life is going to change. It is not only today; it has been so in all ages. Such signs always mean the change from autocracy to bureaucracy, and then the new era begins, the era of democracy.

By the time that this new period has come, the spirit of independence has become ready to meet it. When this spirit is understood wrongly, it becomes a time of great trial to the world and humanity at large. When violence comes, rudeness and crudeness predominate in the social life, disregard of the true spirit of religion, and of consideration for others—these are the degradation of democracy.

Human nature is just like goats and sheep: where one goes, twenty come behind, fifty want to walk behind. So it is with humans: one comes and seeks democracy, and the others follow without knowing what democracy is. It is not a craze. It is not lunacy. It is not a spell. It is the maturity of souls—that is the real democracy. The soul now feels the responsibility, the value of its own power, the latent power and inspiration that it possesses. It is not necessarily a breaking off from church or religion, from law, nor a disturbance. These would be a degradation of civilization.

Where can this spirit, this true spirit, be learned? Is it from socialism? Yes, but only a little. Is it from politics? Yes, but only partially. The view of the politician is a partial view. In the law courts the pleader is the truth, but the other is also the truth. Politics will give education, but the perfection of democracy can only be learned from the real science or religion, from the spiritual ideal.

See the spiritual democracy in Jesus Christ. According to their law, the Jews wished to accuse the people who sin, but he said, "Let him throw the stone, he who has never sinned."[2] That was the outlook of democracy. In that, Christ has suggested human nature: that human nature was everywhere. See the picture of the master washing the feet of his disciples!

Then, in the life of the Prophet, we read of a black slave whom the Prophet's grandson called by his name. The Prophet said, "That is not a good manner; call him 'Uncle,' he is older than you." He taught his followers that in the house of God there is no distinction between sovereign and servant; the place of prayer must not be for the rich people alone. All can pray together, shoulder to shoulder; the sultan and the beggar can meet and pray thus. That is democracy.

Whence did it come? It came from the depth of religion; it came from spiritual law. However humble and low a person may be in occupation and evolution, we are nonetheless interdependent and require another's help and service as they need ours. However much wealth or power or rank we possess, yet

2. John 8:7.

how much is our dependence upon the humblest and poorest person in the world.

The realization that the whole life must be give-and-take, is the realization of the spiritual truth and the fact of true democracy. Not till this spirit is formed in the individual can the whole world be elevated to the higher grade.

25

SPIRITUAL DEMOCRACY

In point of fact democracy is always spiritual, there cannot be a material democracy.[1] But material democracy can be called that system that appears or that claims itself democracy, but which, after examination, in the end proves to be a shadow. There cannot be two goals; there is but one. It is true or false. The birth of true democracy is in the spiritual ideal. As long as there is no spiritual light to guide one's life, one does not know the real democracy.

There are two stages in the life of every individual, in the life of a nation, of a community, of a race, of the world: the minor period and the major period. The minor period is when a person realizes that there are others who have experienced life more than they have, and that is the beginning of their career; they then accept the help and advice of those who have more experience than they do. This is the preparatory stage that leads to democracy. No parents think it wise that from the moment the child is born it should be permitted to act without any direction or advice. What really happens is that when the minor, the preparatory period is despised, then instead of democracy, anarchy comes and takes the place of democracy.

1. A lecture given on November 28, 1921, at the Salle de l'Athénée, Geneva, Switzerland. The transcript of this talk will appear in a forthcoming volume of the *Complete Works*.

True democracy is rising from the lower stage to the higher stage. And false democracy is pulling the ones who are on the higher stage down to the lower stage. A picture of true democracy is to take those with us to the top of the mountain. False democracy is to pull the legs of those who are on the top and bring them down to the bottom. In some respects, people show childishness all through their life. Very often people also have the same character that one sees in sheep who flock together. No one knows where they are going, but one leads, and the rest follow. One person cries democracy, and no one knows where it goes, what comes from it, what the result will be. As every moment in the life of a human being is a cultivation in which one learns something from every experience, so in every period civilization takes a certain direction, develops in a certain direction, builds up something. Then spectators of this civilization can have two attitudes: the one who thinks it is not one's ideal of civilization and wants to break it all to pieces, and the attitude of the other is before wanting to break anything wondering what needs to be broken but also what is good, what can be preserved? These persons can do a great deal of good by this attitude. They see what is beautiful and valuable, and the whole that can be made of the parts that exist.

The tendency to destroy all the beauty and culture of life is not real democracy. Whatever nation or race with that tendency will destroy the beauty and culture of centuries. Of these two tendencies the one is right, the other wrong. The right tendency is the one that comes from a spiritual ideal, the other comes from human egoism. What today is coming up as the democratic ideal comes from a material ideal instead of spiritual ideal. Those, revolting and agitating against others who have some culture, beauty, power, possessions, want to crush it and destroy all these. But democracy born of a spiritual ideal is different. Democracy from the spiritual ideal teaches true human sister- and brotherhood. It teaches true equality of people, recognizing it in the source and goal of every person, which is always the same. A real democrat is the God-realized person, for whom the world is an open page. It is not the one who destroys beauty for selfish purposes.

There is a story about a young man who met a dervish and was very interested in keeping his acquaintance and asked him for the privilege of seeing him again. The young man asked, "Will you please tell me, when I come to the place where you live, where can I find you?" "Where I live is called the place of liars." The young man was very astonished at the answer; he was amused but kept quiet. When he went and inquired after the place of liars, people did not know. They knew of a dervish living in a churchyard, near a tower, perhaps he could find him there. He went and found the dervish there. He asked, surprised, why it was called the place of liars. The dervish said, "Come with me, I will show you." He showed him the grave of the great kings. "This person thought he was a king; here, this one, that he was a general; this one, a minister. Is he a king, a general, a minister now? They were liars."

It is the realization of the beginning and the end, where we come from and where we go that is the real spirit of democracy, the realization of the one life. If there is not that idea of spirituality then there are parties of democrats fighting for political and business interests. This is no real democracy; it is a pretense. That thought, ideal, realization can be changed by change of condition; when a person has not yet come to that stage where they can give their whole life for their ideal, what are they? The thought of selfishness is an idea that closes the door to democracy. Today democracy is claimed by the ones who are working on the basis of selfishness. Today, in reality, it is not just national interest that people should consider, but the interests of the whole of humanity. This should be one's sacred duty.

For a long time nationalism has existed. The war[2] has proved that nationalism cannot solve the problems of today. That every nation thinks of own interest is the nature of the world. There is great good that people can do by their example in life, by an example of the absence of egoism. If any nation can do good, it will be by working not only for its own interests. All others will follow, for it is the nature of the soul.

How can this spirit be awakened? No doubt every activity, like the League of Nations, every institution of this kind is good but not sufficient. What is needed is religious awakening; the awakening of that religion that is of every soul, not of a particular sect or faith. If the spirit of democracy is to be born, it will only be born in the hearts awakened to spiritual life. Every faith, belief, has its principles, right or wrong, good or bad; some follow these, others do not. They are given to humanity for a particular time, when a message is given for that time, for that race. Whenever a spiritual wave has come in the world, in the time of the prophets and great teachers of humanity, it was always a great spiritual ideal to awaken democracy. In the scriptures of Zarathustra, in the Bible, in the Qurʾan, in the Kabbalah it is always the same voice teaching the equality of people and love for one's brothers and sisters.

Whenever social reform has come, however good service it has done, it was never able to kindle the spirit of universalism; this shows that a reformer is the child of civilization, the prophet is the parent. One ideal comes from the heart of an intellectual person; the other from the spirit of God, expressed by the human.

The message of God is not a system that is only given for a certain period, after which the world is deprived of it. It is Alpha and Omega and has pronounced softly or loudly the same words at all periods. Advancement or progress is not stillness and stopping at one ideal or principle. Progress is life, stand-

2. First World War.

still is death. When people become hardened in feeling, when their only interest is in the family or the nation, they do not go further, they are dead. But as long as they are advancing from a family to a nation, to a race, they are alive, they are progressing.

The great disaster that has come upon humanity in the last years is caused by this death; the feeling stopped up in nationalism has burst out in national conflict. It is not only visible in the form of nations but also in religious forms, in communities. Destruction is always vouchsafed when people do not progress. The mystical explanation is found in the Bible: "We live, move, and make our being in God."[3] And it is also said that God is love; we can say we live, move, and make our being in love.

When selfishness eats up that divine spirit that is in a person, that one is dead, the heart is dead, and the person only seems alive. Friends, many people seem to be alive, but rarely do you meet one who is really alive. The condition of living is moving, the condition of death is standstill. The greatest progress is a constant expansion of the divine spirit.

The Sufi Movement regards this expansion in whatever direction as long as the ideal of unity is applied; this is our ideal. It is not a desire of the Sufi Order that all should become members; but the ideal of its members is to invite humans to become members of humanity. Sufism is not a new religion or community; it does not want to add a community to the world. It is an attitude toward life, not taught by any particular principle or dogma; it is to tune oneself to a certain pitch, that the heart can become tuned to God. This is the only religion that exists. This is the only message that Christ gave. There cannot be two religions, truths, Gods, if our mind is clear. But to understand this religion it needs tuning. To fight in order to make you believe this—this is not the ideal. What is necessary now is understanding another person's point of view; to see with two eyes instead of one. Why is there so much misunderstanding?

3. Acts 17:28.

It is because of using one eye instead of two. In the Sufi Order people of different religions are welcome to study wisdom, that point of view where we all unite and understand each other.

It must also be remembered that there is another side of religion, the esoteric side; that part of religion that prepares a person by prayer and other forms to receive the blessing from God from within. For a person to become illuminated, tuned to that illumination, becomes difficult without that blessing. There comes a stage in a person's life when they begin to inquire, "Is this all; or is there still more to understand?" To understand more, what one does in one's religion for that is that one looks for a teacher. It is this need in a person's life that the Sufi Order tries to help and to meet. It is the contact with the teacher, study, meditation, silence, repose, that makes one understand one's own religion, the inner side of religion. The Sufi idea is that in time one may arrive at that stage of understanding where one can hear the voice of God from all sources, all sides, all things, all beings. There is a saying of Saʿdi, "Every leaf of the tree becomes as a page of the sacred book when the eyes are opened and the sight is keen."

26

THE FREEDOM OF THE SOUL (1)

Freedom is such that it is liked by every creature. From this we see that it is the soul's tendency, it is the spirit's longing to become free. Animals and birds that we give education to and tend, however carefully, still have the instinct to avoid being bound.

Where does the desire for freedom begin? Its beginning is explained in a very beautiful way in some ancient stories. The stories from the Hebrew and Arabic scriptures tell us that when God made Adam, God commanded the spirit to enter the body of Adam, which God had made out of clay and water. When the spirit was commanded to enter, it refused, saying, "No, I will never become a captive in this dark prison, I who have always been free, dwelling anywhere and without bondage, without barrier. No, I will never become captive in this place." Then God said to the angels, "Sing." And when they sang, the spirit passed into an ecstasy, it became intoxicated by the beauty of the singing. And while in this state of intoxication it did not know whither it was going. Thus it was that it entered the required place. So when Adam opened his eyes, the spirit was there; Adam was alive.

Rumi said, "The bamboo-flute, which appeals to you so much, moans to you about its separation from its home, the original bamboo." In Persia and in India the reed flute is taken from the tree; so it says, "I am taken away from my source, my home; made into a piece instead of the whole that I was at first." And this pain in its heart is the only thing that appeals to the heart of those who listen. It touches them, and moves them to listen to its longing. There is a very beautiful truth in this.

When we inquire into the tragedy of life, the very first of all causes is this separation from freedom. This tragedy can be seen in all kinds of people. From rich to poor, from the most illiterate to the most educated, every one has this life's grudge. Maybe one confesses it, while another does not. But the grudge is in everybody's life just the same—that we have entered this objective world; for this entry seems to be the cause of all the tragedy of life, the tragedy that one's spirit cannot be satisfied in life, cannot have everlasting happiness, as long as one stays in it.

But if you ask some person that you meet, "What is the cause of your life's tragedy?" that person may say, "Oh, that I long to have some wealth; I am very poor; in the absence of wealth I am so unhappy."

Another person may say, "Oh, I have everything nice, but my relatives are very unkind and inharmonious toward me." Another says, "I have everything but good health." A fourth says, "I have everything, but I long to have a certain peace." Another, "I long to accomplish this art; that big purpose in life; not having done so makes me unhappy."

And if you were to supply to each their life's need, giving money to the poor one, harmony to the one without harmony, position to the one who has it not, a beautiful palace to the one who longs for that, health to the one who has it not, then see how long they would remain happy! It would be only for that moment that they receive their desire, and then they would still feel the hunger for they know not what. One asks one's mind, "What more do I want?" and one's mind says, "You feel so unhappy." And as soon as one asks, "For what?" one's mind answers that one cannot have that which one seeks.

It is in this way that people, all through their life, run after things that are, after all, not the real desire of their soul. Sometimes they think it is their bodily appetites and passions that demand satisfaction, sometimes that it is their intellectual powers; but even were those satisfied, they would still find themselves unhappy. "Perhaps," they think, "it is wealth, position, or honors that are lacking." Or they think, "It is not that I have not got the things I need, but I have not enough of them." If one has a motorcar, one is unhappy because one has no chauffeur.

One's mind, one's reason, always puts forward some other cause for one's unhappiness than the real one, in order that one may be kept in illusion all one's life, in order that all one's life one should run after things that are not the real goal of one's soul. Throughout one's whole life one seeks after things, trying first this, then that. One day one buys this, another that, and after getting these things one still thinks, "Oh, it is something else yet—that is why I am unhappy," and as long as one has not got it, one considers that is the cause. If one has ten things, one wants twenty; if one acquires twenty, one seeks thirty; if one has thirty, one desires fifty, and so on. Indeed if one had thousands and billions, one would want a kingdom; after that a whole universe; and if the whole universe were given one, the heart would not be satisfied, because the demand of one's soul is still not understood. One goes through life mourning and sorrowing for things one cannot gain, not understanding in what lies true gain and true loss.

Therefore, when a seer or those who have realized life look at this world they see that however old a person may be—aged, young, middle-aged—that person is still like a child. Children become very unhappy because they have not got, or cannot get, a toy—a toy to which grown-ups would not attach any importance. To the seers, the desires of ordinary grown-up people are also toys. The things that matter to the world, to them they do not matter. This is the sign that they have realized the aim of their soul.

For the aim of their soul is freedom. Freedom is the soul's true nature; the soul has been free. By nature it is free; it is a captive in mind and in body. The whole tragedy of the soul is its captivity. Words such as *nirvana*, or *mukti*, or *salvation*, or *liberation*—all these names are those of the one aim or ideal of the soul through our whole life; yet people hardly know what it is they aim at. All that they do know is that there is such a longing, that there is this hope constantly there.

Everyone wakes in the morning as if they were looking for something to come. Everyone goes to bed with the thought, "Perhaps tomorrow, or the day after tomorrow I shall obtain my heart's desire." To some the desire is a position, a friend; to others a hope. Everyone is looking out as if waiting for that something to come.

There is a familiar saying, "Wait till my ship comes home." Every soul is waiting for its ship to come, not knowing what that ship will bring, or what sort of ship it is. Still every soul is looking for "my ship"; every soul is unconsciously waiting for the coming of "my ship." One thinks it is the prospering of trade, another of business, another thinks it is the coming of power or position, but everyone believes the ship will come!

The ship is different according to whether it is pictured by the mind or the body or the soul. The ship of the soul is its freedom. Indeed freedom is the real object of all directions of life; if the desire is for wealth, that is nothing but a desire for freedom from poverty; if the desire is for power, that is nothing but a desire for "freedom to act as I wish"; the ideal of every soul is freedom—freedom to work, freedom to act, freedom to think, freedom in every direction.

Not knowing that this is the heart's real desire, from the first day of their creation till today, people still neglect the true freedom, because of their pursuit of freedom in the external life. That has been their mistake. The scanty freedom they have so obtained does not prevent them finding themselves captives still; they have still failed to gain that complete joy and peace that their soul longs for.

Freedom for the body would be the freedom of walking in gardens, of moving about in all things, to its own content. But that would not be freedom for the mind. The mind would still be captive. Suppose the mind has freedom—freedom of thought, of understanding, of imagination, of action—the soul would still be captive. But if the soul is free, the mind is free, and the body also is free.

How do we attain to this freedom? In the Sanskrit language there is a beautiful word for freedom, *taran*, which means "liberation," "swimming," or "floating." And it is such a beautiful idea that both these things, swimming and liberation, are alike in their nature.

How true it is, as the Eastern poets have always said, "Life is a Bhavasāgara, an ocean into which all things are drawn, fall, and are absorbed."[1] It sweeps away all the plants and trees, animals and birds, and all that lies in the path of the flood—all are borne into the ocean. Such is the force and power of the ocean. Similarly, this life sweeps away all the trees and plants, animals and people. Everything that we see is here for the moment, and then swept away. There is always a certain period after which the things that seem so strong have all disappeared. Our ancestors, if they came back, would not recognize the country, the houses, the trees, the manners—everything would be different. All that was familiar to them has been swept away. That is the story of this life. That is why it is called maya, the illusion created before us like a dream in the night. In the morning, it has all gone. All the happiness, unhappiness, pleasures, horrors, whatever we experience in the night—in the morning we perceive it has been a dream.

1. Bhavasāgara, the "ocean of existence."

The whole of creation, when we come to think of it, is, in the end, no longer what we have thought it was: manners, customs, faces—everything is different.

That is the condition of life. It is just like the ocean or sea. The flood comes, and it sweeps off all before it—flowers, fruit, and all. Therefore life is pictured by the thinkers of the East as an ocean into which everything is swept.

The miracle of Christ walking on the water is understood by mystics as teaching a mystery. Walking on this water is *taran*, the same idea that the Sanskrit gives—to float or swim. To float or swim on the water one must have one's head above water. The water that sweeps us away we avoid, in order to be able to keep that existence that our soul longs to save. Our body is alive, our mind is alive, our soul is alive; and it does not want to be nonexistent; it desires to continue to exist. However unhappy or feeble the person, their life is too dear to them to sacrifice. Suicide is only possible under great stress of emotion. All work, all struggles are in order to live. All fights, all disagreements, all money-seeking, all comfort-seeking, are in order to live. All through life it is one struggle to live. But the real life is not realized.

Christ, from first to last, teaches the importance of eternal life. His only lesson was "life." It is the desire of the soul to live; and that life is the real life. A person keeps imagining their life is for eating delicious dishes, for making merry, or for being comfortable for the time being. But when the body has gone, how will you live? What will become of your comforts? When the mind is not there, how will you satisfy the mind? To live in the body or the mind is to live in vehicles upon which the person becomes dependent—vehicles that must pass, and be no more.

Therefore the lesson that we must learn is how to swim, how to float, how to overcome the sinking in the flood of death or mortality. How shall we avoid that? The answer is found when we understand that we are like a person who is traveling in a boat; and the boat is heavily laden. The storm comes on, and the one who is rowing says to the person, "The storm is very heavy, your luggage is very abundant; the best thing will be for you to save your life by throwing off one of your bundles into the water." The person says "Oh, that bundle is of things I have collected all my life, and I cannot throw it out." "Well, if you cannot throw it out you will drown." And when the person has thrown out one bundle, perhaps the storm becomes greater, and it is a case that the last bundle has to be thrown away as well. And the person says, "Oh, this one I can never part with; it contains things I have collected all through my life; they are souvenirs, and you want me to throw these away; things from my grandfather and my great-grandfather—do you want me to throw them away?" The other says, "If not, you will go also. If you want to save your life, throw them away!"

That is what death does with humankind. It says, "You are interested so much in your vehicle that you call your body." So first of all it sends disease. Those who think so much of their body are always ill. That is the first step. They are very conscientious about their body, saying, "This is the one thing I must keep well-preserved." They go on thinking of it too much. And so they feel ill, and in the end they have to throw both bundles away, body and mind.

Others will say, "Oh, I do not care for my body, but for my mind." They take care of their own imaginations, their own standards of thinking: "What you say is a lie, what I say is right." They are occupied with thoughts, with pursuits, with arguments, saying "Am I thinking right? Are you? Is she?" And they are all the time in doubt and constant worry of mind; all the time in a struggle about something that really is nothing. To the seer it matters nothing. And then the flood—death—comes, and they are swept away; the mind goes, the body goes, and the soul returns to its own source. This is a picture of mortality when mind departs from body with the impression of death.

There is a story that explains this subject very well. It is of a king who had a parrot that he loved and liked so much that he kept it in a golden cage, and always attended to it himself. The king and queen both paid such great attention to the parrot that every person in the palace was jealous of it.

One day the king was about to go into the forest where the parrot came from, and said to him, "My pet, I have loved you, and kept you with all the care and attention and fondness that I could; and therefore I should like very much to take any message you would like to give me for your brothers in the forest." The parrot said, "How kind of you to have offered to do this for me. Convey to my brothers in the jungle that the king and queen have done all their very best to make me happy—a golden cage, all kinds of fruits, nice things of all sorts; and they love me so much. But with all the attention they give me I long for the forest; and the desire to dwell among you, free as I used to be before, always holds my mind. But I see no way out of it, so pray send me your goodwill and your love. One only lives in hope. Perhaps some day my wish will be granted." The king went into the forest, and approached the tree from which the parrot was taken and said to the brothers of the parrot, "O parrots, there is one who I have taken from among you to my palace; and I am very fond of him, and he receives all the attention I can give. This is your brother's message." They listened to the message very attentively, and one after the other dropped to the ground and seemed dead.

The king was depressed beyond measure. Spellbound, he could not understand what it was that he said that should affect the feelings of those parrots so much. The loving parrots could not bear his message. And he thought, "What a sin I have committed, to have destroyed so many lives." He returned to his palace, and went to his parrot, and said, "How foolish, O parrot, to give me such a message that as soon as your brothers heard it, one after another dropped down, and they all lay dead before me."

The parrot listened to this, and looked up gently to the sky, and he fell down too. The king was even sadder. "How foolish I was! First I gave his message to them and killed them, and now I give their message to him and kill him also." It was all a bewilderment to the king. What was the meaning of it all?

He commanded his servants to take this dead parrot in a gold tray, and bury him with all ceremonies. The servant took him out of the cage with great respect, and loosed the chains from his feet; and then, as they were laying him out, the parrot suddenly flew away and sat upon the roof.

The king said, "O parrot, you betray me." The parrot said, "O king, this was the aim of my soul, which is the aim of all souls. My brothers in the jungle were not dead. I had asked them to show me the way to freedom, and they showed me. I did as they told me, and now I am free."

There is a hadith that says: *Mutu qabla anta mutu*, which means, "Die before death." A poet says, "Only he attains to the peace of the Lord who loses himself." God said to Moses, "No one shall see me, and live." To see God we must be nonexistent.

What does all this mean? It means that when we see our being with open eyes, we see that here are two aspects to our being—the false and the true. The false life is that of this body and mind, which is only existent as long as the life is within. In the absence of that life, the body cannot go on. We take the true life for false, and the false for the true.

Dying is this: when there is a fruit or something sweet and good to the taste, the child comes to its mother and says, "Will you give it me?" Although it would have given joy to the mother to eat it, she gives it to the child. The eating of it by the child is enjoyed by the mother. That is death. She enjoys her life in the joy of another. Those who rejoice in the joy of another, though at their own expense, have taken the step toward true life. If you are pleased so much by giving another a good coat that you would have liked to wear yourself—if you enjoy that, you are on the first step. If you enjoy a beautiful thing so much that you would like to have it, and then give that joy to another, enjoying it in their experience, you are dead. That is your death. You live more than the other. Your life is vaster; your life is deeper; your life is greater.

Seemingly it is a renunciation, an annihilation, but in truth it is a mastery. The real meaning of crucifixion is to crucify this false self, and so resurrect the true self. As long as the false self is not crucified, the true self is still not realized. By Sufis it is called *fana*, annihilation. All the attempts made by true sages and seekers after real truth are for the one aim of attaining to everlasting life.

27

THE FREEDOM OF THE SOUL (2)

Beloved ones of God, I will speak this evening on the subject of the freedom of the soul.[1] The human being pursues captivity and seeks freedom. There is not one single person whom the word *freedom* does not touch, and there is not one person who does not long for freedom.

And at the same time, if we look at human life with a magnifying glass, whether people seek freedom or not, what they pursue is captivity in some form or other. The ancient people, whose imagery was beautiful, put the idea in a beautiful form. There is a Hebrew story that God made a statue of clay, the first form of humankind, and commanded the soul to enter. The soul refused to enter, saying, "In this dark room I am afraid to enter, an imprisonment, a captivity; do you wish me to enter in my grave?" Then God said to the angels, "Sing and play and dance," and the angels sang and played and danced. And the soul came into an ecstasy, and in the blindness of ecstasy entered into this body of clay, in which it then was captive. This gives a beautiful illustration, an illustration of the soul in the first place, which is a dweller in heaven, and the life of which is freedom. It knows nothing but joy, and sees

1. A lecture given at the Lenox Theatre, New York City, on January 24, 1926.

nothing but beauty. Its own nature is peace, and its being is life itself. It is not intelligent, it is intelligence. It is not a soul, but spirit; it is not human, but divine by nature. And again that soul is in captivity. There is a saying from Persia that no infant is born smiling; the first thing the infant does in coming on earth is crying. It is in exile, it is a captivity. A thousand other reasons people may give for the infant's cry, but you can read in its trembling, as its cry is a feeling of captivity. It is a difficult experience the moment it has come on earth, it is feeling different, it feels that it is audible by nature and yet its audibility is limited. With its two eyes it can see but only so much and no further. Its ears are limited, it can hear but no further. By nature it is the sight itself, it is hearing itself, but now it depends upon the ears to hear, upon the eyes to see, and that makes its horizon narrow, smaller, its world becomes limited.

Someone asked a wise person, "What is the reason of pain?" And the wise person answered, "If I were to say in one word the reason of all the pain you see in the world, it is limitation." Limitation is the cause of it all. One says that, "My means are scanty." Another one says, "My position is not high enough." Still others say, "I lack the love that I need." Another one says, "I have no learning, or no friends." There may be twenty thousand different complaints that come out of it. That is the limitation in one word. And where does this limitation come from? This limitation comes from a heavenly being turning into an earthly being. There is nothing to be surprised at in this life when we see that hardly anyone seems to be perfectly happy. A rich person has their tale to tell, a poor person has their story; a wise person has their complaint to make, a foolish person has their own legend. And so everyone has something to say. And what they all have to say is one thing, and that is limitation.

What one pursues, what one seeks after, is a feeling of freedom, and yet everyone pursues freedom wrongly. The nature of life is such that whenever one thinks, "That will make me free," that itself makes one more captive. And one cannot realize it until one gets it. As long as one has not got it, one thinks, "That is what will make me free." And so life goes on. And one goes on in the pursuit of freedom and what one gets is captivity. With all the talk of freedom today, life is more a life of captivity than ever before. There was never such a thing in the past that in order to cross the boundary of one's country to go into another country one had to trouble with a passport. People were free to go in one another's country. There was more brotherhood at that time than today. It is not only passports, but customs, duties, and many other conventionalities can make one wonder if one is even at home or free in one's own country. People do not enjoy freedom where they live because of the ever-increasing conventionalities of life.

With all the talk on freedom, have they come nearer to it? No. Not knowing the real meaning of freedom, they are coming closer and closer to captivity. People live in captivity because they think little. The more they think, the more they will find that as they pursue the path of freedom, every step brings them closer to captivity.

In all ages prophets and masters and thinkers and philosophers have taught that the ultimate aim of philosophy and mysticism was to attain the freedom of the soul. Different ceremonies, religious legends, and philosophies are narrative of this truth. Whatever be one's longing in life, whatever be one's life's pursuit, one's object to attain, behind it all there is only one pursuit and that is the craving of the soul to become free from all bondages. People do not appreciate this idea when they are absorbed in getting things in life, which things will make them free, because they do not give a thought to freedom, but only give thought to what they pursue for that moment. Perhaps, if they gave a thought to the real condition of life, they would become different, their attitude would change, their outlook would become wider, and they would not attach importance to things they usually attach importance to.

If one asks what kind of captivity it is, I will say, "For a spider the thin threads of the web are a kind of captivity; for an elephant iron chains are a captivity." The stronger the person is, the greater the captivity; the greater power the person has, the greater difficulty they have before them; the stronger the soul is, the greater the load it has to carry. Therefore in captivity we are all equal. When a person sees only on the surface, it appears as if one person has an easy life and the other has to toil all day, as if one has a gay life and as if the other is miserable. But that is the outside. When we look deep into life, in some way or other, whether a person looks cheerful or gay, some captivity is hidden behind. We do not know with that person. In order to understand their life's situation it is not enough to have a glance from outside. We do not know enough to form an opinion. We only see the prisoners; if we saw the prisons, we would be shocked.

One might ask, "Why is this condition so tragic, why can it not be better?" The answer is, "It is natural." What is a human? The human being is a process; the manifestation is a process through which the spirit goes from one condition to another condition, from one pole to another pole. And through this whole process the attempt of the spirit is to find itself. In that process the spirit itself loses its freedom. Freedom is lost in order to come to freedom. That is the tragedy. But at the same time, in the end it is happiness, because for the fulfillment of this object the whole creation was intended.

To every thinking soul, to every feeling heart, tragedy appeals. Why? Because tragedy is going on continually. People would like to get away from tragedy, but what appeals to them is tragedy because the soul is always in that condition; it is longing for freedom when it does not know what it is.

In the Bible and in the Qur᾿an we read, "Die before death."[2] What does it mean? It means that in order to be free, we must

2. Hadith.

first die. The rituals and ceremonies of old all have this secret as the greatest secret, and it is this that is taught through ceremony, philosophy, and mysticism. This is the main secret of all those things.

But is it really dying? No, it is playing death. No one dies really. What dies is death; what lives is life. Life lives, death dies. Therefore, the art of the mystics is to learn how to play death. Call it meditation, call it contemplation, call it concentration, call it worship of God, it is all playing death.

And what is it in one that must die? It is not one's real self; it is the false conception that one has of oneself. It is that false conception that brings about all limitation. One is not really as limited as one seems to be. But because there is a cover over one's soul, that cover makes one limited. That is why one sees no further. One's world is oneself, one's own environments, one's conditions, one's impressions, one's experiences. That is all one knows; one knows nothing beyond. Therefore, what is to be crucified in one is that false self, and resurrection follows crucifixion. One might ask, "How is it to be achieved? How can one play death?" And the answer is that we have played life and we play life every day. For what is it, the life from morning till evening, is it not a play? The more we study it, the more we shall find that the world is subject to change. Conditions alter, situations change from moment to moment. If it is not a play, what is it?

Of course, if one thought it a play, one would not take it seriously. But if we are able to play life, we are able to play death also. By playing death the eyes become open; the soul that becomes captive by the closing of the eyes, that soul begins to soar upward once the eyes are opened.

People say that, "Here is a dead person." But in reality it is the living person. For in order to live, one must die. And what must die? Death must die, and life must live.

28

THE FREEDOM OF THE SOUL (3)

Beloved Ones of God, my subject this morning is the freedom of the soul.[1] In the East it is said that the reason why an infant cries as the first thing after its birth is because it grieves the loss it experiences, and that loss is the loss of freedom. The soul, which was once free and could float into the spheres higher than the birds and could expand and could live as light and life, has become captive in this limited body of flesh and bones when it came on earth, a sphere that is quite new and strange to the infant. Neither has it yet made any connection with earthly beings nor with its atmosphere. That is why the first thing a soul does is to cry. The Sufis, all mystics, have recognized this fact most and have founded their philosophy on this theory, that through every condition in life a person is consciously or unconsciously seeking for freedom.

It may be that one is seeking this freedom from having to work. Another may be seeking freedom by getting away from some influence that surrounds him or her, perhaps another seeks freedom from a national point of view. But they each and all strive continually for freedom, and that which gives the incentive to strive after freedom is that unconscious craving that

1. A lecture given at the Sufi Center, Steinway Hall, New York City, May 31, 1926.

is born with the infant at the moment of its birth. That is why a human being is striving continually, knowingly or unknowingly, to attain to that freedom.

Therefore, friends, our despair, our depression, our sorrow, our worries, they have a thousand reasons. But at the back of all these is one and the same reason, which is that our soul is striving, striving every day for freedom, which is something that perhaps death will give us. People very often commit suicide for the same reason, that they will gain freedom by it. Sometimes they think that getting away from everybody will give them this freedom, but they do not know that whatever effort one has made to get out of a situation, yet one is not free because it is one's self that is in captivity. Apart from all situations outside that give us the impression of imprisonment, even our own self is captive; we are captive in ourselves.

But now I must explain the relation between the soul and the body. The relation between the soul and the body is that of the spark and the charcoal. When the spark of the fire touches the charcoal then it is caught by the charcoal. What they say in English, "it has caught fire," means the fire, which was apart from it, has been caught by it. And so the soul is caught by the body. It can be seen in another way also, that the body is caught by the soul, or better, the body is used by the soul. And therefore the relation of the soul to the body is that of fire catching the charcoal. As the charcoal turns into ashes, so the body has its end, and it is destroyed one day. The fire is not lost, it has disappeared to its own element, to heat. Besides this, it is the sun that is in electricity and gaslight, and in all forms of heat it is the sun that manifests through different processes.

It is the same with the spirit, it is one and the same, like the sun, appearing through different processes as souls. One has become many in different forms, the one appears as many, but it is not many in reality. In other words, the light appears as five lights in the room or as six or as a hundred. But in reality it is one light. It is only in its appearance, because there are so many globes, that each light is limited. In the same way, each human body has taken divine light in it and shows it as a different light; and all these lights seen in many globes are called souls. But we may call them the light itself, for it is the one spirit seen in different globes as different souls. All human beings are one consciousness, they have one source and one goal. At the same time, the spirit is caught by different vehicles.

Now, the condition is that the body holds the soul and the soul holds the body. The soul holds the body in order to accomplish its purpose and the body holds the soul because the day the soul leaves, it will turn into nothing. Therefore, the body is continually striving to keep the soul because it is made for the soul and because it lives for it. Therefore, it is the body's continual desire for the soul to live in it. That being the situation, it is only the moment when the soul feels it has finished its work and it no longer should exist in the body, that it leaves the body. Or perhaps the body has become so feeble that it can no longer hold the soul. So it goes, and as a result there is death.

Very often there are people who wish to die and do not die. The reason is that it is the mind that wishes death, but the body is still clinging to the soul and the soul is still using the body for its purpose although the mind is against it. And therefore death does not come. And there are others who say, now the body is too feeble and it can no longer hold the soul. And yet the mind says, I have not finished, I have not seen my friend, or my husband, or my daughter, and I would like to live until I see them. And it goes on living because the soul, having the impression that something is not finished, keeps holding on to that body that can no longer hold the soul. It holds on as long as that particular desire is present.

Since the soul has been caught by the physical body, there comes a time when the soul awakens. As long as it is asleep, it is in a kind of dream in the physical body. That is the condition of the average person, a kind of dream. The mystic is the one who is awakened. But the most amusing thing is that the average person will call the mystic a dreamer, when in reality it is that person who is dreaming.

During this dream the soul knows nothing but what appears before it, for instance, one's desires, habits, wishes, experiences, environments, actions, thoughts, and impressions. All these things are like a dream the soul is busy dreaming. One person will perhaps dream all their life, and yet another who will wake at an early age or in their youth. But there are souls, as in the case of Jesus Christ, who from childhood begin to manifest their awakened condition. Therefore, it does not depend upon a certain age. Even an infant may be awakened, a rare infant. And it may be that a person will live all their life and live in the dream and may leave in the same dream. And yet there is a subconscious awakening when something begins to say that you are dreaming, that there is something else for you to know. But one does not listen to it.

But friends, sooner or later that time may come in our lives when we waken from this dream, and as soon as we wake from this dream, our first thought is, what is it all about? Why are we here? And, what are we doing here? And where are we to go? What is the purpose of our life? And when this thought comes, then a person begins to feel a little less interested in the things of life. This does not mean that one is less capable of doing them. On the contrary, an awakened person can accomplish greater worldly things than the unawakened person and in a better way. For instance, if our politicians today, and our great merchants and wealthy people, educationists and scientists, were spiritual persons, the world would become different, and they would not be any less than what they are; they would accomplish greater things as scientists, as businessmen, and so on. You must not think that to be spiritual only means having the desire to run away from the world, go into the forest and sit there. Yes, they would not give that importance to things as they appear to one in the dream, but at the same time, they would be more inspired to accomplish things in the world than if they were not spiritually awakened. Everything that an awakened soul does, be it in business, be it in the state, in society or in political life—in all different aspects—has a meaning for that soul, it has a life because that person does it so heartily, not in a rigid way. For instance, we see so many criminals under laws and regulations, so many courts and everything. And when the Prophet Muhammad declared that it was *haram*, prohibited, to touch liquor, fifteen centuries after the Prophet has gone every true Muslim feels in their heart, I must not touch it. One does not say, it is because the Prophet said it, go and drink, no; some go and drink but at the same time with tears in their eyes they say, I am sorry; our Prophet has said, no. I feel shame to show my face to my Prophet, he has said no. That is a different feeling.

The awakened soul, whatever it does or says is living, its impression is greater. Do you think if the generals of today and the politicians and statespeople and business people and people of industry were awakened souls, we would have had the war? By this time we should be past those days of stupidity when people used to kill one another. We are in a different stage of evolution. Today there is no need for war. Humanity is grown up, it is no longer an infant. And even after the war, there is no security of peace. We do not know what will happen tomorrow. If that is the case, it shows that there is something missing. And what is missing is the realization of the dream. People think they are awakened, that they have common sense, and yet they are still asleep.

In the League of Nations, every day there is a new lecture and a dispute and much ado about it, and yet they are in the same boat. They say when things are settled, conditions will be better. But when will they be settled? Not when they are settled outside. It must be settled in us; we must be wakened from this dream we are in; the soul must come to that realization of what it is. Then a better day will come for us.

And now coming to the signs one sees after the awakening of the soul. The first sign is that one begins to see from two points of view. One begins to see the right of the wrong and the wrong of the right. One begins to see the good of the bad and the bad of the good. One begins to see that everything is reflected in its opposite. And in that way one rises above intellectuality, which then begins to appear as a primitive or elementary knowledge. Elementary knowledge says it is this, it is so and such; this is gray, or black, or dark, or light. But as soon as one has gone one step forward, one sees the contrary of it. One sees the dark in the light and the light in the dark, death in birth and birth in death. It is a kind of double view of things. And when one has reached this, then reason has opened to higher reasoning, which is the second sign. No doubt, one's language will become gibberish to others; people will not understand it. They will be confused by what one says. To some it will be too simple, to others too subtle: too simple to those who only hear words without meaning, too subtle to those who strive to understand the meaning and do not reach it.

The third aspect is that in failure one will not feel such disappointment, and in success not such a great joy. In adverse conditions one will not be disappointed so much, in favorable conditions not so conceited. And these continual changes we experience in this world, such as friends turning into enemies, love sometimes turning into hate, sense into senselessness, these little surprises that we experience every day in this world, when things are different from what we expected, all these shocks will not be felt so deeply. Life in the world is full of shocks, there is no end to them. At every turn we make, we find some surprise, all the time something new. When the soul is awakened, we do not feel these shocks so deeply. They come but they do not hit us so deeply. And at the same time, there is a deeper feeling; in spite of all that, there is a deeper feeling. An advanced person is more susceptible to being hurt than the one who is not advanced. Because such a person's heart becomes tender, they feel rapidly; they are living—a rock would not feel it. This awakening of the soul gives fineness on the one hand and strength to sustain one on the other.

And then we come to another stage that develops after the awakening of the soul, and that is the feeling for freedom; and people think this has to be carried out as retirement. Of course, that is a temptation. A spiritual person regards it as a temptation. An awakened soul no longer values the dream as important, and yet that one on the path to retirement will say "I will continue to work because there is still time to be of service"; that is the thought when one is less selfish.

And now coming to the ultimate freedom of the soul. This freedom is gained by concentration, by meditation, by contemplation, and realization. What concentration is needed for the freedom of the soul? The concentration on that object that is prescribed by your spiritual teacher, that by the thought of that particular object you may be able to forget yourself for a moment. And then what contemplation is necessary? The contemplation that this, my limited self, is no longer myself but God's own instrument, God's temple that is made in order that the name of God be glorified. What meditation is requested? The meditation on the thought of God, on the being of God, forgetting absolutely one's limited self. And the realization is this, that then whatever voice comes to you is God's voice, every guidance is God's guidance, every impulse is divine impulse, every action is done by God. It is in this way that the soul is made free, and in the freedom of the soul lies the purpose of life.

* * *

Question: *Are we connected with those we love when we pass out of this life?*

Answer: Certainly, we are connected with those we have loved and with those we have hated. We meet against our wishes those we have hated and by the power of our wish we meet those we have loved. The Prophet said, death is a bridge that unites friends to friends.

Question: *What is the thought, what constitutes the basis of the human will? What is the force that shapes that will?*

Answer: Thought is the willful action of mind. The action of mind directed by will is thought. The action of mind that is not directed by will is automatic action, is imagination. That is the difference between thought and imagination. What constitutes the basis of the human will is divine will. Nothing moves without divine will. Therefore, behind every impulse there is the hand of God directing it. What is the force that shapes that will? That is divine force, almighty power. It is the scheme of the whole plane of existence; that force shapes that will.

Question: *What does Sufi philosophy teach in regard to Christianity?*

Answer: The Sufi philosophy is one thing and belief is one thing. If we explain belief according to philosophy we only break it to pieces. As it is said: to analyze God is to dethrone God. Therefore, Sufis have no particular beliefs in any direction. In the Sufi Order no beliefs are taught. Philosophy is taught that you may know yourself and respect the beliefs of all different religions.

Question: *People give the best of themselves to their work and yet have to fight for their rights.*

Answer: Working is one thing, and fighting another thing. Both things are required in life.

Question: *Do souls keep their individuality after death?*

Answer: No doubt. Because individuality is not made by the physical body. Individuality is covered by the physical body. When the cover goes, individuality remains still.

29

THE IDEAL LIFE

When speaking on the subject of ideal life, the words of the Prophet of Islam may be quoted, where he says, "Every soul has its own religion"; which means that every soul has a certain direction, such as it has made, as the goal to attain to during life. This goal is a certain ideal that depends on the soul's evolution.

For instance, young people in a family understand, "The responsibility of my mother and father, who are old, is on me. It is a duty, and not only a duty, but a virtue on my part, that I should devote all that I earn, and give every service that I can render them in order to be useful to them in their old age." Religion, in the language of the Hindus, is *dharma*, which means "duty." Their idea of virtue is that if they can be helpful to their aged parents by money or by service, they will devote both to them, and they consider that to be a virtue. That is the ideal thing for them to do; so they do it. Perhaps they do not perceive anything beyond it, but that which they do perceive is virtue in their eyes. And that is why they wish to do it, and in it is their satisfaction.

Another person is in business, as the agent of a firm. Such a one thinks, "I am paid by my firm, and the head of my firm is so kind that it is my first duty to prove myself faithful to my firm." Such people labor with enthusiasm and great zeal from morning to evening, seeing a great virtue in serving righteously, although they do not pretend to religion or spirituality. But they consider that as their virtue, and as long as they consider that they are doing their duty, they are following their religion.

Religion, in the East, is not made into a thing apart from one's life, as in the West where business, profession, and other things are one side of life, and on the other side going to church one day a week and saying a prayer before going to rest, together constitute religion. But strictly speaking, life is religion. When you have that ideal before you in whatever occupation you are concerned—business or industry or domestic life or whatever it is—and carry it out, being wishful to be worthy of it, that is your religion.

In the Hindu language, the same word *dharma* means both duty and religion; both are expressed by one word. "This is your dharma" means "This is your faith." How beautiful the thought is! Whatever kind of duty it is, so long as you have an ideal before you and are performing that duty, you are walking in the path of religion.

The Prophet says, "Every soul has its own religion." We, with our narrowness of faith or belief, accuse others of belonging to another religion, another chapel, or church. We say, "This temple is better, that faith is better." The whole world has kept fighting and devastating itself just because of not understanding that each sort of religion is peculiar to itself.

Therefore the ideal life is in following one's own ideal. It is not in checking other people's ideals. If a certain thing is one's ideal, that does not imply that another person will agree that it is best to offer prayers ten times a day. One may be doing better in following one's religion in one's shop, than in going to a mosque and offering up a prayer twenty times a day. Perhaps a person to whom that is ideal cannot see that the other's way is ideal also. Leave everyone to follow his or her own ideal.

Is it right for all people to follow their own ideal? Does the ideal remain the same all the time? No, the ideal grows and improves as people grow and improve with the years.

Sometimes in life a person thinks that it would be ideal to have a beautiful house, and a beautiful estate, and good clothes, and all manner of comforts. From that moment that should be the path one ought to pursue. But then one comes to another ideal. One comes to think, "My surroundings are not sufficient if the people in the town are not happy or in good surroundings." From that time one cares less for one's house and beautiful things, and goes in the town every day and seeks to improve the health and happiness of others. One thinks, "The poor in the town should be looked after." This is one's new ideal. Before one evolved this new ideal one was only enjoying one's beautiful home; one was living up to a lower ideal.

And then, later on, one may come to say, "Never mind about my town; I think of my whole country." The whole nation comes in for consideration, what is beneficial to it, and what are the things that should be improved. One's fortune may not be very great; perhaps the town is not so beautiful as that of one who is thinking only about one's town; but one is thinking about the whole nation, and so one's ideal is still greater. It does not matter to one in which town one lives, one's life is in the whole country, in the whole nation. One becomes the spirit of the whole nation. That is one's ideal.

Are people the same, whatever their appearance? We see now that it is all a matter of one's ideal as to whether one differs from one's neighbor, whether one is heavenly or earthly, as high as the devas, the heavenly beings, or as low as the demons. One's ideal makes one as high as the one, or as low as the lowest demons. One's greatness lies in the greatness of one's ideal.

That which makes us esteem those whom we esteem is their ideal. That which raises one from earth to heaven is one's ideal; and that which pulls one down from the heavens to the earth is also one's ideal. When one does not live up to one's ideal one falls to earth; and when one raises one's ideal one goes from earth to heaven. One can rise to any height, according to the level of one's ideal.

One person thinks, "Oh, it does not matter; if I have a good dinner, never mind what others have"; another thinks, "It is no pleasure to me to have had a good dinner, since my family still starve; it is much more happiness to me if I have only a frugal dinner, so long as my family also are well satisfied." This raises one higher than the person who thinks only of their own happiness. A third person thinks, "It does not matter how I live, as long as I have brought some happiness to the people of my town, or village; that would be worthwhile." That one's ideal is greater.

The trust that is sent by heaven is the ideal given to a human. That is one's charge in life, one's responsibility in life. To take care of this and prove worthy of this responsibility and position that has been given to us—that is that we ought to prove to be our ideal, our religion, our dharma. In the Gospel the "pound" represents the same ideal; at first it is small, but it expands as we go through life.[1]

This explains the fact that the sin and virtue of two people cannot be the same. For instance, there may be two students, and one is sent to a university and is studying for an examination. There are only two months left, but he happens to see a beautiful play advertised. He thinks he would like to see this play, and yet there is so short a time for study. "But then it is only one evening, and I can soon make that up. I will go just this once, and it will make no difference." He disregards the importance of the ideal he had—that of passing his examination. He has changed his ideal to thinking the examination does not matter. So he goes this once, but next day he sees another advertised, and again gives in to his pleasure; and again and again. His fondness for the plays grows; and the evenings go by, and the time comes when he is no longer ready for his examination. So he fails. Seeing the plays was a sin, not because

1. See Luke 19:11–27.

it was a sinful action, but because he failed to keep to his ideal. He was meant to study to pass his examination.

Again, there is another student. She is trying to become a good playwright, or orator, or actor. She sees the same advertisement. She goes to the play and enjoys it very much. Every play she attends adds to her experience, and increases her knowledge. The same action has become a virtue, because by going to the theater and giving her thoughts to the plays she has accomplished her ideal. Therefore it all depends on our ideal whether the same action be sin or virtue. We have to follow and prove ourselves worthy of that ideal, and the farther we go the more does our ideal develop. However small it was at the time, we are always progressing as long as we follow it, and wish to prove ourselves worthy of it. But when we go astray from our ideal we lose the track.

If there be anything wrong or evil in the world, it is this: leaving the track of the ideal that we have placed before ourselves.

A person may say that a religious ideal is the true ideal, or a moral life, or a spiritual life, or a practical life. Many people say it is much better to be in the world, to live in the world; others say it is better to live away from the wicked world, to get away and live in the forests, the jungles, the caves. They say, "This is the only way to live." Others say, "Just make merry, eat, drink, enjoy life." Others say, "The good life is in the service of others; as much service as we can give, as much kindness, as much love—that is the ideal."

If you ask a hundred people, you will get a hundred ideals. Everyone thinks that everyone who follows that ideal is the best person, and whoever is contrary to that ideal is a wicked person. Sufis, mystics, ascetics, with all their high ideals, have been killed, beheaded, and tortured by different religious authorities because the religious authorities had a different ideal, and were convinced their own ideal was right, and the other wrong. They said, "My church is the only church that exists, the only one that can teach you the real truth." Is it not true that every church or every faith in which there is a willingness for others to join, thinks that its ideal and its belief is the best to follow? That is people's foolishness. They wish everyone to follow the same ideal as theirs. They do not know that the prophets whom the whole world may follow, often could not get their brother or their wife or their child to follow them!

If you read the history of Abraham, Moses or Muhammad, you will see what happened. It was difficult for their own people to follow them, however many followers they may have had; because every soul has its peculiar ideal, and it wants to go on toward it.

True preaching would be to ask everyone to develop their own ideal, however wrong it might appear to be to the outsider at the moment. Let them develop their faculty of doing right in their own judgment. You will see that in time they will develop the real thing, because in them is the light of God and it will never misguide them.

Once I was with a sage whom many people went to see. He pleased them all, and he was not fond of disputing or discussing, because to a sage there is nothing to discuss. Discussion is for those who say, "What I say is right, and what you say is wrong." A sage never says such a thing; hence there is no discussion. But the world is always fighting and discussing and disputing.

Many would come and try to dispute with him; but he did his best to avoid dispute. I was very fond of hearing his way of dealing with enquirers. My friends were ready to discuss what is the ideal life. He said, "As you think it." But my friends were not satisfied with this; they wanted a discussion. They answered, "Do you think this worldly life, with so many responsibilities, strife from morning to evening, can be the ideal life?" He said, "Yes." "Do you not think that the life you lead—retirement and seclusion—is the ideal life?" He answered "Yes." "But how can we give up our present life, our responsibilities to our children, our occupations, and all these things that take up so much time; how can we leave that life in order to follow your ideal life?" He said, "Do not leave it." "But if we do not leave it, how can we get on in the spiritual life?" Then the sage asked, "What do you mean by the spiritual life?" "We mean by spiritual life a life like yours." He said, "If you think my life is a spiritual life, be like me; if you think your life is the spiritual life, keep to it. Which life is best, it is not possible to say. If you think your worldly strife brings you happiness, just keep to it; if you think my life gives you happiness, give yours up. Whatever makes you happy and makes you think you are doing right, do it from that moment, and see what is the result. If it gives you more happiness, go on regardless of what others say. If it gives you happiness, if you are satisfied while doing it, while reaping its effect, then it is all right. Go on with it, and you will always be blessed."

Therefore when the question of the ideal life comes up, no one on earth can tell you that this particular mode is the ideal. Those who presume to tell you so say absurd things. They only tell you what they think ideal; it is not necessarily the ideal for you. Whatever you think best, follow it. You are on the right path, in whatever direction it may lead, whether to heaven or to earth; both will lead to the same goal in the end, if pursued to the end.

30

THE JOURNEY TO THE GOAL

The word *journey* may be applied to life. As life has two aspects, so it is either a journey or a goal.

Why should life be called a journey? Because it is a changeable experience, because there is a change in nature, and there is a change of experience. One goes from one experience to another, and that is also the meaning of the word *journey*—going from one place to another; passing from one experience to another. The whole life, the external life, is nothing but a succession of experiences, one after the other, night and day. That is why it is called a journey.

But there is a part of life, the life from which this life of changes has sprung, the life that is everlasting, that is eternal, the life to which everything and all things return—that life is the goal. Therefore life is not only a journey, it is a goal. The goal is the stable part of life, the source of life; the manifested life called creation is the journey.

In this way we see there are really two journeys. There is the journey from the goal to the life in the world, and there is the journey from the life in the world to the goal. And both journeys are natural. As it is natural to go from the eternal goal, so it is necessary to go from the changing life to the life that is unchangeable.

Which is the more desirable thing in life—to seek for the goal or to dwell in this changing life? The answer is every person's desire is according to their evolution. That which they are ready for is desirable for them. Milk is desirable food for the infant, other food for the grown-up person. Every stage in life has its own appropriate, desirable thing. The desire to attain to some goal must be there before reaching it. When one does not feel the desire, it is not necessary for one to seek it.

All things are worthwhile when you seek after them; then only do you have their value; then only are you happy to have them. You do not need the things you do not know and do not desire. You need them when you know them and desire them.

The law of nature is that this external life develops gradually, stage by stage—through rocks, through vegetables, through animals, through the human. Its depth is intelligence, which is named *ʿilm* by the mystic. The joy of the whole life is the fullness of intelligence, and intelligence comes to its fullness in the human kingdom. It is in the latter that life and the primitive intelligence have their eyes opened to see and understand and think. "God slept in the mineral kingdom, dreamed in the vegetable, woke in the animal, and became self-conscious in the human." But in the human stage we find that every person has not the same capability of thinking and understanding and knowing. The word *man* comes from the Sanskrit word *manu*, which means "mind." It is one's thinking quality that distinguishes the human. Therefore the real human is the thinker, one who is capable of thinking. The more thoughtful, the more awakened the mind, the more fullness of that attribute for which the whole world was created can be found in the human.

When we begin to think, the thought comes, "Why was all this created?" The answer comes: all this gradual development is toward one single development, that of human life; and in human life, the development of mind. Through the whole universe that which has really developed is the mind, which begins to know the use of all things and all forms, their secret and the way in which all things and all forms are controlled. Another question comes to the thinking mind after realizing the secret of all things and all forms, and after knowing the way in which all forms and all things are utilized, "Is this enough? Is there not something else that one wishes?" One finds that there are four different desires: (1) the desire to know; (2) the desire to love and be loved; (3) the desire for joy; and (4) the desire for peace.

After the toil of the day there is a desire to rest and be away from people. Then there is the desire to get a certain amount of pleasure or joy in things one feels delighted in, as by going to museums and theaters. Another finds comfort and happiness in loving and being loved. The scholarly minds who wish to know and understand things have happiness and joy when they understand them.

If any of these four desires are absent, one is unhappy. One realizes that the world is engaged in four different kinds of occupations. To one person they are repellent and undesirable, to another they are desirable. Everyone has their own occupation in which they seem to be happy, but that of another seems useless to them, or foolish, or undesirable.

In Sanskrit these occupations are called *kama*, *artha*, *dharma*, and *moksha*. The occupation of kama is love, affection, attachment, or infatuation to such an extent that nothing else matters in life—money, position, nothing. Kama is the thing one wants; it is one's single occupation.

Artha is the occupation in which people are after money; they wish to be rich, to have property, to make trade prosper. Love does not appeal to them. They call the lover crazy, foolish, out of his or her mind. They say, "Everybody will love you if you have money. It is crazy to go after love."

Dharma is the occupation of pursuing duty. Such persons say, "These things are not right. The right thing is to do one's duty." Perhaps one is interested in one's family, in family duty, to mother, father, wife, or children, saying, "This is my virtue"; or in other persons, the people, the nation, the poor, or the rich. Whatever these consider their duty they give their life for. They may be a soldier, a teacher, a merchant; but they feel justified according to how they do their duty in each. The person who is after money thinks such a one is a fool. The lover thinks that same one is a fool too. For them the first thing is to convert persons to their church; to do something good for their nation, city, or village.

The fourth occupation, moksha, is different still. This is to work for paradise, for heaven, for heavenly peace. "What is the use of bothering about your duty? The whole thing is heaven; that is the happiness to look for. All things will change, all will go—wealth, the earthly beloved—they are all changeable. But paradise, the happiness one can get hereafter, after all the suffering here, that is the unchangeable." Such persons are pious. They suffer all their life; they go through all kinds of pain; they are seeking for that paradise. The lover may say, "How foolish; my paradise is on earth. My beloved is my love. What a foolish person to sacrifice all, and who knows what will come hereafter?" The other says, "I can create my paradise with my wealth."

These four paths are diverse; and everyone considers his own the best and wisest.

The Sufi looks on all with tolerance, and knows that each is for each. The path of the lover is for this one, the path of seeking for wealth for that one, the seeker after paradise is following his or her path—it is all a journey. It is only that there are four different routes by which the journey is made. The Sufi sees the same goal at the end of each. The lover has to meet the seeker after wealth, and both have to meet the one who has done his or her duty. Therefore, at the end of their journey, there is a certain place where they can meet. What does it matter if you do not go by that path? Let each choose the way that belongs to their own temperament and tendency. Therefore Sufis do not trouble. They give no preference to one or the other. They see the journey of life being made along one or another of these roads. The saying of Buddha, "Forgive all," comes true. Forgiveness does not come by learning, it comes by understanding that a person should be allowed to travel along the path that is suited to their temperament. As long as people are journeying with open eyes, let them journey.

The great thing is that one should journey with one single desire. There should be the single desire: whether to love a beloved, to collect wealth, or to do some good for the world of humanity, or to attain paradise; there should be the desire to journey to the goal.

So many do not know which is the goal or what it is. One thinks wealth is the goal, another paradise, another the beloved. They do not see that there is a still further goal. They are naturally prompted by the desire to get to the goal, and yet are not conscious of the further goal.

As it is said in the Bible, "Seek ye first the kingdom of God, and all things shall be added unto you."[1] The desire is for that kingdom of perfection, the goal of everything. How can one desire that of which one does not realize the meaning? Desire comes by knowing the thing to be desired. If you do not know what the goal is like, how are you to be attracted to it?

Rumi, the great Persian poet, speaking about this, says, "Every soul is a captive on earth." And this captivity is in the limited physical body, which one calls one's individuality or personality; and the nature of the soul is peace and joy and freedom. In this captivity it lacks these things. That is why the soul begins to think, "I want this, or that"—paradise, duty, a beloved, wealth. Reason may suggest, "This is it," and the soul goes after it; but having acquired it, it begins to feel, "No, this is not the thing that I wanted." All this shows that there is a constant desire of the soul to find its own nature; and until it finds it, it is always busy looking for something that it does not know. Is it not true in the life of every individual in this world that, whatever desire one has, during the time one has

1. Matthew 6:33.

not attained it, one is very unhappy, and eager and anxious to achieve it? One is longing, and suffering, and doing all one can to attain it, but when once one has succeeded, one does not feel happy. No, there is at once a new desire. If one has a thousand, one wants a million. If one has done one duty, there is another, and after that another. So it is with love affairs; so it is with paradise. One will never feel contented and satisfied, because at bottom it is not the desire that one is really concerned with. Though one crosses the boundary of the wall of the desire one finds oneself again with a new desire. And this itself proves the fact that there is only one fundamental desire underlying all others—that desire for spiritual perfection.

One is not capable of setting out on the journey to the eternal goal unless the four desires and occupations have been surpassed. In the first place the motive limits one to a certain routine along certain lines of accomplishment; and it does not allow that person to accomplish anything beyond the scope of that particular motive. As long as a person has the longing to attain to any particular motive that person cannot go further. That is why the sages of the East have always said, "Rise above the earthly motives." They have said, "Get your motives in life accomplished and then that itself will lead you to a stage from which you can rise above them, and above the earthly desires of the body." They have never said, "Stop, and go into the jungle, and see life from our own point of view." Everybody's path is for him- or herself. Let everyone accomplish his or her own desires so as to be able to rise above them to the eternal goal.

There are four different paths recognized as leading to the attainment of that goal. The Yogis call them by the names, *hatha yoga*, *raja yoga*, *mantra yoga*, and *bhakti yoga*.

Hatha yoga is the path of abstinence. This is a form of self-control. You read of how people practice different postures, sitting quietly and trying to slow down the circulation or follow a certain rhythm, or quieting the nerves by a certain kind of breathing. This is all a process of mastery of the body and mind. Sufis call this mastery *walayat*.

It is not study alone, it is practice that gives help in controlling the nerves of the body, the rhythm of the circulation, the control of the mechanism of the body. Perhaps you have heard that many a time the adepts are able to stop every pulsation of the body at will, for a few seconds at a time. There have been experiments made by doctors (at the Religious Congress at Chicago[2]) verifying this power. However surprising it may seem for the external pulse to be controlled in this way, what would it seem like if we could see still more deeply into the life of the adept! The control of mind is so much greater; words can never explain it; it must be one's own experience. The control of the self means the control of everything.

What does it mean when we see a person fail time after time, or another person succeed time after time? It is just a matter of holding the reins of our affairs in our hands. When there is no rein there is failure. Failure means that there has been lack of self-control, whether it be a failure in affairs or in health. Illness always comes when a person has lost the control of self. It is because this is the main ideal of metaphysics that hatha yoga has been considered of the greatest value. All the miracles and all the wonders that have ever been known and done in this world are by those who have been able by abstinence to control themselves, and therefore control life. However much were said about it, it would still not express it. To begin with, people are puzzled by it; and they wonder whether they are to believe it or not. That is why in the East the adepts never speak of their experiences in the spiritual life. They only tell their disciples to do and practice it for years. "That will make it clear to you," they say.

2. World's Parliament of Religions, 1893.

The other path on the spiritual journey is raja yoga. This is the path of life, going through all life's experiences and accepting its responsibilities. On this path there are four stages:

1. *Brahmacharya-shrama* is that path when one works with intellect. One wishes to know about things, reason about them, and understand them. It is the intellectual attainment of knowledge.

2. *Grihastha-shrama* is the attainment of knowledge by the experience of the responsibilities of life—of home, children, servants, neighbors, friends, and enemies; the experience of living among them, doing one's duty to them, loving them, being kind to them, and taking upon one's shoulders every kind of responsibility; the experiences of welcoming the neighbor, the friend, with a smile through all distress and despair, and amid all difficulties. This itself becomes a lesson.

3. *Vanaprastha-shrama* is the service of the world, of humanity. Here the work is to consider not only one's own family as one's responsibility, but also one's townsfolk, race, the world at large.

4. *Sannyasa-shrama* is retirement, love of solitude and silence, and contemplation and resignation with regard to all the things of this world.

By these four stages of development perfection is gradually attained.

Mantra yoga, strictly speaking, is the attainment of perfection by means of wisdom, and understanding life, and seeing through it. The best word to use for such a person is *seer*. One sees into life, into the depth of life, through a person, through an affair, through a thing. Not only outside, on the surface, but through, by means of concentration, as with a torch, as with a light in the hand that illuminates the thing seen. This seeing is called *jñana*. The journey through life is made by that means.

In mantra yoga a person comes in touch with the mysticism of sound and begins to see and understand; one begins to see that one gets power by sound, that in every vowel, word, composition, one finds there is a certain effect or element, because the whole life and the whole manifestation is the outcome of what may be called *vibrations*. The scientist today says, "Life is motion." But the mystics have said so for thousands of years. At the same time they have worked with the sound God, or vibration God.[3] They have worked with life according to the law of vibrations, and have seen what great power vibration has. The whole of what is called mantra yoga is based on this law of sound or vibrations. But this is a very large subject.

Bhakti yoga is the most important yoga, especially for those who have the quality of love and kindness, because all beauty that there is in life is after all what we call love. From it all the virtues spring. The whole beauty of life is in it. The English song says, "The light of a whole life dies, when love is done."[4] The whole life's light is in love; and when the heart is void of love, one is living and yet not living; one is dead. When the heart is asleep, one is as dead in this world, for one can only love by the heart. But love does not mean give-and-take. That is only a trade; it is selfishness. To give sixpence and receive a shilling is not love. Love is when one loves for the sake of love, when you cannot help but love, cannot do anything but love. Then one is not forced to love; there is no virtue in that. One does not love because another does. It is there; it cannot be helped. It is the only thing that makes a person alive. If a person loves one and hates another, what can that one know of love? Can you love one person fully if at the same time you cannot bestow a kind glance on some other person? Can you say you love one person fully when you cannot bear that person to be loved by someone else as well? Can you hate a person when love is sprinkled in your heart? Love is the water of the Ganges; it is itself a purification. As the Bible says, "God is love."[5] When

3. Nada Brahma.
4. "The Night Has a Thousand Eyes" by Francis William Bourdillon; see chapter 1, note 4.
5. 1 John 4:8.

love is awakened in the heart, God is awakened there. When one has journeyed, one has reached the goal as soon as one's heart has reached love.

The Sufis say, "The Kaʿba, the divine place, paradise, is the heart of the human being." That is why they have respect for every heart. Every heart is their Kaʿba, their shrine. The human heart is the place toward which they bow, for in this heart is God.

31

THE PRESENCE OF GOD

Speaking about the presence of God, I should say that everything present seems to us real, and that which is absent seems to us less than real; and therefore the conditions in life that are facing us seem for the moment to be real, and have their fullest effect on us. If they are joyful, if they are sorrowful, if they bring us happiness, if they bring us unhappiness—in all these circumstances they are the ones that are real that moment; when they are not present they are only a tale that is told.

During the night, while people are dreaming, whether it be a dream of horror and fear, or not, it is real to them for that moment; or whether it be joy, it is real for that moment. When the morning breaks, and their eyes are opened, then they call it a dream. The experience has become absent. It was only during the presence of the experience that they took it to be real. Once it has passed, they call it a dream.

Now, if we can only think: our disappointments, our sorrows, and our pleasures and happiness and joys at different times in the past—are they nothing to us now? At the moment of intensity of experiencing pain, it seemed as if we could not live a moment longer; but when it is past, the pain gone, and we look on it today, it is only a tale that was told. If a thousand years have passed, it is only a dream, a story. True, there is some impression that we are holding; but that which is past is past.

What counts with us is the present, what is before us just now is the only thing that counts.

People have different ideas about God. To some God is the Creator. That means God was present when the world was created, but now God is absent. To some, God is the Judge; God belongs to the Day of Judgment. Therefore God is absent just now, since they perceive there is no justice in the world. To such persons there is a hope that some day they will be placed before the Judge of the world and then they will know that God perhaps is really there; at present God is not. Then there is another who may think, "God was present when God created me, but God is not before me now. God is not present where I am, for God is in heaven; I am on the earth. Therefore I am not in the presence of God."

In this way it is clear that not only unbelievers in God, but even the believers in God, who look upon God as a heavenly Being who dwells in Heaven—both are absent from God just the same.

Then, coming to the philosophy of presence, we find that what we see and hear and experience with our senses around us, about us, and in our surroundings is what we call "present." That which our senses cannot perceive seems to be absent. But in reality there is something else present besides all that we perceive; and in spite of the presence of all the things of our comfort or pleasure or happiness, people generally are unhappy because of an unconscious longing for it. One can be in great agony living in a palace, surrounded with all pleasures; and in spite of the wealth and attentions one receives, one may yet be unhappy. And there is a possibility that a person may be very happy even in the absence of all means of pleasure, happiness, luxury, and comfort.

What is the meaning of this? It is that the world outside is a more distant world to us than the world within; and there is a world within that is immediate to our being, and that is the first we are conscious of. Although we are in the presence of the world without, we do not recognize that world within. And yet its effect is just the same. This means that a person who lives in happy surroundings and luxuries and sources of pleasure and comfort may be envied and imagined as very happy, and a lucky person. In reality, however, that person may be very unhappy. The external world has given that person all they wished, but the inner world, the inner being, is unhappy. There is, then, something absent, and the person wants it to be present. There is something missing inwardly. That shows that the inner presence is required; the external presence is not the only comfort.

But we ask, "The inner presence of what?" Many will say, "We know we are unhappy at different times in spite of wealth, comfort, happiness, friends, or beloved." Perhaps they will not believe that it is some other lack, the lack of a divine ideal, that makes them unhappy. Others consider that life requires a scope for progress, and that it is a lack of scope that causes the greatest unhappiness. Such persons think, "I cannot prosper in the work that I am doing, I cannot be any better than what they are." Such a thought is worse than death. Life is unlimited, and it wants a scope to expand and rise. Without the scope, life is unhappy. You find this not only among human beings, but also in nature. Look at the constant progress of sun and moon, rising and reaching the summit, the zenith, and then setting. See the rising of the crescent, and how it progresses till it becomes a full moon. That means there is a scope between the crescent and the full moon. This progress is the only thing that gives happiness or pleasure or joy in life; its absence means nothing but death.

However disappointed people may be at not being in a particular profession or in a particular calling or rank in life, they develop enthusiasm and energy as soon as they see some scope for progress. Their disappointment is only when they see no more scope. Though they were in the depths of the earth, it would not matter as long as they could think, "I shall some day rise to some height."

Another wonderful thing that we see, which supports this philosophy, is the tendency of everything in nature to rise. The tendency of earth is to rise as mountains and hills. When we go and see the mountains and hills, how high they are, our heart also seems uplifted; as we climb them our heart becomes uplifted; as we look up to them from below, it seems as if the earth itself is desiring to rise and go upward.

Then, when we look upon the perfection of water as we see it in the sea, the ocean, it also rises as waves; and every wave, as it lifts upward, seems to be stretching its hands upward as if to say, "Take me up, take me up, higher and higher." It is the same desire that is behind all nature, making it strive to rise upward and to reach something higher.

So it is with fire. They call people sun worshippers, or fire worshippers in Persia. In reality, it is only a symbol to show how in its blaze the fire wants to ascend. It shares the desire of all things to go up.

So it is in our own life. A person who is after wealth desires to be richer and richer, better and better; the person who is in a high position desires to rise higher and higher. Whatever the goal, every heart's desire is to reach higher.

But these are all external desires. The external surroundings and environment cannot suffice the purpose of the human, because there is a higher world. We may call people wicked because they always delight in doing evil, and in causing another person harm, and in being unkind; but were we to study their nature we should find that they also have a dislike for evil and for wickedness; it is only that their sense of justice has not yet awakened. If evil is done to them, they feel it; it is only the evil they do to another that they do not feel. They are in the intoxication of doing the evil, and therefore do not feel it. That they do not like it when another does it to them shows that they also seek goodness.

There is a desire for goodness in every heart. When a person thinks of goodness, loves goodness, admires goodness, and looks for goodness in every person in the world, that person, so to speak, collects good. When you recognize the goodness in any person it is like collecting the seeds of goodness and sowing them in your heart.

But when people look for evil, then they can see nothing but evil in every person. In that way they become so accustomed to it that their world becomes full of evil. They have contemplated it, looked for it, and created it. You will always see complaining people complaining about this one or that one having done wrong. You will find, perhaps, that they have a record of a thousand people having done wrong. The world is a record in their heart, a record of all those who have done wrong or evil. If you study them you will see they have as much evil as they have recorded, perhaps more; because if they have evil in them, they collect a thousand evils; they become a storekeeper of evil, and yet discontented with evil. When people tell other people about evil, they think they themselves are so good, so free of evil. This side of human nature we see even in children. One child will come and tell how naughty the other is, thinking, "I must be called good." Such a tendency grows and develops; the life gathers the wickedness of all people; the heart becomes impressed; in time the evil is stored up. That which is the store becomes the treasure, the world within. The people who store evil cannot see good; because there is no good in this world that has not a little spark of evil in it; there is no evil in this world that has not a little spark of good. If people only tried to find the spark of good, they could find it; and if people seek to find a little spark of evil in every good, they can do that also.

Someone says, "That person is very good." The neighbor says, "Yes, that person is good, but you do not know this about them; let me just tell you what they do." Is there no one who will not gainsay when another praises a person? There has never been anyone in history about whom somebody has not spoken evil.

What is really good? The answer is, there is no such thing as good or evil; there is beauty. That which is beautiful, we call good. That which is ugly compared with the beautiful, we call evil, whether manner, custom, idea, thought, or action. That shows that this whole phenomenon of the universe is the phenomenon of beauty. Every soul has an inclination to admire beauty, to seek for beauty, to love beauty, and to develop beauty; even God loves beauty.

In all ages the various religions have given different standards of good and evil, naming them virtue and sin. The virtue of one nation has been the sin of another; the virtue of the latter the sin of the former. Travel as we may through the world, or read the histories and traditions of nations as we may, we shall still find that what one calls evil, another calls good. That is why no one can succeed in making a standard for good and evil. The discrimination between good and evil is in a person's soul. Every person can judge that for themself, because in every person is the sense of admiring beauty. But people are not satisfied with that which they do themselves; they feel a discomfort, a disgust with their own efforts. Many people who continue some weakness or some mistake, or who are intoxicated by some particular action that the world calls evil, or they themselves call evil, yet go on doing it—a day comes when they also are disgusted. Then they wish for suicide. There is no more happiness for them. Happiness only lies in thinking or doing that which one considers beautiful. That act becomes a virtue, goodness; the goodness is that beauty.

What is beauty? One sees beauty of form, and beauty without form; beauty of thought, beauty of feeling, beauty of ideal. Not only does one see beauty in the flowers and fruits and trees, but one sees still greater beauty in imaginations and thoughts. One feels one could give all one's wealth or life for a beautiful thought or a beautiful dream.

A great many rewards have been given in ancient times to the poets, the writers, the thinkers, expressing their beauty in poetry and writing. At the same time one comes to the realization that sufficient rewards can never be paid for beauty of thought, or beauty of imagination. But there is a still greater beauty—the feeling of kindness, of self-sacrifice, of devotion, of love. The beauty that has been so impressed upon the world, that never dies—that is seen in the life of Christ, the forgiveness, the love for humanity, the gentleness, the humility—nothing can be compared with it, it is so great. Therefore it cannot be limited to name or form or to the external world. There is beauty of thought, and great beauty of feeling, of sentiment, of kindness, of self-sacrifice, of selflessness. And yet there is a still greater progress—the seeking of the source of beauty. As it is said in English, "The gift is nothing without the giver." There is no doubt a beauty in listening to the composition of a great musician, but there is at the same time a desire in the heart to meet that composer, and thank them personally. What a satisfaction—you have not only heard the music but seen the composer. You can say how delighted you are, and how much you are pleased with their music. Or there is a very good picture that you have admired. Yet your still greater delight would be to be able to tell the painter, "How much I have enjoyed it; this picture has really pleased me." So it is with the love of goodness: that constant gathering of goodness, the constant comfort of looking for goodness in everybody, the constant consciousness of doing good to another, the constant delight in one's own goodness. There is no limit to such progress. One may say, "This goodness belonged to my father, to my mother, to my beloved, to my friend, to my acquaintance, to a stranger." But when it is all summed up—to whom does it belong? Is there nobody whom one can thank for it?

A person may see different places and palaces, beautiful gardens and museums, and meet people of all kinds; but would that be the person's last desire? No it would be to meet the king or queen! "If only I could greet the sovereign, since all the goodness that I have seen and admired makes me wish to see its representative."

A person may have corresponded a long time with another at a long distance. In every letter you read delightful things and admire the thoughts so much. Will not your greatest pleasure be to see that person, and be face-to-face with that one?

So in the end it is the desire of every soul to be face-to-face with that Owner of beauty, to whom all beauty and goodness belong.

Now, whether we look at this subject religiously, or philosophically, or scientifically, from all three points there is no difference. There is only the one conclusion: that the whole life, with all its manifestations and variety is nothing but the manifestation of one life. The believer and the unbeliever will both agree that there is one life behind it all, one source of all the manifestation, one constant life that is as a stimulus, a food, a source and goal for the whole manifestation. No one who sees this with sentiment, thought, feeling, and admiration will deny for one moment that it would be the greatest happiness to come into touch in some way or other with that source of all beauty and goodness that one has sought all one's life and always admired in one's progress along the path.

No doubt there may be some souls who are so absorbed in their daily wants and present pursuits as not to feel inclined to make this search after this source. But at the same time an unconscious yearning to get to that source is always present. If it is not to be face-to-face with the Lord, it will be an ideal: if you are fond of music, to see the composer; if fond of painting, to see the artist; if of reform, to see the leader of reform; if of great people, to see the greatest person there is. Whatever one may be fond of, one will be always very glad to see the person who is identified with that beauty that one admires.

But how can one be face to face with the Deity, the Formless, the Nameless, whom one can never picture, never dream of? This is a wise question. Unless it is solved, one is a pretender who claims to be face-to-face with one's Lord. And the answer is, "Is the Deity a separate Being, or is the Deity formless, nameless, above all limitations?"

No doubt it is the fact of the desire for the presence of God that accounts for the human tendency to make idols and worship them. It was the desire to see the Deity and worship the Deity that made people stand before the sun and worship it, to stand before a tree and worship it. But this could not satisfy, because it was worshipping a limited thing. In reality, the first lesson in the presence of God is, as a philosopher says, "If you have no god, make one for yourself." How true it is that before you come to the real conception of God, the first thing is to build God in your heart. The word *god* has the same origin as the word *good*, no doubt. But its original in the old Hebrew means "ideal."

What is ideal? Ideal is that which we make. We say we make an ideal. When we think a person is so very good we think of their goodness; and that goodness surrounds that person, and our artistic tendency and idealistic tendency help to paint that person's goodness as beautifully and as nicely as we can. We can make it thoroughly good by our artistic faculty. That is called ideal. When one wishes a person to be wicked, one paints their wickedness and all the badness that is there; one makes them an ideal of wickedness. When one thinks of one's mother or friend one paints till one makes the ideal of goodness. No one can paint it for you as well as you can for yourself.

There is a saying of Majnun, the great lover of Persia. "Oh, Majnun," they said, "your girl is not as beautiful as you think. You are sacrificing your life; you grieve for ages and ages for that girl; but she is not so beautiful." Majnun answered, "You should see my Leila with my eyes; it is the eyes of my heart you need. My heart has made my Leila." That is called ideal; and the ideal of perfection, of course, makes it beauty.

The ideal of perfection is the ideal of God, and you will turn to it in your troubles or worries or fears. If there is a fear of death, yet you have that ideal by your side; you feel protected. If you are disappointed in anything, still there is that ideal by your side to reassure you; you say, "I do not mind, I am not really disappointed; for you are present in my heart; I feel your presence; you have become my ideal." In trouble, in pain, in poverty, in difficulty, in being friendless, in all these things—and no one in the world can be without them—there God is beside you. The older you grow, the more you feel: "As long as I can be of use to the world, so long will the world want me. As soon as I can be of no service, of no use, then the world gets tired of me, it does not want me. The world is after that which is not myself. If I am wealthy, the world is after my wealth, not me; if I am in a great position, the world is after me because of my position, not because of me. The world goes after false things. The world is false. The only safety from it is to have that ideal of God alive and constantly present. With that ideal I can be satisfied, and have rest and peace; not only on earth but even in the hereafter I shall be in the arms of the Divine!"

No one can ever be so dear, so close—neither children, husband, wife, nor friend—as this perfect ideal. That ideal will never fail. God will always be with you here and hereafter. You belong to God. From God you came; to God you return. By feeling the presence of that ideal always in the heart, one feels every springing of every beauty, every impulse, every thought, every imagination, everything that comes out of oneself, everything one sees all around. One identifies it all with God in the end. To the person who creates the presence of God the whole life around becomes one single vision of the immanence of God.

32

THE SPIRITUAL HIERARCHY

In the Qur᾿an we read that God is the light of the heavens and of earth.[1] That explains to us that if the Creator is the light of the heavens and of the earth, if the Creator is light, then the whole Creation is the Creator's light also. Therefore if we wish to know the secret of the nature of the heavens or of the earth, we can learn it by studying the nature of light. There is nothing more attractive to our eyes than light, nothing more elevating. Every heart feels full of delight in the light of the sun.

The nature of light is to throw out its rays. The nature of the light of God is the same. If we study the rays minutely we shall see that from whatever angle we view them there is one central ray shooting forth with more intensity and with much more light than all the others. That means there is a central ray. Actually the emblem of the cross, which is a most ancient emblem, is derived from a study of light. The first glance shows the one central ray; the second glance develops that ray into a horizontal line; the two lines now form the figure of a cross.

But light is everywhere. Whether electricity, or gas, or candle, it is the same. But light in its perfection, as in the sun, can be observed better than the small forms of light. Science has come to understand that the light of the sun is in all things.

1. Qur᾿an 24:35.

Religions have all understood this from the first. The Hindus and Egyptians taught it. All over the East worship of the sun was the first to come into existence. Only later were the sun worshippers considered infidels, or heathens, or pagans. But as sun worship is the natural religion, it is true that every religion can be traced to it. The external light was the first thing that impressed the human heart with the idea of God. No doubt the inner light helped, but even that is light. Therefore both the external and the inner light reveal the mystery of the source and secret of all religions.

We can see the same thing in different aspects of life. For instance, the falls and springs of water, the different channels, all show one big central current of water, which scatters as it falls. It touches different rocks, spreads into many streams, and yet unites into one big stream. In vegetable life we see the same. A tree with fruits and flowers and so many leaves and branches, has yet one central part of its being—its stem. The life of the stem is the life of the whole tree. It is not so much that the fruits and forms appear from the tree as that the stem is repeated over and over again. Every branch is a stem to smaller branches. That again shows how the light that we call life takes a main channel for its expression, and spreads through different organs, the small channels or boughs.

We see it in the human form. There is the spine, which is the stem. The breath runs through the center of the human body, although the hands and legs and face and different organs have different directions. This central life is more important than any other part of a person.

Then we see it in the life of people. Perhaps in every house there is someone whose sorrow means sorrow to the whole family, whose pleasure or happiness means a portion of pleasure or happiness to all the others. Perhaps a whole town moves at the strength and energy and enthusiasm and initiative of one person. A whole nation moves through the person of the day. However many wise people there are, however intelligent and capable they may be, there is still one person as the stem, through whom the whole activity is kept going. It has never been otherwise, whether the age was aristocratic or democratic. Even if the age was one of democracy, a democrat has nevertheless been in the place of that stem, just as in the age of aristocracy an aristocrat was in that place. No nation, no town, no city, no family exists that has not that one soul on whom the happiness, unhappiness, degeneration, or evolution of the whole depends.

Once, being asked whether one person's influence or understanding could be better than five persons', it was evident to me that the questioner thought that in these times one individual is no better than another. But the answer is, "Five persons? That is very few. There are some persons who know and understand more than five thousand!" In all ages we find musicians, poets, others of the greatest repute, who were seen by thousands of people who did not understand them. Millions of people may have adored them after they were gone. Poets, reformers, scientists have been considered crazy for thinking of something impossible. Yet they have been the greatest people in the world. Was not such a person equal to fifty thousand people? Surely.

Even today we can see, in everyday life, how people argue and dispute without coming to a conclusion. Then perhaps another comes, and sets the whole thing right. The discord of thousands of people can be broken, and thousands of people could be united into one harmony by the presence of one person who unites them all.

Whether the democrat accepts it readily or not, it does not matter. Even in a democratic land like Russia there is the influence of a leader just the same. Whatever nation you go to there will be one person equal to thousands.

This natural condition is the basis of ancient civilization. It is the reverence and honor that is given to age—the old person has experience. However intelligent a person may be, it is the aged person's experience of life, the life that one has seen, that tells.

Honor has been paid to learning. The learned person was respected because that one understood more. Honor was paid to goodness. If a person showed goodness to their family, proved to be honest, and virtuous, and right to their neighbor, people had respect for that one also, and made that person a leader in the village or town. The social life was based on that appreciation of virtue, intelligence, and experience. Hence came the custom of the king, queen, rajah, chief, pasha, sultan—whatever name they received, they received it by virtue of their goodness, kindness, education, experience, or manner. They became the leader of those who wished to become like them.

Those who believed in religion had faith in their church; they believed in their tradition. They had a regard for it. Others had the faith in their ruler. In the story of the dervish and the procession of the king[2] we see how easy it is, under the delusion of democracy, to go against all custom, education, authority, experience, and age. Keep away from that delusion, and we find the real democracy, that which comes from showing an ideal to others, honoring and respecting that ideal ourselves. It is a crude spirit that says, "I do not care for your education, your experience, your age; I do not care if you are thousands of years old." That is the false democratic spirit. The true democratic spirit feels within itself that there is nothing one cannot be, and at the same time appreciates, respects, and understands all that it sees in age, experience, goodness, righteousness, piety, or virtue. To follow such a spirit means evolution; not to follow it means degeneration.

So we come to the idea of the religious hierarchy. It is natural for those who admire art to admire those who have painted beautiful pictures. Those who have a taste for music naturally admire the composers of the past, who have given their lives to

2. See chapter 24, p. 202.

the observation and contemplation of music, and have benefited us by that deep pursuit of music, and enabled us to start from the point at which we begin today. This inclination is inherent: to admire, respect, and feel grateful to the masters of the past. We feel the desire to be near to them and get still closer.

It is the same in all directions of life. There is always the desire to get near to those lives that have helped humanity in music, science, reform, philosophy, or religion. Whatever we know today is the discovery of thousands of years. No country or nation can say, "We were the only discoverers of this, or that." No, the discovery of the very least thing is the discovery of the whole of humanity. How could we understand language, were we not taught? Books, reading, civilization, seeing life—all has helped so much that no one can say that something is only due to a particular person or nation. The whole of humanity shares in everything that we think new today.

In the case of the spiritual cults, we find how all the mystical and occult schools gratefully recognize the masters of the past who have given their experience, sometimes by giving away their efforts, sometimes by giving away their happiness, sometimes leading a very hard and restricted life, sometimes renouncing all the happiness and wealth and possessions of this world, rejecting all temptations of life by going to live in mountain caves or forests.

Every cult of mystics has used certain names. There are certain names in the cult of the Hindus under which they recognize certain masters. We find them also in the Semitic races, mentioned in the Bible, the Kabbalah, the Qur'an. Naturally, the human mind has its limitations. If we had no limitations we should be perfect. Still it has always happened that people have recognized as masters only those who are found in their own tradition. They recognize the spirituality, or greatness, or blessing only of those whose names they can find in their own tradition. In the tradition of the Kabbalah there are the names of Abraham and Moses; in the Christian tradition there is the name of Jesus Christ, and after him those of the saints; in the tradition of Islam come other names again, Muhammad and many Muslim saints. In India, there are Brahma, Vishnu, and Krishna. And as there was no convenient means of communication in ancient times, it was only natural that the tradition of one country should not be known to the others, and that the tradition of one country should become corrupted as it passed to another. The names used in one nation thus came to be different from those in another. Brahma, Abraham, Bahram in Persia, are all related names. If you tell some people that one name is really the same as another, they will not accept it, because they do not wish to think another tradition is the same. Those of their own tradition are the only ones.

There is no blame in this, seeing the human tendency to revere, appreciate, be grateful, and link up to their piety, virtue, goodness, spirituality, or power. It does not matter as long as the greater thing is recognized. If one does not recognize it now, one will perhaps do so later. In just the same way no particular school or group of scientists has been the only help. When we perceive the depths, we see that every person in this world has been helped in their evolution, and all have helped each other. When we look deeply into life we see how a person is illuminated from another, how one learns from another. Whatever the name of the teacher, there is still the one stem of life and light. As long as the tree of this manifestation exists, the stem will exist. The names are all names of one current of life and light that runs through the tree. The one spirit of life is given different names, the sacred names; and we more easily recognize the current by the particular name to which we are accustomed. So far we are right, but the mistake we make—and it is to our loss—is to ignore or deny the same truth because it is given to us in another form and in another name. We limit it. We say the truth was only in that period when such and such teachers came to the world, and that after that the truth was stopped. But the spirit of illumination can never stop as long as life goes on. Illumination has been continued from the first to the last, and will always be continued until the manifestation stops; so long will the spirit of illumination continue to spread out its rays.

We accept some forms and ignore others. It is the natural tendency of humankind. It is this that accounts for so many religions. Even if one cannot see things in that light, one can at least be tolerant of other people's religions. One can respect the religion because one sees others respect it, even if one has no respect for its teacher. After all, spiritualism means respect, advancement. One shows one's evolution according to one's respect, one's consideration, one's thoughtfulness. If we could only develop that faculty in our mind, it would not matter not believing or recognizing the spirit of guidance shown in different human forms. If we held our own teacher or master in the greatest esteem it would do a great deal of spiritual good. All the wars of ancient times and all the inharmony of the world are usually caused by religious differences, and the differences are caused by humans' failing to understand that religion is one, truth is one, God is one. How can there be two religions?

The tendency to regard highly the teachers who have passed is natural, because when such persons have passed they are unapproachable, and the goodness of their spirit can be recognized. When the spirit is in physical form, it becomes difficult to recognize spirituality in them and give them the same esteem as given to one who has passed. Sages and teachers in all ages have usually been recognized after they have passed. In their lifetime they were neglected and even met with opposition.

The mystic understands that the illuminated souls, the guiding souls, are on earth too. They were not only in the past; they are here now also. Were there none on the earth now, how could illumination be continued? It is the present that is the best, not the past. What is present today, will be the past tomorrow. So the mystic does not lose the opportunity of recognizing the spirit in the present as well as in the past.

The Sufis use such terms as *wali*, *nabi*, *ghauth*, *rasul*, *qutb*. But names do not matter, though the grades are necessary grades. One person's influence may be in a village, another in a county, another in the whole country.

What is the sign of such souls? Of course in the East it is believed that some persons bring good luck. We say somebody, or some child in the house, this guest or that friend has brought good luck. The good luck may be brought to one person, or it may be to ten, or fifty in one's life. That shows there is some influence, and we can recognize it as beneficial, good, harmonious, to five, ten, a hundred, a multitude. The soul is as great as the circle of its influence.

Human beings are all in limited form; they are so tall or so short; the soul is much wider. One person's influence may hold a thousand people. There is a saying in Gujarati, "It is possible that the world may be saved by the virtue of one; it is possible by the sin of one that the whole ship may sink."

We see that also in practical life. An incapable foreman in a factory will bring nothing but disappointment; an inefficient manager in an office or shop will bring nothing but bad luck. One person's influence, capability, knowledge, enthusiasm, initiative, strength of mind, willpower, are perhaps far greater than those of a thousand people. When we look at it from a spiritual point of view there is one person's soul emitting a blessing and goodness to thousands.

There are two forms of this. First, there may be a soul in a very humble guise, so that nobody would think that soul could possibly be at all spiritual, or pious, or good; it may be a soul working as a servant, one who scrubs the floor; yet there is such a great influence of goodness and light and blessing in that soul, that unconsciously wherever it goes, it brings some blessing, some goodness, light, harmony, joy, and peace.

In the East this has always been believed and still is today. Therefore a child is taught to be careful not to offend anybody, however humble or weak they seem. We do not know what is hidden in their humbleness or weakness. That person may be uneducated, or possess no money, position, or sign of high birth, or anything bringing notice in the eyes of the world; and yet a beautiful soul is hidden there like a beautiful gem lying for thousands of years under a rock until someone finds it and puts it in a crown to be worn by a sovereign, where everybody can see it.

A person who welcomes everybody, and sees virtue in everybody, has faithfulness and consideration for everybody; this person's soul develops so that in time others perceive its light. Wherever the light is, it can be perceived.

In the second case, it is not necessary for the jewel to be so hidden. Sometimes it is not. It is not hidden where there is a task in life that a soul has to do. There may be a task to give a divine message, or to uphold a country or nation that is going into degeneration. One may have to guide it through its difficulty, keep its harmony and peace.

As in the days of Noah, so there may be need of a warning. That soul comes to give it. The light that is mostly hidden now comes forward to bring something to light that is in the depth of life. At one time such a soul was called a prophet, or teacher, or godhead, or incarnation. Others claimed to be prophets, or healers, or warners. But in the time of humankind's maturity, of the whole world's maturity, such things are not so named, and yet the work is needed. The personality has been the sign, the evidence; the message has been the sign, the evidence of its truth or falseness. There was a time when the world was not capable of seeing. Humanity was not realized enough to recognize the message. Hence the claim of prophecy had to be made. But now the world can recognize, sooner or later, what is right and what is wrong. The warners, the masters, the messengers of today will not claim; they will only work. They will leave their work to prove for itself whether it is true or false.

Those who view life mystically consider not merely that they are one with the teachers of this or that tradition of the past, but they consider that in every soul there is a spark of that teacher. No soul is without the light of that spiritual teacher. Therefore they have regard and respect not only for the spiritual hierarchy, but also for the spark of that light that has made a spiritual hierarchy in every soul. So they regard with respect and reverence every human being in the world.

The whole vision of life, the whole manifestation becomes one single evidence of the sublimity of God.

33

SUBLIME KNOWLEDGE

Beloved Ones of God, I will speak on the subject of the result that is attained by sublime knowledge.[1] In the first place, the result of spiritual attainment is so vast and great that words can never explain it for the very reason that all that words can explain is limited, is learned or taught or bought or sold, and that which cannot be learned or taught or bought or sold is something higher, which cannot be put into words. The first thing one begins to see in oneself is that words such as "I cannot" or "It is impossible" or "I am helpless" or "It cannot be done," these thoughts cease to exist. A soul naturally becomes positive and will say, "If it is difficult today, tomorrow it will be easy," "If it cannot be done just now, afterward it can be done." This optimism comes not only in imagination, but it springs from the spirit; its root is in the spirit and it strengthens a person immensely in accomplishing things. The fear of death that every person has, more or less, disappears, and if fear of death disappears, there is no other thing that frightens a person, for that is the thing that frightens one most. Many say, "I am not frightened of death," but they will not continue to say that when death is before them.

1. A lecture given at the Sufi Center, San Francisco, February 26, 1926.

A story is told in India about a woodcutter who used to say in his times of self-pity, after having worked all day long, "Oh, what life! What a terrible life, having to work all day long in the hot sun cutting wood; I wish I were dead." And sometimes he used to say, "O Death, why do you not come? I would rather die than live such a life." And one day Death took pity on him and appeared before him. And the moment he looked at Death, he was so frightened that he began to beg him to leave him for some time in this world, that he would never invoke his name again, that he would very much like to live a few more days on earth. So it is with everyone. They call death when death is not present, but when death comes, then they are frightened. It is the spiritual soul who as a result of spiritual attainment begins to rise above all fear. As Ali has said, "Fear no longer remains in the heart of the spiritual ones." For fear is like the darkness, and the illumination is light. When illumination comes, obscurity disappears.

When people have arrived at spiritual attainment, their doubts cease to exist. And without spiritual attainment, however intelligent one may be, one still has doubts. And very often, the more clever a person, the more doubts that person has. And you will find that among the most intelligent ones, they cannot make a decision. They cannot make up their mind, for they doubt. And doubt is the decay that destroys every action. And there is only one thing that raises one above doubts, and that is not belief, but conviction. And conviction comes by spiritual attainment.

You will very often see a most learned person, who has studied many books and who is most intelligent, say, "I suppose it is so" or "It can be so" or "It may be so." The mystic never says that. The mystic says, "It is so" or "It is not so." There is conviction. It is spiritual attainment that gives conviction to a person. Have prophets and sages said, "There may be a hereafter, there may be a soul," or "Perhaps there is a Judgment Day," or "Perhaps there is a God"? No. They have said, "It is so." It is not that they have said, but they have known. Besides, the soul begins to see a way to immortality, and it therefore does not doubt or fear. It looks with open heart to what is coming.

Spiritual attainment also makes the sight penetrating. In other words, before the eyes of the spiritual person, objects and people unfold themselves. They reveal their nature and character and secret. It is just like a master chemist; whatever drug that is there, that chemist knows how to utilize it, how to make medicine out of it, how to prescribe it. In the same way, everyone stands before the spiritual soul with the record of their nature and character together with their past and present and future. Every person is like a written letter. But a letter is no comparison, for a letter is dead; here is something living, something communicating and most revealing. A letter can reveal very little, but a person reveals a thousandfold more. All that words can never express is confided to the spiritual soul in the twinkling of an eye.

Very often people are deluded by the great compassion, by the graciousness, fineness, and saintliness of a spiritual soul. They see in their negativeness a lack of power, but it is not really so. On the contrary, behind the refinement, behind that saintliness and that sympathetic and compassionate attitude, a great power is hidden, a power of resistance, a power of accomplishment. Only they do not make the most of their powers. But the greater you are, the more spiritual you are, the less you use your powers. It is like a child soul and a ripened soul. If you give money into the hand of a child soul, that person will go in the shops and different places and will buy things that attract it; it will waste that money, and in a short time it will have nothing left. But a ripened soul who has got the same amount will use it more slowly, more thoughtfully, and make the best of it, giving happiness to him- or herself and to others with it. And so spiritual persons neither make use of their inspiration nor of their power in little worldly things. They are more economical than if the same power, or one-hundredth of that power, were in the hands of an unrefined soul. For instance, someone who knows all about their surroundings would abuse that insight if they were still inquisitive and so small as to speak to everybody about what they saw. And it is the same thing that everybody does. People are most inquisitive when it comes to knowing about another; they care very little of knowing about themselves. Therefore, the smallness of one's nature must first be shaken off. When one rises morally above the tendency of giving one's thought and time in knowing people's conditions and affairs that do not concern one in any way, speaking about them, forming opinions about people, when all this is given up, then a person becomes entitled to spiritual attainment. And those who are childish enough to use their powers, if they had any, in doing wonder-workings or in accomplishing things of an everyday worldly nature abuse spiritual power too.

The other day a scientist asked me if there were any way of raising a pen that was lying on a table by spiritual magnetism. I said, "Nothing is impossible to a mystic. But why spend time to raise the pen, when there are so many human beings to be raised higher? This would bring about a much better result than raising a pen."

What people want to do today is that they want to get spiritual insight and power and use it for their material advantage. They think, "If we can make things more profitable in our worldly life, that is worth doing." That is like spending pearls to buy pebbles. They would do better to pay for pebbles with pennies than to spend spiritual pearls on pebbles.

What business and industry and all other things require is effort, perseverance, qualification, intelligent working. If you do it that way, you are successful. But to try and think that spiritual attainment must be only for worldly success is a very small aim to be accomplished. Spiritual attainment is success itself. All things come to the spiritual person; if one is a businessperson, one is bound to be more successful. But one must not try to attain spiritually in order to succeed in business. The accent must be on spiritual attainment and all things will follow as a matter of course. As Christ has said, "Seek ye first the kingdom of heaven and all these things shall be added unto you."[2] Therefore, in all professions, whether one is a writer or a poet or a political person or an inventor or in any other profession, spiritual attainment will always help in every direction. But it must not be attained because you need to be successful in a certain direction. Because that makes the course longer; then it takes a longer time. Besides, there is no greater success than spiritual attainment because it is the finer success, a success that reflects in everything you do and brings about fruitful results. Therefore the ancients have called it the philosopher's stone, that whatever the philosopher's stone touches, whether it is iron, copper, or brass, it turns into gold. In other words, whatever the heart of the spiritual person touches, it turns into life.

Morally a person who has spiritual attainment need not cultivate sympathy, for sympathy comes without one's cultivating it, as a matter of course. A spiritual person cannot be other than sympathetic. It is a continual outflowing of love that manifests by spiritual realization. It goes out to the wise and foolish both, to good and wicked both, as Christ's forgiveness was always ready for the wicked, his affection always for the good.

It is love manifesting in different aspects as compassion, forgiveness, kindness, graciousness, as affection, as sympathy—it is one and the same. And in the end spiritual persons do not see in another person a separate entity. Their realization makes them feel, "It is myself." Therefore, they cannot wrong another person once they begin to see the other person as themselves. And no one in the world seems to them to be different and distinct from themselves, but they see in the other the various aspects of their own being. It is in this way that the spiritual soul expands and attains to perfection.

2. Matthew 6:33.

34

INTELLECT AND WISDOM

Beloved Ones of God, my subject this evening is intellect and wisdom.[1] Often people confuse these two words: *intellect* and *wisdom*. Sometimes they use the word *intellect* for wisdom, sometimes *wisdom* for intellect. In point of fact, these are two different things altogether. The knowledge that is learned by knowing the names and forms in the outside world is the knowledge that may be called intellect. There is another source of knowledge, and that source of knowledge is within oneself. Saying it is within oneself might confuse some people. One might think that within oneself means inside of one's body, but this is the ignorance of humanity of itself. Humankind has a very poor idea of itself, which keeps it in ignorance of itself. If one only knew how large, how wide, how deep, how high is one's being, one would think, act, and feel differently. But with all this length and width, depth and height, when one is not conscious of it, one is as small as one thinks oneself to be.

The essence of milk is butter, the essence of the flower is honey, the essence of the grapes is wine, and the essence of life is wisdom. Wisdom is not necessarily a knowledge of names and forms. Wisdom is the sum total of that knowledge that

1. A lecture given at the Sorbonne, Paris, February 25, 1924. This version of the talk was published in *Social Gathekas: Sufi Wisdom on Social Harmony and Service* (Richmond, VA: Sulūk Press, 2020).

one gains from within and without. Intellectuals are those who will argue and will dispute, but very often upon a subject that they themselves do not know fully. And very often you see among those who dispute and argue, that they dispute for the very reason that they do not know it fully. Their argument on the outside makes one feel that they know it, but the very reason that they argue shows that they do not know it. Those who know do not need to argue; they know it. For the very reason one knows, one is so satisfied that the satisfaction does not give one the hunger of that person who argues.

In the first place, the trace of wisdom in nature can be found in studying instinct: the art of weaving and making a nest among the birds; the art of swimming among the fishes; the art that exists in nature; and besides that, the science that exists in the animals and birds who know their medicine when they are ill. In the ancient traditions of the Oriental people there exists a belief that the first medicine was learned by the bear. The reason is that the bear knew when it was ill, where to go, and what to find as an herb or as a remedy to take in order to bring about a cure. By a deep study of this idea, no scientist will deny the fact that among the birds and animals there exists an instinct that, in their illness and distress, they too find the medicine.

Therefore, what we call intellectual study is a collection of knowledge that has been given to humankind as a study to learn; and one understands it as an intellectual study, something to depend upon. But that is not all the knowledge; that is a limited part of knowledge. There is another fact of knowledge that can be drawn from the essence of life. That which is called instinct in the animals and birds in the lower creation, is the very instinct that, when developed in a person, becomes intuition. It is not true when the psychologist says that all the child knows is what the child has learned—whether a favorable attitude or an unfavorable attitude, whether a good manner or an ill manner. If two children were brought up from different parents and different races without being trained in manner or wisdom, you will find that both will show their manner and tendencies differently. If one were to think how much one learns from the outward world and how much one learns from within, it would not be an exaggeration if I were to say that ninety-nine percent one learns from within, and one percent one learns from without—if one learns. It is not true that outwardly the learned person becomes the great person or personality in the world. It is the inward learning that helps one to become that. By this I do not at all mean that outward learning is not required. Outward learning is the qualification of expressing the learning that one gets from within in a better form. But at the same time, it is from inner learning. If anyone has ever learned anything, one has learned from there.

And now the subject comes of how one has to pursue this. How does one pursue the wisdom that is within? By first realizing that intuition exists in oneself. It is not every person who perhaps even believes in an intuition. And among those who believe in intuition, they are not all those who trust in their intuition. No doubt they have a reason not to trust, because many times an intuition seems to be a futile knowledge. But if I were to say what is the reason that intuition proves to be wrong, I will say that it was not an intuition but that it was thought. Every person is not able to catch the first impulse, and the activity of mind always goes from one thing to another. Therefore, as soon as from within there comes one thought, it goes to another; and therefore, mind thinks it has thought an idea. And therefore, one thinks that: "I thought like this"; but really speaking, it was not an intuition. But after an intuition, one goes a little further in thought, and one thinks one has an intuition. In this way one begins to distrust intuition, and when one distrusts one's own intuition, one has no confidence in oneself. And to me the meaning of faith is self-confidence. The one who has no confidence in oneself, whatever be that person's faith or belief, it is not substantial. If a person would come to me and would say: "I believe in you, I trust in you, but only I cannot trust in myself," I would say: "I appreciate very much your trust and belief, but I cannot depend upon you." But if another person comes and tells me: "I trust myself and do not know yet if I can trust you," I should say that there is a hope for that person. For I will know that person has taken the first step already. The person has to take the next step. Those who cannot trust their own intuition are perplexed; they do not know what they want. They will always depend upon outer things that give them reasoning; and the things of outer life, which are subject to a continual change and all subject to death and destruction, are not dependable. These things are called by the ancient Hindus an illusion. A person who thinks that: "I am a positivist because I depend upon outer reason," is depending on something changeable and subject to death.

But now a question comes: How are we to know that it is an intuition? The thought waves are just like voice waves. It is quite easy and possible that a thought of another person happens to float in that horizon in which one is conscious. And one hears it and thinks: "It is my intuition." Very often what happens is that a person feels a depression without any reason, a person feels humorous without any particular reason. Very often it is a kind of floating thought or feeling of another person that passes through one's own mind and being, and for that moment one begins to feel happy or unhappy without any reason. And it happens very often to all people during the day, that there come thoughts and feelings and imaginations that they have never thought or that they have no reason to think. It would then not be right to call these things intuition. Water that is to be found in a little pit is not the water that is in the depth of the earth; and therefore, the thoughts that come and go, floating on the surface, are not to be depended upon. Real intuition is to be found in the depth of one's being. In the first place, one must learn to believe in the existence of such a thing as intuition. The next thing is to be able to follow one's intuition, even at the cost of something valuable. Even if one were deceived for some time after, one will not continually be deceived. Therefore, in the end, one will find oneself on the right path.

But the third thing is to make the mind one-pointed by the help of concentration, which would help one to perceive the intuition properly. Just as in hearing the ears are so made that the voice waves make a resonance and become clear, so also the mind must be made a kind of accommodation or mold in which the intuition may become clear. The difficulty is this: that outwardly the work of the ear is different from the work of the eyes. The mind does both kinds of work: seeing and hearing at the same time. But besides this, the mind is perceptive and also creative. But it cannot at the same time both perceive and create, for creating is expressing and perceiving comes by receptivity. In the Sufi terms there are two temperaments among humanity: the *jalal* temperament and the *jamal* temperament. The jalal temperament is expressive, and the jamal is receptive. And the temperament that at the same time is receptive and creative, that temperament proves to be without result. It is this temperament that is called *kamal*, a temperament that has no result. That is why many people would like to hear, and there are many other people who would like to speak. There are many people who would like to act and be active; there are others who would like to see others act, and sit.

The one who works is pleased with working. The one who is sitting is pleased to sit. Both enjoy what is akin to their temperament. Therefore, that one is creative who acts; the other is receptive who sits. But one can master one's life by taking these two different faculties in hand and trying both: at times to be creative and at other times to be receptive. The one who is creative needs, no doubt, an action and a knowledge of action. But the one who is receptive wants concentration and the attitude of mind that is receptive. The mind can become a receptacle of knowledge that comes from within. If we look among people, we shall find that among a hundred persons there are ninety-nine who are creative by nature, but only one among them who is receptive enough to receive from intuitive faculties.

The difficulty with the mind is that when one wishes to receive, the mind wishes to create. When one wishes to create, then the mind wishes to receive. For Hindus, the mind is like a restive horse. A horse, unless you have put a rein upon it, will not be controlled and will not take the direction that you want it to take. Therefore, in order to attain the wisdom that is as the essence of life and that is to be found within oneself, it can only be attained by first making the mind obedient. And the mind can be made obedient by concentration. People have easily understood when you tell them about voice culture, and how necessary it is, in order to sing well, to produce the voice. Also one can easily understand what it is to learn physical culture in order to make the muscles strong. But when it comes to training the mind, in the first place a person asks: "Is there a mind? I thought that there was only a brain." And if it happens that people believe in the mind, they do not know what can be done with it. Anything else they will find more valuable than the training of the mind. They might think that it is the work of the lazy people, who have all sorts of luxury to give time to it. It is the greatest mistake that one makes by keeping away that culture, which is the most necessary to begin from childhood, as a training. And sometimes a person asks the question: "Does a child not learn concentration when it goes to school?" And my answer is: "Quite the contrary. Children mostly lose their concentration in school." When little children begin to learn mathematics and go from one to a hundred, they lose their concentration. Children never have an opportunity to sit quiet for one moment. They have not often an opportunity to think of one thing for a moment. What, therefore, becomes of them? Children become nervous. Today one sees that nervousness is to be found everywhere. If people have equipped themselves with a certain amount of education, they are found to be nervous. Besides, after the education, the education has to be made use of. If the mind is not under one's control, how can one use it? It is one thing to learn, and it is another thing to make use of learning. It does not suffice the purpose to learn a song. By that, one cannot be a singer; one must learn to produce one's voice also. And so it is with intellectual knowledge. A person has become a qualified person by studying for a long time, and if that person cannot use a knowledge, what is the use?

There is a sufficient number of learned people. What today we want is people with masterminds: those who do not only see the life without, but within; who do not only draw inspiration from the life without but also from the life within. Then they become the expression of this perfect being, which is within, hidden behind this life of variety. I do not mean by this that everyone learned becomes a kind of super-being. I do not at all mean that a person should be able to perform wonders or to perform miracles. I only mean by this that a person may live a fuller life and may become a human being in order to bring about better conditions in the world. What do we want? We want human beings. It is not necessary that all people must become most religious or most pious or too good to live. We want wise people in business, in politics, in education, in all walks of life—those who do not only live on the surface, and those who do not only show belief in matter, but those who believe in life within and without. It is such souls who will produce beauty. It is these souls that will harmonize the world, who will bring about the condition that we need today. We want not only the knowledge of matter or spirit, but we want it living in all walks of life—in one's business, in one's effort, industry, in every art or science one is busy with—that one might use the wisdom that is perfect in oneself. When the individual and the multitude will find beneath their feet a solid foundation on which they stand, from that day we will begin to say that now we can hope for a better condition in the world. It is toward this ideal that every effort of the Sufi Movement is directed. It is to attain to this mastery of mind that the facilities have been given by the Sufi Movement to those who wish to study and practice in their lives.

35

SIMPLICITY AND COMPLEXITY

Beloved Ones of God, my subject this evening is the secret of the spirit.[1] We read in the *Gayan* that, "Simplicity is the greatest beauty."[2] People today have made life so complex that whatever they seek after, they want to find in complexity. All things in life that have importance, beauty, and value are simple, and simplest of all things is the divine truth. The one who cares little for it says, "It is deep waters to go into," and the one who cares much for it thinks, "It is so difficult that it would be the hardest thing to find it." In this way the lover of truth and the one who does not care both look for complexity. Knowing this nature, the wise have guided people gradually to the truth. Nevertheless, the message that Jesus Christ gave, the teaching that Prophet Muhammad brought, the message that Moses has given, all the different prophets who in their times have given the message of God and truth, have given it in perfect simplicity. Today those with knowledge—say professors or doctors—may complicate that truth and give it a form that is not understood. The general tendency is that when people do not

1. A lecture given at the Waldorf Astoria, New York City, December 20, 1926. In the *Complete Works* (1926, vol. I), this talk was given the title "The Secret of the Spirit."
2. The saying is in the *Vadan* as "Simplicity is the living beauty," and can be found in the *Complete Works, Sayings 1* (1989), 382.

understand something, they say, "Yes, it is something"; the very fact that they do not understand it makes them think, "There is something in it."

Can there be any truth that the human soul has not known? If the soul had not known it, it could not be truth, for truth is not a knowledge, it is the very self of a person. The truth is not a newly invented theory, not a dogma, not an idea; it is reality itself. At the back of it is the human self. Therefore, it is simple. But it is not simplicity that people seek; they are longing for complexity. Anything that will confuse, they are glad to take interest in. If it is simple, they say, "I know it already." In the *Gayan* we read that, "I have come to tell what you already know, for it cannot be too often repeated."[3]

And now we come to this evening's subject, which is the secret of the spirit. What is generally known about the meaning of the spirit is that it is the source and goal of all things and the essence of life, that spirit from which the whole of manifestation comes and the same to which the whole manifestation is drawn. We also use this word in the case of a person who has passed from this earth. This is another meaning of spirit. From a metaphysical point of view, it is the mind and the soul and their working that is spirit. There is another meaning of spirit we know in everyday language: influence, power, radiance, enthusiasm—those are also called spirit. What I would like to explain today is the nature and character of the spirit that manifests as what we call manifestation or life. Many ask the reason for this manifestation, "What was the reason at the back of this creation?" The reason is beyond all reasoning. There is no reason. It is love's nature itself that cannot but manifest. It is its nature. It is beyond reason. When poetically expressed, the great ones have said that God was alone and God was lonely,

3. A version of this saying is also in the *Vadan*, and appears as "Be not disappointed if I tell you about things which are already known to you. Realize that they can never be repeated too many times," and can be found in *Complete Works, Sayings I*, 360.

and in order to see God's predisposition, which is love, in order to experience it, God manifested. It is poetic and it is true. But the process of manifestation can be understood by knowing the nature of manifestation, that the spirit is likened to the sun and what we call souls are the rays of the spirit. If the spirit is eternal, the souls are eternal. If the sun is eternal, the rays are eternal because the sun and the rays are not two things. The rays are the unfoldment of the sun, and souls are the unfolding of the spirit.

In manifesting, the souls enter into three spheres. No sooner a soul comes out as a ray, it enters what may be called the angelic sphere. In order to make it intelligible, the wise of the ancient times have pictured angels in human form. Nevertheless, it is in order to make the human being that the whole creation was made. It was not only the angels, but rocks and shells, fruits and flowers, birds and beasts, all show in their form a preparation, a preparatory stage of the human being. As we read in the scriptures, "Man was made in our image."[4] The whole creation was a process to make that image that was the image of the human. The human being was the finished image. Therefore, God was recognized in the image of the human.

The nature of the beings of this sphere may be explained as those who are happy, innocent, musical, lyrical, poetical, pure, and worshipful. Among human beings, when we see that nature, we say, "Here is an angelic soul." Perhaps one person shows this more concretely than another person. It is not necessary that, in order to be wise, one should not be innocent. It is not necessary that an innocent person must necessarily be an ignorant one. The most foolish can be ignorant; the most wise are most innocent because they hear all things and do not hear. The foolish are innocent because life does not speak to them; their heart is closed.

4. Genesis 1:26–27.

The soul in its further journey pierces another sphere, the sphere of genius, in Oriental terms, the sphere of the jinns. The souls represent the qualities of this sphere in intellectuality, in inventive genius, in poetic gift, in musical talent, in art, in science, in all things that belong to the mind. It is for this reason we call that person a genius. The word *genius* comes from *jenat* in Arabic.

After this sphere, the soul manifests in the physical sphere, where it adorns the physical garb that is the human frame. One may ask, "Is it necessary that every soul that shoots as a ray from the spirit must pass through all these three spheres?" Yes. One might ask, "Does it not remain in any sphere longer?" Yes, it does too. It remains or it goes further, as when some of us in art, in science, in learning, in the pursuit of knowledge go so far and no further. And so it is with souls. Those who are satisfied in one sphere, they remain there. They may live like any creature of the lower creation would live: they drink and make merry and are quite happy. There are others who feel uncomfortable until they have penetrated into another sphere where they are more contented. Some are not satisfied in that sphere and look for another sphere. If we human beings here have this tendency, it is the tendency of the soul. Wherever it finds interest, joy, and pleasure, it remains; it settles there. But again, every soul is bound to its goal, it *must* go there. But the condition is that in order to get to the goal, it must return. The condition of that return is that it must give up the garb of the particular sphere where it is in order to enter another sphere. It is not allowed to enter into the inner sphere with the outer garb. Plainly speaking, each of these three spheres, angelic, jinn, and physical, have each a particular garb. That garb may be called the body of that sphere that the soul has to adorn. And when going back, it must give that garb to the same sphere from which it borrowed it. And this giving of the garb to the sphere from which it was borrowed we recognize as death. Since humans do not know their soul and are only acquainted with the garb, after the garb is given back, one says that is the end of life. But it only begins. It begins one act of the play that is the further journey to make.

But there are three different ways of going back, or one should really say going forward. One way is the way of the drunken person, another of the person who is asleep, and the third is the way of the person whose eyes are open.

The way of those who are drunk is the general way. What is life? Life is drunkenness. Whether they are in business or in enjoyment, or whether in a profession or in any other interest in life, what is it? It is a wine. Those ones are drunk. After drinking the wine they know nothing except that particular intoxication. They are intoxicated in the life they have lived. That is their world: ambition, aspiration. They are taken back against their wishes like a drunken person, who is drinking. Somebody said, "Come along, you can no longer drink." They cannot help it, their mind is in the drink. This is the general way that a soul goes toward the goal.

And then there is the way of those who are asleep. They know not what death and life and birth mean. They do not know why they came here, why they are going from here. They are happy because they are asleep. They are taken wherever they are taken.

And then there is the third way, and that is the way of those who journey with open eyes. Those with open eyes will see all the beauty on the way. They are the ones who will enjoy the journey, who will appreciate the beauty of traveling. For them, every step forward has a new experience, a greater joy, a particular blessing.

This process by which every soul comes forth and returns is this very process that the mystics of all ages have realized here on the earth; and the true meaning of mysticism or spiritual attainment is to know fully, here on the earth, of the way that the soul has manifested and is bound to return. The question is: How do the mystics know this explanation of the journey we have made? To understand this it is necessary to make intelligible to your minds that this journey is an idea. In reality, the soul has never been away. One end of the soul is attached to the goal; the other end is manifest. When you look at the center of the line, it is one line. Neither is God human, nor is human God; and yet, human is God and God is human. The difference is in how we look. And if the human soul is attached to the goal, then it has not departed from any sphere it has once penetrated. It is still there. But one is unconscious of those spheres that one has gone through because one is so open to this visible sphere that one's soul has closed its eyes to the sphere within. As heaven is not a place where the virtuous are sent; heaven and hell are within. All the higher spheres of which people talk are within. People never realize nor imagine that they could find the higher spheres within themselves.

The analysis of the spirit is simple: the spirit is fine matter and matter is the dense spirit. It is only a difference of words. All difficulties that arise come from a difference of words. Words are to cover truth, not to explain it. And it is not truth that can be explained in words. The spirit is likened to water; matter is likened to snow. Water and snow are the same, it is only the condition of water that makes it snow. It is a condition of spirit that makes it matter. It is in this process that people must realize, it is through this process that people must come to the understanding of the great fullness of the purpose of life and all that they seek after through life.

There is a story among Hindus that the lord Indra, the god of heavens, had fairies in his court called *upsaras*. And their work was to dance at the court of Indra. Once one of them went on the earth and saw an earthly mortal being, and she was so much in love with him that she lifted him up and brought him to the spheres of Indra. And when it was known that the mortal man was brought there, Indra commanded that the mortal man should be dropped on the earth to live the mortal life and the fairy should be sent to the other end of the world to overcome her karma, to pass through her karma. This story conveys that every soul is born to dance before the throne of Indra, which is God. In reality, every action of beauty, of harmony, every action of love, of kindness, of compassion is the dance of the soul. But when the soul becomes conscious of this dance, then the presence of Indra becomes clear before that soul. To be in the presence of Indra is to be in the presence of God. It is the greatest joy and happiness, which nothing on the earth can give. As Rumi has written in his *Masnavi*, where the soul is likened to a reed flute, "Why does the music of the flute appeal to you? Because it laments, it cries, it longs for that spirit, for that being which was its stem. This reed was cut away from its stem and holes are made in its heart. That made it cry. It cries to rejoin the stem."[5] So it is with every soul. The restlessness, the uncomfortable feeling every soul feels, it is always for one and the same reason, though each one gives another reason. One would like to possess earthly wealth; another suffers by the contempt of friends; another says, "I cannot approach my beloved"; another has troubles at home; another has a case in court. But in reality, there is only one trouble, and that trouble is the sorrow of the spirit. As it is the inclination of every river to go and meet the sea, so it is the inclination of every soul to go and meet the spirit.

At this time, when materialism prevails all over, people say that there is a great hunger after truth. Yes, it is natural that people should hunger after truth. The very fact that there is so much materialism shows that every soul feels uncomfortable and begins to long for spiritual attainment. But how do they pursue spiritual attainment? Generally there are two kinds of seekers. There is one kind who is curious, who wonders if there is anything or not, if it is really true that there is a soul and a hereafter. They look for some phenomena in order to be sure. They use psychometry, palm reading, clairvoyance, and all

5. From the prologue to book 1 of the *Masnavi*.

such different means. There are hundreds and thousands wandering about in madness, looking for phenomena. And there are others, who are perhaps more intellectual, who say, "I have read this book on occult science. Have you read it?" because they saw in the newspaper, where it said, "We recommend this book." After one book they read another, and the end result is that they become more and more confused.

Dear friends, is this the way of learning? Is it not enough that from childhood one has to learn in school? And after having read all those books, all that is there to be read, where does one arrive? At confusion. One does not know which is real and which is truth.

There is a story of a seer in Punjab who became a great poet and saint afterward. When as a child he was sent to school, the teacher gave him the first figure to make, alif, which is a straight line. And the other children who were learning, they learned many figures. But this child continued to learn this same figure of alif. The teacher said, "Have you not finished it?" He said, "No, I have not yet learned it." He was sent home because the teacher said, "He is too stupid." At home everybody was annoyed with this child who could not learn more than this one line. This lad went away and lived perhaps in the wilderness, in the forest, for a long, long time. One day he came back in his old village where he had been at school. He said to the teacher, "I think that I am beginning to know that figure." Many children had come and gone since he had been there, so the teacher could not recognize him at first. He said, "Shall I write it?" As he made this sign, there came a split in the wall. The teacher said, "Here is a man with a miracle." He said, "That is the way one learns in the wilderness." In everything he had realized this one line, alif: in the trees, in the plants, in the birds.

Friends, there is one thing that is learning, and there is another thing that is unlearning. In other words, rising above what we call worldly learning. Very often what we call knowledge keeps our soul away from the knowledge of the soul, a knowledge that is most essential because the knowledge that comes from learning is so complex. People think, "That must be truth; if it is more simple, it cannot be truth. All what we value is complex." In this way one covers, with one's own tendency, the truth in oneself, which is one's own being.

36

DEPENDENCE

Beloved Ones of God, I will speak this evening on the subject of dependence.[1] There are three different ways in which a person depends upon another. One way is that of a child who has been put in the situation of being cared for by its parents. The child has not sought it, has not asked for it, nor does it even know that it depends upon them. And yet it is put in a situation where it depends upon the parents.

And there is another aspect of dependence, where one depends upon someone to whom one has given one's confidence, one's trust. That depending is different; one has chosen it, and in order to depend in that way, one must have some reason also. One says, because my friend is sincere, because I trust in this friend, because I can give my confidence to this friend, because it is my relative or because this is someone whom I know I can depend upon. It is just like depending upon a ship to carry one through the sea. There is every reason for one to depend upon the ship. One knows that this ship has sailed perhaps a hundred times from this port to the other port, and it has come back safely, and everyone knows it. Therefore, this is a dependence based on reasoning, and this dependence is the one that we see in life.

1. A lecture given at the Summer School in Suresnes, July 11, 1926.

But then there is a third kind of dependence, one that was better known by the ancient people. In this age of materialism and of commercialism, that dependence seems to have disappeared. That dependence is to depend upon the unknown.

When one reads in the Bible that even the lilies are clad by nature, and when one reads in the *Masnavi* that even the smallest insect is taken care of by Providence, one thinks, but if we did not do anything today we should still be taken care of just the same. But then a person thinks that bread is going higher in price, what will become of me tomorrow? That person cannot think of dependence upon the unknown. Today people think that if the lilies are clad, I should be clad according to the latest fashion. This all shows that we have become too artificial; and, far from following this principle, we cannot even believe in this principle.

There is a great deal of pessimism from all parts of the world, and the more civilized the country, the greater the pessimism and the greater the strife. For instance, what one thinks in Europe, how much one strives and how much one is anxious to live in Europe, cannot be compared with the person who lives in America. There one does not know about one's job for the next week, if one will continue it, if one will find it. The competition is increasing every day to such an extent and life's mechanism has been made so artificial that one cannot believe in dependence on the unknown. It is not that the support of the unknown has been taken away from people. But life has become so difficult that it is difficult for even the idea of the unknown to reach people.

When you think of hundreds and thousands of people today not knowing from day to day what they will do, anxious how they will get on in life, it shows to us that it is not progress. A progress that can make people worried and anxious so that they cannot depend upon life—how can you call that progress? And if it is progress, it is not on the natural line. Progress means ease, relief, peace, happiness, less strife, less struggle—that is progress. Progress does not mean greater struggle, greater uneasiness, greater anxiety, and greater worry.

There is a very good example. I knew a person whose father had such enormous wealth that he could sustain a hundred generations very comfortably, and this person was anxiously looking for some work. He came to ask me about it. I said, "I am very surprised that you are looking for some work and want to do something. What are you looking for?" He said, "Some business, some industry, something to produce. That is the only real field of production: one where you can produce money." I said "Is there no other field of production where you can produce something better than money. You have enough to last for generations." "But what will people say, I must do something," he said, "and I can only think of doing that, nothing else."

There is much that can be done in the world for the poor, for the needy, for the ignorant, for those who are not yet awake but are still asleep, for the conflict between nations, for the prejudice that exists between races—there is no end of work one can give one's thought to instead of thinking, no, I must produce some money and that that is the only thing that can be done that is accepted by the world.

If a person does not do this, then people think there is something wrong with the person. And what has it done? It has wrecked the nervous system of the present generation. And after a hundred more years, you will see that the race will begin to suffer tremendously from it.

Working beyond the limit, from morning till evening, and then what do they gain? Some of them perhaps can collect money. But many of them have only a loaf of bread in the evening after a whole day's toil; that is all they can get.

And besides that, today the difficulty between capital and labor does not happen because there is money on one side and poverty on the other; it is not true. The truth is that for humankind, there is no other ideal left except money. And wherever there is a lack of it they feel it, because they do not see anything else.

If you go to the capitalists, their God is the same. If you go to the laborers, their ideal is the same: money. All the different morals and arguments and theories and discussions are meant to civilize the world, but how will they civilize the world as long as the ideal of the world is money?

There is a very large number of people who do not wish to make a home and do not have family, for the same reason, because they are waiting for money. Imagine hundreds and thousands and millions of examples of this, waiting for that time when there will be enough money to live in a society as artificially as is done today. The ideal of home in ancient times was quite different. The home of each person was a palace for that person, whether made of straw, reeds, bamboo, brick, earth, or marble. Everyone's home was a palace. If they had a simple bread and water, they were thankful to have it. They did not think that because another person had a home of marble they should not marry unless they had a home of marble too, that they should wait all their lives until they had a marble home. And what is this attitude destroying? It is destroying the happiness of the world; it is spreading discontentment, and the lack of money, without reason, is felt more.

Then what comes as a result of this is the desire to snatch the money from one another's hands. All the different ways of making the economical conditions of the world better will not prove satisfactory as long as the ideal of the world is not raised high, as long as people do not look at the spiritual ideal as something greater and worthwhile, forgetting for a moment the things of the earth. A pessimistic person would come and say to me that suppose I went and sat before the city bank and raised my hands in prayer and said, "Million francs, million francs, million francs. I depend upon you, million francs!" will it come? To such a person, Prophet Muhammad answered very nicely when he said, "Shall I depend upon God?" He said, "Yes, but tie your camel to the tree. Do not let your camel walk loose and then depend upon God. First tie your camel, then depend upon God.

This was a practical hint the Prophet gave, but at the same time, when we come to think about dependence upon the unknown, we go into a much deeper subject and a subject of the greatest value in our everyday life. It is true to say "Tie your camel to a tree," but at the same time, do we not see that very often with every strife and struggle and worry and anxiety, a person gets nothing in the end? And very often we see that to a person who does not strive and struggle, the hand of Providence comes naturally and says, "Here you are, here is what you want" In the East there is a saying that when God gives, God pours it through the roof, so that it comes into the house, and this is true also. We do not see it because we do not want to see it, because we do not open our eyes to see it. But it is not a story, it is everyday life.

Do you think that strife brings money, or struggle brings the things that you want in life? Do you think that anxiety produces what you wish for? Never. On the contrary, very often a person may lie awake in bed for nights, for months on end, and say "Million dollars, million dollars," and does not get it. Or a person may go out and work from morning till evening to gain a million dollars and does not get it. And yet there is another one who gets it very easily.

America is the best example of this philosophy; people with nothing have gone there and worked and have got everything. This shows that when it comes, it comes amply. And when it does not come, it does not come. Does that not show that somewhere there is a key to it, a treasure house from which you can draw? It shows that there is a hand of wisdom working behind all things. And one who does not look for it, does not depend upon it, does not recognize it, makes a great error because all through life one lives with the treasure yet does not know of it.

But now if you look at it from a metaphysical point of view, you will find that some action is necessary, not only depending upon, but some development in, one's own self. Even among the so-called spiritual people of today, many of them never think about it. They think of occult sciences, of psychic things, of intellectual ideas. But when it comes to dependence, this is an idea they do not know of.

The other day I was visiting a very large city and there the head of an occult society came to see me. He had perhaps a very large following in that country. And would you believe what the first question he asked me was? He said, where does the support of your society come from?—this from a so-called spiritual person. And I told him. And I saw his expression—it was pessimistic. He could not believe it. If I had told him that I have magic, and by that magic I can get as much as I want, he would have believed it at once. But when you say God, God does not mean anything to them. Magic means everything to them. If I would have said thought power, we have an engine of thought power going on; he would have believed it. Tell them about any organization that is working for money, they believe it. But when you say that God is the source of all, then their mind is blocked; because they have never used their mind in that direction, it never goes there.

In order to depend upon anyone, you ought to have faith in that person, and your dependence upon that person is a mechanism that gives that person that responsibility. When we look at nature's phenomena, we find most beautiful examples of this. The little sparrows who do not yet know how to fly and who depend upon their parents; not only the mother but also the father brings grain in its beak and gives it to them. It is a most wonderful phenomenon to look at it from this point of view, that what is it? It is dependence. The young ones cannot fly, they depend upon the parents. And the day they begin to fly and take grains themselves, then neither the mother nor the father has any inclination to share their grain with the little ones. From that day they leave them alone. This shows that if you look for the grain and say, my mother and father must look for me also, it cannot be, and it will not be. The day you have awakened to the sense that you are looking for your own grain the mother and father have lost their responsibility. You have exactly the same relation with the unknown. As soon as you begin to depend upon the known source and on your own faculties to get all you wish, that unknown becomes more unknown to you. Just as the parents of the sparrows withdraw and do not appear to the young ones, so God disappears more and more. The more one looks after oneself, the more the unknown source disappears. But is it disappointed with you? No. Is it cross with you? No, it is only an automatic process. Naturally a mother whose heart is always focused upon her little ones is watchful of every move and every little tumble that child makes. But for how long? As long as the child has not gained control of itself. The moment the child has taken control of itself and moves about, then the mother puts her mind on something else. It does not mean that her love has decreased. It only means that the moment the child is able to move about without depending upon the mother, then that much responsibility is removed from the heart of the mother. It is exactly the same thing with the heavenly Mother and Father.

Sufis are the best examples in the world of dependence on God. One will find numberless examples in the history of the Sufis of how they have practiced this dependence upon God as a spiritual practice. And you might ask how have they practiced it? Not only for their food, but for everything in life, they have developed dependence in their nature. While everybody is looking for independence, they have practiced quite the contrary thing, dependence. And the wonderful results that they have achieved by practicing this are worth studying: dependence on life with food and without food; dependence for health without considering it, without attending to it. And in this way they have not only made themselves independent of the world, but they have made the unknown known to them. It is in this way that they have found the nameless, the formless, the unseen, the unknown God.

In the terms of the Sufi this is called *tawakkul*, and *tawakkul* means dependence upon God. And now you might think, well, it is good that some people say I will wait, I will wait. I will not work, and I will just depend upon God. I am doing a little work, but my whole dependence is on God. And there are others who do nothing and say I will just wait, but it must come. All these different ways are weak; there is no strength in them.

There is a story of a peasant woman. Her son, when he was fourteen or fifteen years old, came to his mother and said, "Mother, tell me what I must do. I must do something in the world. People ask me to do something. But which is the best thing to do in the world?" The mother said, "Son, I do not know. I know so little about the world, but people say that the best thing is to search for God." He said, "Mother, will you tell me how to search for God, how to do it?" She said, "I do not know, Son, I never have done it myself. But people say that those who search for God, they have to go to the wilderness." So the son said, "Yes, Mother, then I must go to the wilderness." It was a great pain to the mother that her child was leaving. But at the same time, she wished the best for him; if that was the best, she thought, let him go. And he went.

He came back after a very long time, and he came to his mother and she asked, "Did you find anything? He said, "No, Mother, I found no one, I lived in the wilderness." "But how did you live, my son?" He said, "When I was hungry, I took some fruits and nuts and ate them. And when I was thirsty, I went near the little streams of water and drank there, and I slept under the trees, and so I was wandering about in the wilderness." So the mother said, "So you did not depend upon God; you depended upon fruits and nuts, and what you could get." So he said, "Mother, I shall try again."

She said, "That is the reason why you could not find God." He said, "Then what shall I do about food?" Well, she gave him a little piece of board, cut in the form of a large cake, and told him to put it around his waist, and when he thinks that he is hungry, he can feel the board and he can feel that there is something. So he went in his way again to search. After a long time he came back again to his mother. He said, "Here I am, Mother." "Did you find God?" "No, not yet." "Well," she said, "what did you live on?" "Whenever I was hungry, I touched this board, and I felt I had food." "So you depended upon this. Therefore, you could not find it. You depended upon something that you touched and felt and thought this is my food."

Then he went for the third time without the board. When he came back the third time he said, "Mother, I have not yet found it. The mother said, "What did you live on?" "Nothing," he said. So the mother said, "Now is the time, my son, that you are ready to go to a murshid. Now you must find a teacher. When he went to a teacher, as soon as the teacher looked at him, he thought, how wonderful, he is standing near the shrine of God. There is only one step to take. The teacher was most impressed and asked him, have you loved someone in your life? This lad from his childhood had lived at home. He was the son of a shepherd, a peasant. He did not know anybody, he had not seen anyone. He said, "I have loved a cow." The teacher said, "That is alright, think of that cow that you have loved. And he thought of the cow. All the murids who came and went from the teacher, every day they had fifteen minutes of silence, or ten minutes of silence, or half an hour. And then they went to do all things in the world. The young man was sitting where he was told in the room and thought of the cow. There was to be a gathering of all murids and the teacher sent for him. But the boys said, we do not hear any sound in that room, the room is closed. The teacher went himself and opened the door and saw the boy sitting there absorbed in meditation. The teacher called him, "Farid," (for that was his name). He answered, but instead of saying yes, he answered like the cow: "Mooo." The teacher said, "Come out." He said, "My horns are too large to come out of the door." The teacher said to the murids, "That is called concentration; when you will be able to forget yourself in the thought that you have before you, the way this man has, that day you will also come near God's shrine."

Dependence upon the unknown is a most difficult thing to practice. And if one can practice, there is no greater virtue that one could practice in this world. That is the way to the spiritual goal, and that gives us the secret of the whole philosophy: that the more you depend upon God, the more God becomes dependable.

37

FRIENDSHIP (1)

Beloved Ones of God, I wish to speak this afternoon on the subject of friendship.[1] It is a word that we all use in our everyday language, and yet it is something that could take one's whole life just to realize its meaning. However learned a person may be, however pious or spiritual a person may be, however more experienced a person may be, if one has not learned the nature and the character of friendship, one has not learned anything. This is the first thing we have to learn, and this is the last thing we have to learn. We so often make use of this word, calling every acquaintance a friend or professing to be somebody's friend, but the more we realize the meaning of it, the less we are able to claim to be a friend. For everything we are tested in life, we are examined, we are tried; but to go through this examination of being a friend is the most difficult thing in the world.

And what is the reason for this? Why is it so difficult to be a friend? One could think that it is the easiest thing in the world. The reason is that there is in ourselves something that is always against being a friend. And what is it? It is the self, the ego, which the Sufi calls *nafs*. So long as this ego is standing and it lives, a person cannot claim to be anybody's friend. And as one

1. A lecture given at the Summer School in Suresnes, June 21, 1925. This lecture also appeared in the *Social Gathekas*.

is not anyone's friend, one is not even one's own friend; for one learns friendship by being a friend to another. Selfish people may seem to be a friend to themselves, but it is on the surface, not in reality. They have not learned yet how to be a friend, so they cannot be a friend to themselves also.

In our pursuit after truth we are inclined to learn a great many things—the nature of life, the secret of life, the character of life—and to understand the meaning of friendship. It seems so easy, so simple, that we never trouble to think about what responsibility it is to be a friend. The great error we make in our lives is that we begin to claim friendship before we have learned the meaning of friendship. In this world of illusion, where in the end of the examination we find all things of little importance, of little worth, if there is here a sign of reality—something that one can depend upon and something in which one can recognize a sign of eternity—it is in the constancy of friendship.

As people are absorbed in the active life of the world, they have a desire for friendship, but they never practice it. But this tendency can be found even among the animals. I have heard this story as a personal experience of a hunter, that one day he was shooting at little birds in the forest, and there were two birds sitting on a branch of a tree. One bird was shot and dropped on the earth. And as this man was at a distance, it took him a little time to arrive there; and during that time what he saw was that the other bird, the mate, which was sitting on the branch, came down on the earth to look at the other bird, its mate. And it touched it with its beak and found that it was dead. By the time that the man arrived, he found both birds dead. "From that day," said this man, "I gave up hunting, for I have seen friendship among birds that one cannot find among humankind." It is a simple lesson, and it is a lesson that we have to learn. And today, when nations are against nations, and races against races, communities against communities, one religion against another religion—at this time friendship is so much needed. Besides, the first lesson of spirituality that one can learn is friendship. One says, "But friendship, a personal friendship, means nothing. A person does not become spiritual by a personal friendship." And the answer is, yes, one begins one's spiritual accomplishment by learning how to be a friend. For a person who is really treading the path of friendship need not go anywhere to learn morals. Friendship itself teaches sincerity, gratefulness, tenderness, sympathy, appreciation. All these things that we must learn in this world, friendship teaches us. And once a person begins to learn these things through friendship with one person, naturally that person shows to others the same virtues that have been acquired by going along this path. Naturally, the one who has learned how to sing beautifully will sing every song that is given to that one beautifully. A person who has cultivated the heart by friendship will naturally be inclined to be friendly with others. It is not the belief in God that leads us to the goal, nor is it the analysis and the knowledge of God that brings us there; it is the friendship of God. For one who learns the lesson of friendship in this world, this lesson develops, in the end, in the friendship of God. But when a person exacts from a friend all that the person does for the friend, then it is not friendship, it is business. It only means I give you a shilling, and you give me twelve pence. When people judge their friend in their heart, the spirit of friendship is not awakened; a friend never judges. When people talk to another about their friends, when they blame the friends and criticize them, those people do not know what friendship is; the meaning of friendship is too sacred to realize. All other relations and connections in this life are empty if friendship is not at the back of it to strengthen it. Between mother and daughter, father and son, brother and sister, husband and wife, teacher and pupil, all these connections need a spirit behind it, and that spirit is the spirit of friendship. When a daughter says, "Oh, I am friends with my mother," there is something beautiful about it. Besides the connection of a mother and a daughter, when she says, "She is my friend, she is my chum," it is a different thing; it makes that connection living.

In every relation it is the same. When there is friendship to bind the relation, it makes it secure, it makes it lasting; it is that which gives it a life. It is true that love is life, and life is symbolized with water. Water is the symbol of life. When one wants to bring water from the ground, one has to dig for it, and the first thing that one finds is mud. And if one was disappointed that: "Oh, by digging for the water I have found mud," one has fooled one's own self. For at the bottom of the earth there is water. It can be found, but one must have patience to dig for it, to dig deep enough to find the water.

If someone has made a friend, it is not something that one has made to order, that must just fit in according to one's expectations, according to one's wishes. Every person has individual characteristics, and as long as the spirit of forgiveness is not developed, friendship cannot last. It is a continual forgiveness that helps friendship to endure. Much can be learned by study, but not unselfishness. Unselfishness can be learned only by one thing, and that is by treading the path of friendship; and it brings beauty into one's life. A friendly person, whether in business or in a profession, in whatever capacity that person stands, gives you a feeling of warmth; in other words, an atmosphere of life. You are always glad to meet a friendly person in a shop, in a factory, in an office; in whatever position that person stands, it does not matter. When this spirit is awakened, you can feel that person in the person's words, in their voice. You can feel it in the expression, in the atmosphere, that this is a friendly person. There is something that goes out to meet the other person, a continual tendency to harmonize with another.

Once this spirit is developed, this ever-complaining tendency vanishes. If not, then this world is full of thorns; everywhere one wants to lean one's hand against, there are thorns that prick. One will have no peace, no happiness, whatever one's position in life may be. If we want to make our life easy, if we wish to create happiness in our life, we must try to crush that ego, that nafs, that thought of self which keeps us continually obsessed in our own thought and in our own affairs.

By rising above it we will learn the spirit of friendship, and then, for us, the same world that is full of thorns will become full of roses. For some souls the same world is heaven that can be as hell to many others, for friendship changes one's point of view. Unfriendly people, as soon as they see another, see the other person from their own critical point of view. They have their preconceived ideas, and therefore, they are not allowed by providence to see the good side of the person. But for those in whom a friendly spirit is awakened, they always overlook little errors, faults, little mistakes. They naturally rise above, for their sympathy and their love help them to rise above the faults of humanity. That story of Jesus Christ, the friend of humanity, before whom the greatest sinners were brought—the attitude of the master was always forgiving. Those who brought them were unfriendly; the master was friendly.

Life is as we look at it. If we wish to find faults, we can find faults in the best person in the world; and if we wish to find good points, we can find good points in the worst person of the world. It is as we see life. Someone went to Jami, the great seer of Persia, and asked if Jami would accept him as his disciple in the spiritual path. Jami asked him, "Have you loved, have you learned the manner of friendship?" He said, "No, not yet." Jami answered, "Go in the world again and learn it. The first lesson in the spiritual path that you have to learn is the manner of friendship. Once that is learned, then all other parts of the spiritual journey will become easy."

Friends, all these difficulties, such as wars, revolutions, disagreeable experiences in nations, fights among parties—where does it all come from? It all comes from that one thing, and that is the lack of friendship. And the most wonderful thing is this: one party is against another party, fighting for years perhaps, but if you investigate the particular ideas of that party, they are not even friends among themselves because of the unfriendly spirit that develops in them from fighting against the other party. They cannot be friends, even among themselves. It is a kind of intoxication. But when this is gone, then they fight among themselves in education, in religion, or in any other way that is possible. The best thing one can do is to introduce the spirit of friendship. But you will ask how can we introduce it, because this is something that cannot come by only reading some books about it. There are so many societies and institutions of kinship that everywhere one hears about it every day, about increasing kinship; but they prove to be everything else but kinship. Therefore, that is not the way. The way is that an individual must be brought to understand fully that the essence of morals and of religion and of education is one, and that is the manner of friendship.

Sufis of all ages have named it *sulūk*, which means "beneficence." If there is a best education, it is beneficence: how to bring pleasure and happiness to another. And one can begin to learn it by understanding fully, and by practicing, at the same time, friendliness.

38

FRIENDSHIP (2)

Beloved ones of God, this evening I wish to speak on friendship.[1] Relationship is cherished by contact, kinship is maintained by reciprocity, but friendship is developed with love. There is no other relationship that can be compared with friendship, for it is in learning the law of friendship that one understands ethics, morals, and also the relation between man and God.

There are three principal things to be understood in connection with friendship. The first thing is understanding without words. If there is no understanding between two persons, words can never help it. You may speak and speak, and discuss and discuss; it will only go from bad to worse, and argument will never end. As it is said in the *Vadan* "Why? is an animal that has myriad tails. When you give it a bite, it drops one tail and another comes up." Can argument bring about an understanding? Never. Argument only increases argument, and so one can go on till two persons can turn their backs on one another. Understanding is a gift of God; understanding is a soul's unfoldment; and understanding is the greatest fortune one can have in life. And it is with understanding that the foundation of friendship is established. And it is in the un-

1. A lecture given at the Summer School in Suresnes, July 25, 1926.

derstanding the friendship is secure. Without understanding there is no friendship.

And the next thing is a disinterested attitude. When people think that by friendship they can get this benefit from the friend, or that the friend can benefit from them, that is just like burning the roots of friendship. And today in these material times, so few of us understand what friendship means. When there is a question of friendship, the first thought is, what can I gain by the friend? Can his or her influence be of some use? Can the friend be helpful in our business? Can that friend help in my industry? Can this friend be of some use? That is no friendship. Whenever there is a thought of friendship with self-interest, that means the ruination of friendship. Every little thought of profiting by it means destruction; it never can form into a friendship, it will only form into a business relationship. It will last as long as a business relationship will last. It will prosper as long as the business relationship will prosper. It will exist so long as the material interest exists. Then it will vanish. Such a relationship can never be called a friendship.

In this world every individual is helpless in some form or other, and every other individual is of some use in some form or other. And unconsciously it can happen that a friend depends upon a friend for their own interest, and even if it were unconsciously depending, it would still turn out to be a wrong attitude. It cannot bring about fruitful results, for friendship must be built upon a solid foundation, a foundation where there is always a desire to give, to be helpful to the friend, to be serviceable to the friend—with no thought of taking, always a thought of giving, and keeping nothing back. A real friend holds their life cheap before their friend. The one who considers anything more important, more precious than friendship, that one has not yet learned the first lesson of friendship. There is no sacrifice too great if it is made for a friend. If a sacrifice is not made for a friend, then for whom should a sacrifice be made? A person would never learn how to make any sacrifice if it were not for a friend.

In the first place we take the word *friendship* so lightly, and we confuse a friend and an acquaintance. An acquaintance is someone whom we have seen, and they have seen us, and we recognize one another. We may have been introduced at a dinner party, but that acquaintance cannot be a friend, that person is just an acquaintance. But we use the word *friend* so freely in everyday language that we have lost the meaning of friendship. Generally, anyone whom we have seen at a reception or party, we call a friend. Or anyone that belongs to our club we call a friend as well. To have two friends or three friends or four friends, or even just to have one friend in life, is the greatest fortune. If you can say I have one friend in my life, it is the greatest fortune.

And the third important thing in friendship is the overlooking. No person in the world is faultless, and no soul in the world is perfect, and if on your part there is no desire to overlook a friend's shortcomings, there can be no more friendship. Friendship is maintained by recognizing one idea: that human beings are imperfect; they have their faults and their shortcomings. There is something lacking in them to overlook, and when you go on doing so, there is always the possibility of them developing those qualities that are lacking, because you add to the friend those qualities that are lacking in the friend.

Sometimes people meet once and they feel they are friends. And so friends meet. And sometimes people know one another for months and years, and so they grow to be friends; and in the end the fulfillment of their knowing one another and coming together brings about what we call friendship. It develops as a result of knowing one another. No doubt there is another odd case that sometimes happens, and that is when two persons, daggers drawn for many, many months or years, throw their daggers away and become friends forever. But it is an odd case. I myself have seen people who have been enemies, working against one another for years, and from the day they became friends, they have been the closest of friends. They have stood by one another, they loved one another, and they were the thickest of friends.

Those who say, I was a friend, or someone was my friend but now we are not friends, they must also know that they have never been friends. It was a presumption on their part. It was a confusion, it was a false impression. Can you be a friend and not be friend afterward? Can friendship be such a false thing? Can gold be gold once and not gold another time? Gold is gold. It never changes, it is the same. Constancy in friendship is the soul of friendship, and that custom where a friend writes to another friend "Yours as always," means it is a dead friendship. If a plant remains as it has always been, it does not grow, and that which does not grow is not living, and that which is not living is dead. People very fondly write to one another "Yours as always," in other words: yours as I have always been; I would never like to progress; I never would come closer to you; I am the same as I have always been. And when a person thinks, "I am too good to you, I have been too kind to you, I have been most devoted to you," that person forgets that kindness, goodness, and devotion are larger than the horizon. No one can be too good, no one can be too kind, and no one can be too devoted. And when there is a discussion between friends, and one says "I have done so much for you, I have suffered so much for you, I have had so much pain on your account, I have had such a difficult life for your sake," that one is entering into business. They want to keep a diary of what they have given in the form of love and kindness and goodness and sacrifice. A friend does every sacrifice that they can and never thinks about it. They do not even allow their mind to ponder upon that subject. Thinking about "what I have done" is a business question. It is against friendship to weigh and measure what you have done for me, and what I have done for you, how you have behaved toward me, how I have attended to you. True friendship means to do what one can do and forget about it. Real friendship means regard, a deep regard for the pleasure and displeasure of the friend.

Is there anything in life that is more delicate than friendship? To think that no word should hurt the friend; that no action should harm the friend; that not the slightest shadow of coldness may fall on the heart of the friend; it is most difficult. If a person has learned the manner of friendship, that person need not learn anything more. That one knows everything. That one has learned the greatest religion. For the same way one has with one's friend is the same way one will make a way to God. And remember that the one who has never learned the manner of friendship will never know the way to God. That one may be God's worshipper, but that one cannot be the friend of God.

There is an attitude that one generally sees in friends, and that attitude reveals a divine secret. That attitude is the tendency of the friend to cover any fault of their friend that is spoken or brought out before another person. And not only to cover it from the sight of others, but to cover it from one's own sight too. One never thinks about it, one never looks at it, one interprets it differently, and thus one turns the wrong of one's friend into right, and every little good point of the friend, even though it may only weigh an ounce, one makes into a pound. One appreciates it so much, admires it so much, raises it so high, and considers it so great that another person cannot imagine that this little idea, this little merit can be valued so highly.

Perhaps I shall tell you a little story that will give you an idea of this. In the beginning of my spiritual pursuit, when I went to my murshid, there was no end to my enthusiasm. There was no end to my devotion. There was no end to my excitement about it. I told everybody I met how I felt about the personality of my murshid. This feeling made such a great impression upon my teacher that once, in answer to my deep feeling, my murshid said, "Friendship in the path of God, friendship in the path of truth, is greater than any friendship in life." With this deep feeling, with this great enthusiasm, I once met a very learned man in Hyderabad, and I told him about the deeper things of life, and he was so interested to hear from a young man such deep thoughts. He said, "I am very interested, I would so much like to see more of you." I said, in my great enthusiasm, "If you saw my teacher, you would think that there is no one in the whole world to compare, how great he is, how wonderful is his personality, how blessed is his presence, how inspiring his glance, how peaceful his atmosphere." He said, "I would like very much to see him. Where does he live?" I told him in such and such place. He said, "There? I have lived there for twenty years! What number? Which place?" I said in such and such a place. He said, "Oh! It is just next to my house. What is his name?" I said it. "I have known him for twenty-five years! I never thought he was so great." I knew in my heart that in twenty-five years he had not seen that which I had seen in a few months. It is friendship that shows one, it is distance that keeps one's eyes covered.

If you are friends and if you cannot understand one another, then you are not yet friends. You think you are friends. And if you understand, then all the beautiful points in both of you are made a thousand times more clear because of that friendship. In friendship there is no limitation. You cannot say there is only so much. You can say there is all and more than all.

And now we come to that most mysterious expression and yet one that is known to all in the religious path: the grace of God. What is it? It is the friendship of God. It is the friendly emotion of God. It is not the judging quality of God. When God's grace comes, it does not come by saying, "Are you worthy, are you not worthy, do you deserve it, do you not deserve it?" It comes. It comes as the emotion, as the love, as the devotion, as the admiration comes from friend to friend. With no limits; there is no limit to it. It is all right for some to say that because in the past incarnation they have done so much evil that this time they have a bad life with much suffering, or that in the past incarnation they have done so much good that this time they have become rich. And it is all right for others to say that when they will go to hell for their sins they will be whipped and thrashed and put into the fire. But when you look at the grace of God, you forget all these things; no rules, no laws, no deserving or undeserving are distinguished anymore. There is only one thing, and that is love, love that stands above law.

God's grace does not come to the pious. God's grace does not come necessarily to the people who are very good. Nor does it come to the people who are very occult or mystical. It comes as love comes from friend to friend. When love comes, it sees not what is wrong about the person or what is right, just as a friend's love comes to a friend without a conception of right and wrong. It is an emotion, it is a rising of the wave. It is a divine feeling that comes. It rises as a stream, and it falls upon the person in the form of a thousand gifts. It may be as inspiration, it may be as comfort, it may be as health, it may be as peace, it may be as rest. It may show itself in a thousand different forms.

Moses was one day passing and he saw a pious man after his prayers, worried about life's difficulties. And the man called to Moses, and said, "Moses, will you ask the Lord why I am put in this state, why I have suffered all through my life when I have kept up my prayers and I have done all the good one can do? Is there ever going to be a change in my life?" And as Moses proceeded on, there was a drunken man sitting there, and he said, "Come on, Moses, come here. Ask God what is he going to do with me? I would like to know." So Moses took both messages. And when he came back, he said to the first one that, yes, those who suffer here, for them there is better in the hereafter. The man was contented. It was worthwhile, he said, that I have gone through all this pain and that I will have a better life, a better place will be given. And when the drunken man asked Moses, he said, the worst place that is there will be given to you. And the man laughed heartily and took the glass and bottle in his hand and began to dance. He said, "How happy I am that God thought about me! I am, such a wretched creature that nobody would look at me, and God, the creator of the whole being, the whole universe, should even think of me! I do not mind where he puts me, as long as he thought of me, that is the greatest happiness; now I begin to think that I exist!

After some time had passed, Moses saw in his vision that they had changed places. And Moses went to God and said, "How is it that you had intended one thing, and there happened another thing?" And the answer was that, "Moses, at the time when we intended, it was so, but afterward it changed. This man thought that his virtues had won a best place for him, and that man thought that he did not even deserve God thinking about him, that is what pleased us."

Friends, whether it is the pleasure of the human being, or whether it is the pleasure of God, it is a different matter. God aside, you cannot say what will please your friend. And if you can ever say, it will only come when you really know what friendship is. If not, you may presume that you are a friend, and all your life you may try to please your friend, and you will not be able to do so. It is the same with God. You may do all the possible good actions and make a thousand prayers, and yet, if you do not know what pleases God, you cannot please God. But it does not come from knowledge; it only comes from friendship. Friendship is an automatic action. It is an innocent devotion, an unconscious outgoing, a pure feeling with depth, with life. Automatically that feeling brings about grace. Therefore no one can say why this person is the friend of the other person. We cannot be the judge of it. We cannot understand it. And so no one can say why God is pleased with this person or with that person. We cannot say. It is therefore that sometimes we see people who do not deserve to have so much wealth. And there are others, if they had some wealth, they would really make the best use of it, and yet they have not got it. There are others who seem not to be deserving of that position or rank they have. And there are others who perhaps in our eyes deserve more, and yet in the eyes of God it is different. It is because they deserve it and we do not see why or how they deserve it; and it is the same thing with friends.

When someone said to Majnun "Majnun, Leila is not beautiful, why are you so devoted to Leila," Majnun said, "To see Leila you must borrow my eyes." When we judge people, do we see with eyes of God? Do we see what feeling God has toward them? And when we cannot see, we have no right to judge others and why they are in this position in life or why they are in that position in life. And friends, this tendency of judging why these people are rich or why these people are in a big position, why these are in a big rank, it is all a kind of battle with God. And there is this one principle to learn: that with a friend I should do my very best to the end to prove worthy of that friendship. And the one who with God thinks that I will do my utmost to regard the pleasure and displeasure of God, without any thought of reward or without any thought of an answer from God, that is the person who really knows the meaning of friendship.

39

THE FOUR PATHS WHICH LEAD TO THE GOAL

My beloved Ones of God, I would like to speak this evening on the subject of the four paths which lead to the goal.[1]

There is one path that may be called the way of the intellectual. When an intellectual person has risen above intellectuality, then that person may be called an intelligent person, for a difference can be made between an intellectual person and an intelligent person. An intellectual person is one who has gathered knowledge by impressions, by studies, and is the ruler of the domain of one's intellect. What one has learned, what one has studied, what one has experienced, that is what one has in the book of one's mind, and that is one's world. No doubt it makes a person captive to a limited horizon of knowledge, and it is rising above that knowledge that may be called intelligence. But, no doubt, it is the intellectual person who is capable of being intelligent. The intellect is a cover over intelligence, and when this cover is taken off, then a person becomes intelligent. Intelligent are those who perceive for themselves, who learn for themselves, who understand for themselves, who

1. A lecture given at the Summer School in Suresnes, August 23, 1925. This lecture also appeared in the *Social Gathekas*.

recognize things by themselves, who are pupils and who are teachers within themselves at the same time.

When once people have risen above the boundaries of their limited knowledge, then the higher knowledge begins to come to them by itself. They begin to learn more in one moment than an intellectual person would learn after having read all the books in the library in six years' time. When once intelligent people have got an insight into the hidden laws of nature, they begin to see a way opening to the higher knowledge. Their reasoning changes its nature; it becomes the essence of reason. They do not see things from the reason they have learned from the world, but they begin to see the reason of all reasons, the reason that is covered by ordinary reasoning. There is a question: How can one be intelligent? The answer is that human beings are born intelligent; it is afterward that they cover their intelligence, and they are glad to call it intellect. Then they are recognized to be learned and think they have got some knowledge. And it is at that point that they make their intelligence limited; and as long as the intelligence is limited, they cannot see further than they see.

There is a time in people's lives when they are learning. And there comes a time when they themselves are the knowledge. It is at the time when a soul becomes knowledge itself that it begins to have glimpses into the hidden laws of nature. And this illumination may develop so that one may see the whole manifestation, clearly and fully, in the light of intelligence.

The Qur᾿an says, "God is the light of heavens and of the earth."[2] And if there is any spark of God that could be found in humanity, it is its intelligence. Naturally, therefore, when this divine light that is hidden in humanity is once brought to blaze, is once risen as a flame, it illuminates one's path to perfection.

2. Qur᾿an 24:35.

And the second path to perfection is the path of righteousness, is the path of duty, is the path of good action. People may not be intelligent but may be conscientious in what they do and what they should do, so that they may always use their good will to do righteous action; and by doing so, they are fulfilling that law of harmony that automatically raises the soul to perfection. Very often one wonders about friends and relations whom one thinks are goodness itself, and their actions are righteous actions, and yet they never seem to show any tendency toward religion or meditation. And often a person thinks: "What a pity! Will they arrive at spiritual perfection?" The answer is yes, it is possible that they will arrive at that perfection before the seeker who makes too much fuss about it and does little. They will arrive at that perfection before the person who talks too much about spiritual things and knows little. They will arrive sooner to that perfection than the person who is clinging to the outer things of religion and spirituality, merely by righteous actions and by good deeds. They may not know it, but automatically it must work because they are taking the path of righteousness that surely will lead them to perfection.

The third path is the path of discipline. It is in the path of discipline that concentration is necessary, that meditation is necessary, that contemplation is necessary. All different forms of discipline are necessary in order to bring about the realization that is the ultimate goal. The path of meditation enables humankind to experience different planes of life, but not always the way people say: by classifying, by saying this plane and that plane, this grade and that grade.

The real experience of the inner life cannot be very well classified. For instance, to a meditative person, if another person asks if there are seven planes of existence, the meditative person says, "Yes, it is so." But the other person says, "I have read in a book on Greek philosophy that there are nine planes of existence. Can it be true?" "Certainly." But another one comes and says, "I think that there are only three planes." The meditative person says, "Certainly, I do agree with you." The meditative person does not say this to please the other; those who meditate are able to see planes of existence as five, nine, seven, in as many forms as they like, because they actually see them. For instance, go to a beginner in music and ask how many notes there are. The beginner says there are seven notes, and then there are semitones besides. Yes, but to very experienced musicians who have perhaps given all their life to music and have come to understand the essence of sound, if you asked, "Is it not true, as the Chinese say, that there are twenty notes in the octave?" They say, "Yes, it can be true." But if you say, "But Indians say that there are twenty-four notes in the octave," they will say, "That is true, too. It is as you look at it." It is not that the octave has twenty-four notes. It is as you look at it; therefore, you see it that way.

All that people learn intellectually of metaphysics keeps them limited to book learning. They derive no benefit but a passing interest to be surprised, to know that there are so many different planes of our being. They do not go beyond. If people have to see them to know what they are, they cannot see them; but by the way of meditation they can realize them. And by that realization they can give an interpretation of any philosophy. Whether it is Buddhist or ancient Greek philosophy or Vedanta philosophy, any philosophy you put before them, they can give their interpretation, for they know what they have experienced through meditation. No doubt the way of self-discipline is a very difficult way. It is a way of mastery. It is the way of power, but it is a hard and difficult path. Imagine, if you practiced discipline by sitting in one pose or posture, how difficult it is to keep doing it for a long time. Imagine if you make a vow—I will not eat fruit, sweet or sour—how difficult it is. Imagine if you make a vow of silence, of fasting, a vow of standing so many hours or walking or keeping up at night—for part of the night or the whole night—it is not always easy. Self-discipline is learned by going against one's inclinations, one's own inclinations. One might ask, are they not natural inclinations? Why must one go against them? The answer is that one cannot say which is one's own inclination. All inclinations are borrowed here, and what one calls natural is that to which one becomes accustomed. The word *natural* is a word that one can study for years and years and years, and one will find, at the end of the study, that there is no such a thing as natural.

There are natural inclinations to pleasure and comforts that clash with the still greater inclinations and deeper inclinations we have for greater power and strength, for more light, and for more life. So the inclinations can be divided into two aspects: the innermost inclinations and the inclinations that one feels in everyday life. There is always a conflict between them. The innermost inclinations are sometimes undermined by the outer inclinations. And by learning self-discipline, one learns to suppress the outer inclinations in order to give a way for the inner inclinations to rise and to flourish, which in the end culminates in what we call mastery.

The fourth path to perfection may be called the path of devotion, a path that cannot be compared with any other path in its value, in its depth. The reason is that devotion strikes straight to the spirit of God. Not everyone is capable of this path, for in some persons the heart is closed by the head quality, by intellect. And in some persons the heart quality is foremost. The first step in the path of devotion teaches selflessness. It makes one unselfish. And if I were to explain what devotion is, I would say that devotion is the tuning of the heart to its natural pitch; in other words, the healthiest condition possible in a person is when devotion has blossomed. It is devotion alone that covers the false self of a person, be it for a human being or for God. If truth is ever to be seen, it is in devotion; for the world of the heart is a different world than the world where all live. Its law is different, the weather there is different. Its sky is different, its sun and moon different. The nature of that world is different; it is a world in itself. By devotion, heaven is brought to the earth. And yet how very often a person says, "But is it not a simple devotion?" It is in simplicity that the greatest subtlety is to be found.

For it is the heart of the devotee that is liquid, compared to the one whose heart has become crystallized. It is awakened to sympathy; it is open to appreciate all beauty. Krishna has said, "I am with my devotees."[3] And therefore, if one asks: "Where is God? Is God in the sixth heaven or in the seventh, or in a certain paradise or palace in which people imagine God to be?" The paradise or the palace or the dwelling place of God is in the heart of the devotee. No doubt, for a person to rise to a devotion to God is not easy. It is therefore that the Sufis in all ages practiced devotion gradually by their sympathy for their teacher, by their devotion to the divine, and by the culmination of that devotion in God. It is devotion that raises the object of its devotion or its ideal to the highest heaven. It is by devotion that rocks have been turned into gods. Someone asked a Hindu. "By the worship of a god made of rock, what do you gain? Is it not a god that you have made?" "Yes," said the Hindu, "my hands have made this god of rock, and my devotion has given life to it. If you believe in the formless God and have no devotion, you have not yet reached God. God is far away from you. My God is before me. Your God is far away from you." As the Bible says: "God is love."[4] If God is to be found anywhere, God is to be found in the human heart. And when is God to be found? When the heart is awakened to sympathy, to love, to devotion.

3. Bhagavad Gita 10:9–13.
4. 1 John 4:7–8.

40

HUMAN EVOLUTION

Beloved Ones of God, I will speak this evening on human evolution; that it is not only that the human race has evolved as time has passed, but as the human race evolves period after period, so individuals evolve in their lifetime.[1] In other words, the human race evolves gradually in a world's lifetime, and individuals evolve, if they evolve at all, during their individual lifetimes. It is possible that the human race may take an opposite course, and instead of evolving, it may go downward, and so it is with individuals also. But a person who is really evolving will not go back. If the person went back four steps, they would feel uneasy and discontented and would go forward again. Perhaps the person will go back a hundred times and a hundred times will go forward again. What I mean to say by this is that the person who has once experienced the joy and the pleasure and the happiness of evolution, will not be content with going back, the person may go back, but they will feel the discomfort of it and so they will go on.

No doubt, the rhythm of every person's evolution is different. As you will have read in the *Vadan*, one soul creeps, another soul walks, another soul runs, and another soul flies. And yet they live on the same earth, under the same sun, and they are

1. A lecture given at the Summer School in Suresnes, September 12, 1926.

all called human beings. How strange it is that at the present time a new spirit has awakened in humanity, and people do not distinguish the evolution of a personality. But what they do distinguish is the nationality. Every country you enter the first thing they ask you for is your passport. It does not matter what evolution you have, and it does not matter what your soul is experiencing, as long as you have a passport that distinguishes you as the subject of this or that country, that is the important thing. And very often people make a great virtue of saying, "I am as good as you." But imagine the insolence of it. The better you are, the lesser you consider yourself to be. If you are better, you cannot say that I am as good as you. That means the consciousness of the present-day person is inferior. One says "I am as good as you" because unconsciously one feels inferior in one's mind.

The other day I happened to see a distinguished lady who told me that a maidservant who was in her house for twenty years, and who always had such a good manner and such a sympathetic attitude, had suddenly changed. Now, will you tell me the reason for this? She is insolent, she is inconsiderate, she has lost that sympathy, she is more keen about the money she receives. She thinks now whether she does more work or less work than she ever did before. I said it is the spirit of the day. They think that they are evolving, but instead of evolving they are going down. But it is not that they are going down, they are pulling down others with them so that instead of making equality of higher spheres, they want to make equality of the lower sphere.

And one might ask whose fault it is? We shall say it is the fault of nations and of races, and of the education and many other excuses we shall give, but it is the times. It is the spirit of the times. It is no one's fault, but at the same time it is not necessary to go through a condition in a kind of intoxication; it is better to awaken to the knowledge of that condition. It is better to become acquainted with the real condition of humanity today. When we study human nature from a metaphysical point of view, we shall see that the origin of human nature is the same as the origin of all other beings. And the central theme of that origin is intolerance. Without reason, a person's first feeling is that another should not exist. Later that feeling becomes modified, and the person becomes more sympathetic, becomes more harmonious, becomes more considerate.

But that first feeling a person has is that another should not exist. And one might ask, where does this feeling come from? In reality there is one life and there is one being. And this world of variety is made of one being. It is the manifestation of the one. But at the same time in this world of variety, one being loses that consciousness of being one, that here in this manifestation there comes the consciousness of being many, and therefore one being stands against another being. Friendship, sympathy, harmony, attachment, devotion, all these come afterward as one evolves, but these are not one's first tendencies. The first tendency is a kind of jarring influence. For instance, how happy you feel when you are sitting in the train alone. And as soon as another person enters, you think well, this is a great crime, I would rather he had gone to the other compartment and left me alone. It is a natural feeling in a restaurant when you are happy eating alone and a stranger comes. That one may be an angelic person, but as soon as they come and sit next to you at the same table, you ask why? Have they not got any more tables? I mean to say that this feeling comes to harmonious people: I am not speaking of the inharmonious ones. Therefore, is there anything to be surprised at if in the history of the world there have been so many wars and battles? And for what? For nothing. And you must remember that humankind is more fond of war than of peace. They like peace after the war. If they had loved peace before the war, there would have never been a war.

What is the soul? If there is any explanation that can be given of the soul, it is the feeling of a knowledge or a feeling that

"I am." The feeling of one's existence, that is the soul, that part of one's being that feels that I exist. And what is the ego? Ego is what is gathered around the soul, and that is the knowledge of oneself. When a person says, when a person feels, "I exist," that is the feeling of the soul. But then one goes further: I exist as what? I exist as a physical body, as hands, as feet, as head, as a tall person, as a short person, as a thin person, as a stout person. That feeling of oneself as being a tangible and perceivable being, it is that knowledge around the soul that makes the ego, and that ego is called the *nafs*. And there are many friends in this world and there are many enemies, but the best friend and the worst enemy is our own ego. It is a best friend when it becomes a friend, but first of all it is the worst enemy. Every offense that a person takes, every insult that a person feels, every impetus of doing something, and every desire of accomplishing something, it all comes from the nafs.

And what is this ego like? It is like the rose and like the thorns that are around the rose. It takes the place of thorns when it is not cultivated, and it becomes a rose when it has become refined. But there are two ways of making it refined. The one way is to humble oneself and to crush one's desires; it is a process of crucifixion by which a person refines the ego. It is a hard grain and it must be ground till it becomes a thin powder out of which a paste is made. And when it remains in a condition of a thorn, there come more thorns, and more and more, till it increases its thorns in such a way that everyone that touches that person is dissatisfied. And now you can find among your own friends, you can think of it and you will know the truth of it, that there are friends who you would think you would be most thankful if they kept away from you. You love them, you like them, but you would be very glad if they would keep away. What is it? It is the thorns that hurt, thorns they unconsciously keep and that hurt. And in what way do these thorns manifest? They manifest in the form of words, in the form of actions, in the form of desires, in the form of manner.

Why do you become annoyed with certain people in life, even before they have uttered one word? Because the thorn is pricking. Perhaps that person will say, "But I have not said anything, I have not done anything." But that person does not know that they have thorns; there are perhaps so many that even before a person utters one word or even moves, that person's presence pricks you. But it is a natural outcome of the ego. Either ego develops thorns or it develops into a rose. When it develops into a rose, then everyone is attracted to it, because of its beautiful petals, its delicacy, its fragrance, its color, its softness, its structure. Everything about it is attractive, everything about it is healing, everything about it is appealing.

Therefore, for every soul there are these four stages to pass through in order to come to the culmination of the ego, which means to reach the stage of the rose. In Sufi terms the first stage is called *ammara*. And in that stage a person is rough and tough, crude and thoughtless, and inconsiderate. Such persons are interested in what they want and in what they like, and naturally as such, they are blind to the needs and wants of others. In the second stage, people are nice and good as long as their interest is concerned; as long as they can get their wish fulfilled, they are nice and kind and good and harmonious. But if they cannot get their wish and cannot have their way, then they are rough, and they are quite changed and crude. And there is a third stage, when people are more concerned with the other person's wish and desire, less with themselves, and their whole heart is seeking for what they can do for another. In their thought, another person comes first, and they come afterward. That is the beginning of turning into the rose. It is only a rosebud. And then this rosebud blooms in such persons who entirely forget themselves in doing kind deeds to others.

There is a little story that explains this idea much better. The king of Bukhara, who had just given up his kingdom and wanted a retired life on the spiritual path once went to a murshid, to a teacher. And the teacher said, yes, I will accept you among my group of pupils, but the first work you have to do is to take the wastepaper basket outside of the town and empty it every day. So this man had to carry the wastepaper basket after having dusted all the rooms. And the other pupils, when they saw someone who was once a king and had so many attendants and had such a comfortable life doing such work, they felt very sympathetic to him, and they said to the teacher, we pray you will make one of us do this work and not give this work to him anymore. The teacher said, the time has not come yet, wait. But they seemed very anxious. The teacher said, well, one of you go in the street; and he instructed him how he must act. So one of the young men went in the street when the king was carrying his wastepaper basket and pushed against him, so that the basket fell down. And he looked at this person and said, I would have showed you when I was a king; of course, now that time has passed, so I will now take this. And he bent down and took all the garbage and put it in the basket and carried it away. And the young man came and gave report to the teacher. And the teacher said, did I not tell you the time is not yet ripe? And again the teacher told the young men to do the same. And when next time they did the same thing, the king did not say one word, but he looked at him sternly. And when the report came to the teacher, the teacher said, it is not yet time. And the third time when they did the same thing, he did not even look at them. He quietly put everything back in the basket again and carried it away. And when this report reached the teacher, the teacher said, now it is the time. Now he is ripened enough to be taken in the spiritual path. In the Eastern language it is called *ghisna nafsi*; *nafs* means the ego, and *ghisna* means the grinding of it.

And how do you grind it? You grind it by sometimes taking yourself to task. When the self says, "Oh no, I must be treated like this." 'Then you say, "No, what does it matter?" When the self says "He ought to have done this, she ought to have said it like that, he ought to have worked like this," You say "What does it matter, either this way or that way? Every person is what they are; you cannot change them, but you can change yourself." That is the grinding. When a thorn shows itself, and you grind it as soon as you see it, that same thorn by being crushed will turn into the rose, for the thorn also belongs to the rose plant. Besides, when a person says, I will not occupy this position, I will not eat this, I hate it, I despise it, I cannot bear it, I cannot look at it, I cannot endure it, I cannot stand it—these are all little thorns. A person might not know it, but they are thorns. And when they are crushed, then the rose comes out of it. How easy it is for people to be inclined to learn occultism, how easy it is for people to say, we want to know about mysticism. Or even if there was a bigger name, they would like to take an interest in it, thinking that by reading books, you can understand it; by learning lessons, you can learn it; or by doing particular practices, you can know it. It is everyday life that teaches us; every moment of the day and night we are up against something that our nafs, our ego, rebels against. And if we took that opportunity to crush it, to keep it down, in some years' time our personality would become the rose.

Now the question is: For whom shall we build the throne of soft cushions? For our own vanity's sake, that we are better than others? No, for the pleasure of others, and not for our vanity. As soon as a question arises of whether I should be better than others, whether I should be more spiritual than others, whether I should be more wise than others, then there is "I," and that is wrong. What does it matter what one is, as long as one is able to give pleasure to others, to make life easy for others, because this is the world of woes. There is no end to the troubles, from the sovereign to the pauper, from the richest to the poorest person; there are endless troubles hanging around every individual. And if you can be of a little use to anybody, you can better learn mysticism; for the only mysticism is when a person thinks that they please God by pleasing humankind.

But then there is another way. Perhaps I have told this story before, but still this story explains it more. And this story is expressive of a higher attitude. The story is about Ayaz, a slave who was brought before the king, and the king wanted to take him in his personal attendance. There were ten of them. And the king had to select one from the ten. And the king gave each one of them a cup of fragile glass, thin glass, and asked each of them by turns to throw it down. So when each slave came before him, the king said "Throw it down." All ten did it, and then he called one and said, "Why did you do this?" That one said, "Your Majesty told me to do it." To another, "Why did you do it?" That one said, "Because it was the command of your Majesty." Another one, "Why did you do it?" That one said, "Because it was your Majesty's desire." All right. All nine of them answered in the same way.

And then came the tenth one, who was Ayaz. And the king asked, "Why did you do it?" He said, "I am sorry, pray, forgive me." The king said, "This is the one who has some sense. They repeated to me the same thing that I knew myself. They said, 'you told me to do it.' I knew what I told them; they said nothing new to me, but this one has said something different." Now let us take the same attitude before God and other people. There is one person who says, well, I have sinned because you have put me in this physical world. You have brought me here. You have given me the power to do it. It is you who has made me do it. You are all-powerful; why did you give me that wish? And there is another person who is sorry, who is sad, who repents, who kneels down and who says, it is true that all that comes, comes from you. And all is in your power, and without your command nothing moves. Knowing all this, I kneel down and ask pardon for my sin—that is a different person. There is a difference between these two persons, one is crude and rough and abrupt, whose thorns are protruding, the other one is like the rose.

Then the story goes on that the king was so pleased with Ayaz, by his wonderful help and attendance, that he made him the treasurer, the one who would keep his precious jewels in his charge. Many were against him, seeing that a slave has been brought to such a position. And they went to the king and said, he certainly robs, he certainly steals some jewelry from the treasure house. He goes there and closes the doors and he remains there for hours. The king said, "I cannot believe it." But they said, "You can see with your own eyes." The king replied, "Yes, I will." So the king went near the jewelry house and a hole was made in the wall, and he was looking through the hole to see what Ayaz was doing. Ayaz went into the house and closed the doors and opened the cupboard, and he took out from there the clothes that he was wearing as a slave. He kissed them and pressed them to his eyes, and he put them on himself, and he looked in the mirror and said, "Ayaz, do you know who this is? This is yourself. Remember what you are, what you were. Do not forget that the king has given you this big position, and so many people to work under you that you may not forget what you were first. Keep your modesty, keep your humility, keep your humble manner. Do not become drunk with this worldly position that comes one day and goes another day. It is a passing phase, it will pass. But you were this, what you see before yourself. Be grateful to the one who has made you this; pray for him and appreciate what the king has done to you and thank God for all he gives to you, which you do not deserve."

After saying this in a sacred manner like a prayer, he took these clothes and put them in the cupboard. And the king was so impressed that he was waiting outside, and as Ayaz came out, he embraced him and said, "For so long you have been my treasurer, but from today you are my minister. You have taught me the lesson of having the same attitude as you have toward God, the only king of the whole universe."

It is in this way we can crush our ego. Every time that it shows its pinprick to us, every time that its thorns come before our eyes we should crush them and say, "What are you. Are you not thorns? Are you not the cause of unhappiness for others and for myself as well? I do not want to see my own being in such a form, in the form of thorns. I want my being to be turned into the form of a rose that I might bring happiness, pleasure, and comfort to others."

If there is anything in the spiritual teaching, if there is anything in finding truth, if there is anything in self-realization, it is the refinement of the ego. Because the same ego that begins by being our worst enemy will in the end, if developed and cultivated and refined, become your best friend.

GLOSSARY

ammara: The first of four stages to pass through in order to come to the culmination of the ego; in this stage a person can be crude and inconsiderate.

artha (Sanskrit): Occupation; acquisition of wealth.

bhavasāgara (Sanskrit): The ocean of existence into which all things are drawn, fall, and are absorbed.

Brahma: Hindu creator god.

brahmacharya-shrama (Sanskrit): The path when one works with intellect.

Brahmins: The priestly caste in Hindu society.

dharma (Sanskrit): Duty, religion.

Gayan: "The Song of Divinity" by Hazrat Inayat Khan.

grihastha-shrama (Sanskrit): Attainment of knowledge by the experience of the responsibilities of life—of home, children, servants, neighbors, friends, and enemies.

haqiqat (Arabic): Reality; the stage in which one begins to realize the truth of the whole being.

iman (Arabic): Faith.

Indra: Hindu god of heaven, ruler of the devas.

jalal (Arabic): Power.

jamal (Arabic): Beauty.

jñana (Sanskrit): Knowledge, wisdom, realization; seeing into life, into the depth of life.

kalpa vraksha (Sanskrit): Tree of desire.

kama: Love, affection, attachment.

kamal (Arabic): Perfection; state of suspended activity.

majzub (Persian; Arabic: *majdhub*): God-intoxicated dervish.

mana, manu, manusha (Sanskrit): Mind.

ma'rifat (Arabic): Knowledge that enables those who have arrived at it to call God "Truth."

maya (Sanskrit): Illusion.

moksha (Sanskrit): Liberation; also paradise, heaven, heavenly peace.

mukti (Sanskrit): The one aim or ideal of the soul through our whole life.

Mutu qabla anta mutu (hadith): "Die before death."

nafs (Arabic): Self, ego.

Rumi: Jalal ad-Din Muhammad Balkhi Rumi (1207–1273): Persian Sufi poet and founder of the Mawlawi (Mevlevi) order.

Sa'di: Musharrif al-Dīn ibn Muslih al-Dīn (1213–1291): Persian poet, one of the greatest figures in classical Persian literature.

sannyasa-shrama (Sanskrit): Retirement, love of solitude and silence, contemplation and resignation with regard to all the things of this world.

shariat (Arabic): Stage where the God-ideal is impressed upon humankind as authority.

sulūk (Arabic): Beneficence; also search for truth.

tariqat (Arabic): The stage where one finds what really matters.

tawakkul (Arabic): Dependence upon God.

vadan (Arabic): Represents the voice of the soul expressed through sound.

vanaprastha-shrama (Sanskrit): Service to the world, to humanity.

SOURCES

Note: The first edition of *In an Eastern Rose Garden* in 1921 was compiled by Dr. O. C. Gruner from talks given by Inayat Khan in the years 1918–20. The transcripts of the original twenty-nine chapters in that volume—as well as chapter 25, "Spiritual Democracy"—remain unpublished. Eleven additional chapters were added to the fifth edition published in 1962. The original transcripts for ten of these are listed below and can be found in the *Complete Works of Pir-o-Murshid Hazrat Inayat Khan, Source Edition* (New Lebanon, NY, and Richmond, VA: Omega/Sulūk Press; London and The Hague: East-West Publications; Katwijk, the Netherlands: Panta Rhei Publishers, 1982–). The *Complete Works* volumes are also available online at www.nekbakhtfoundation.org. Chapters 34, 37, and 39 also appeared in *Social Gathekas: Sufi Wisdom on Social Harmony and Service* (Richmond, VA: Sulūk Press, 2020). The original transcripts of the earlier talks will appear in future volumes of the *Complete Works.*

26. The Freedom of the Soul (2)	1926, vol. I, 210
27. The Freedom of the Soul (3)	1926, vol. III, 14
33. Sublime Knowledge	1926, vol. I, 478
34. Intellect and Wisdom	1924, vol. I, 122
35. Simplicity and Complexity	1926, vol. I, 44
36. Dependence	1926, vol. III, 342
37. Friendship (1)	1925, vol. II, 44
38. Friendship (2)	1926, vol. III, 521
39. The Four Paths Which Lead to the Goal	1925, vol. II, 557
40. Human Evolution	1926, vol. IV, 460

BIOGRAPHICAL NOTE

Hazrat Inayat Khan was born in Baroda, India, in 1882. Trained in Hindustani classical music from childhood, he became a professor of music at an early age. In the course of extensive travels in the Indian subcontinent, he won high acclaim at the courts of the maharajas and received the title of Tansen-uz-Zaman from the Nizam of Hyderabad.

In Hyderabad Hazrat Inayat Khan became the disciple of Sayyid Abu Hashim Madani, who trained him in the traditions of the Chishti, Suhrawardi, Qadiri, and Naqshbandi lineages of Sufism, and at last blessed him to "Fare forth into the world."

In 1910, accompanied by his brother Maheboob Khan and cousin Mohammed Ali Khan, Hazrat Inayat Khan sailed for the United States. Over the next sixteen years he traveled and taught widely throughout the United States and Europe, building up the first Sufi order ever established in the West.

In London Hazrat Inayat Khan married Ora Ray Baker. They raised their four children in London during the First World War and afterward in Suresnes, France, where a little Sufi village sprang up around their home, Fazal Manzil.

The doors of Hazrat Inayat Khan's Sufi Order[1] were open to people of all faiths. Appealing to experience rather than belief, Hazrat Inayat Khan's discourses and spiritual instructions illuminated the twin themes of the presence of God in the depths of the human soul and the interconnectedness of all people. Numerous books were compiled from Hazrat Inayat Khan's teachings during his lifetime and posthumously. In September 1926 Hazrat Inayat Khan bade farewell to his family and disciples and returned to India. On February 5, 1927, he died and was buried in New Delhi.

1. Known today as the Inayatiyya.

INDEX

E

F

G

H

I

N

O

P

Inayatiyya

A Sufi Path of Spiritual Liberty

Sulūk Press is an independent publisher dedicated to issuing works of spirituality and cultural moment, with a focus on Sufism, in particular, the works of Hazrat Inayat Khan and his successors. To learn more about Inayatiyya Sufism, please visit **inayatiyya.org**.